MW01240996

TO DAKOTA AND BACK

THE STORY OF AN ORPHAN TRAIN RIDER

TO DAKOTA AND BACK

THE STORY OF AN ORPHAN TRAIN RIDER

Judith Kappenman

Lulu
2010

Published by Lulu
http://www.lulu.com

© 2012, 2010 by Judith Kappenman. All rights reserved.
Printed in the United States of America.

ISBN-13: 978-1-300-22284-2

Note on sources:

Letters are fiction with the exception of John's letters to Bess on pp. 106-108 and the letter from Craig Donahue to his father on pp. 227-228. Newspaper articles are fiction with the exception of articles from *The Enterprise* (reprinted courtesy South Dakota State Archives). The debate in the United States Senate found on pp. 26-28 is fiction.

Photo credits:

Page 118: Home for Catholic Children, Harrison Avenue, Boston. Courtesy of Daughters of Charity Archives Northeast Province.

Pages 119-124: Family archival photos.

To my grandfather, John Donahue, for instilling in me love and gentleness.
To my mother, Kathleen Kappenman, for insisting that her father's story be told.

Acknowledgements

I am grateful for all those who have helped me in telling the story of this wonderful man: first my mother, Kathleen, who insisted that the story be written; next, my siblings, especially Sharon, who remembers so many stories; also my three Donahue cousins. I am indebted as well to South Dakota folks, especially Ethan natives, including Eva Lingemann and Mary (granddaughter of M. J. Coyne) Tystad.

I am grateful to all the leaders and participants of various writing groups, workshops and retreats, especially the members of the Western Massachusetts Writing Project at the University of Massachusetts, and the writing/response group led by Diana Callahan; to a number of teachers including Lucile Burt, Anne Herrington, Janet Sadler and Margaret Szumowski; to my religious community, who gave me a sabbatical year enabling me to begin research and writing; to the Springfield Cultural Council for its generous award in 2000, enabling me to travel to conduct research; to readers Sister Kathleen Keating and Bonnie Moriarty; to my editor, Janet Sadler; and especially to Bruce Penniman, who guided me through the publication process and designed the book.

This book has also been made possible with the help of the many archivists, librarians and volunteers who offered invaluable help in my research: Phyllis Danehy and Robert Johnson-Lally in the Boston Catholic Archdiocesan Archives; Ken Stewart at the South Dakota Historical Society; the countless number of people who helped me in public libraries (Springfield, West Springfield, Boston, Pittsfield, Mitchell, South Dakota); the Elms College and University of Massachusetts libraries; the Connecticut Valley Historical Society; the National Archives in Pittsfield and Waltham; and the Davison County Records in South Dakota.

But most of all I am grateful to my grandfather and grandmother who lived life to its fullest and shared their love so freely. They taught me how to live. They are the inspiration for this story.

Prologue

In a farmhouse in Worthen, South Dakota, in 1900 John Donahue sat in the rocker near the hearth with a book on his lap. But he wasn't reading. He was taking a final look at the Coyne family and this farmhouse where he had spent so many years. *Who were these people? Strangers.* He felt as if he had just met them. The parents stood near the stove, the farmer rocking on his heels with his hands in his pockets as he regaled his wife with stories of his recent trip to Chicago to sell the cattle, while she, stirring the pot, nodded occasionally. *How amazing it was that the two immigrants, one Irish and the other German, both fiercely independent and strong, would marry.* For all these years they treated him coldly with never any sign of affection. He thought of the food Mrs. Coyne deprived him of over the years so she could give more to her own children.

He looked at the two older boys as they sat at the table: Robbie leaned over a schoolbook while Charley polished a leather harness. Their sister Anna scrubbed clothes, stooping over the washbasin in the corner. So much like her mother in looks and behavior. The three older children would always have a special place in his heart. Willie and the baby Ed played with their toys on the rug near the hearth. When he'd arrived there had been only Robbie and Charley.

He turned his attention back to Michael J. Coyne, standing by the stove with his head thrust forward, now gesticulating as he talked. In his late thirties, the man had a square, sturdy body with broad shoulders. He had a full head of wavy brown hair combed straight back. He had wide-set eyes, a firm jaw and an aquiline nose. He was a happy man whose face easily broke into a smile. He was a man who laughed often when he was the center of attention, but he could be harsh, even severe when it came to farm work or the pressures of making money for his family. *This man was the only father figure I've had.*

Rosa Coyne was about the same age as her husband. Childbearing had thickened her body; hard work in the kitchen and labor in the garden (occasionally also in the field) had given her strong muscles, especially in her hands and upper arms. Her dark hair, worn in a bun on the top of her head, was already flecked with gray. Her broad face with the small tight lips seemed to fall into a downward curve for, as a joyless woman, she rarely smiled.

John thought how over the years he'd learned a good work ethic from them. He'd learned how to do everything on the farm and in the house: care for the animals, do the fieldwork, carpentry and cooking. His gaze strayed to the open door where the dog lay asleep on the doorstep. The Coynes taught him to treat animals – even the dogs and cats – not as pets but as workers. At first he'd been frightened of the animals. As a small child, the size of the horses and cattle had daunted him. The teeth of the dogs and cats had threatened him. Even the grunts of the pigs and the clacking of the hens held menace.

How would an outside observer describe this young man, on that warm April day? John Donahue at age twenty-three had a full head of dark red hair, parted on the right, topping a noble head. His brilliant blue eyes, rosy complexion, and benign expression made him quite attractive. He was glad he shared the same Catholic faith as the family who took him as an orphan. Still he felt like a wayfarer, though he had actually lived more than half his life here on the harsh Dakota plains, working in the fields, the barn, and the house. He no longer remembered much of his early life in Massachusetts.

Before lunch, he had packed his few belongings and sat on his single bed, looking blankly around, wondering why he didn't feel sad. In fact, he'd be glad to be gone from here – to be on his own, to make his own life. Nothing in the house belonged to him except the few clothes and books he had placed in his small carrying case. He had walked the few short steps to the wardrobe, opened it and fingered his fine wool overcoat. He had bought it after his first year of teaching, his first store-bought coat. He had caught a glimpse of the past in that touch, back to the years when Mrs. Coyne had made all his clothes, many from Mr. Coyne's hand-me-downs.

He moved to the narrow window and looked out to the yard, remembering an early winter day when as an eight-year-old he had come shivering from school, hugging his thin jacket to his chest. When he'd been sent from Boston in the spring, a winter coat was not included with the clothes the Home gave him. The farmer had met him in the yard with his cryptic, "Put your books in the kitchen and join me in the barn. You're late."

He'd said, "Yes, sir," through chattering teeth.

Mr. Coyne had asked, "What's the matter, Boy?"

"Nothing. Just cold." He'd felt too cold even to move.

"Don't be such a baby. You get working you'll warm up fast enough. Come on, Boy. Move it," Mr. Coyne shouted at him.

John walked into the house where a blast of hot air in the kitchen greeted him. He dropped his books on the kitchen table. "*Nein,*" Mrs.

Coyne bellowed, pointing to his books and then upstairs. *"Oben. Oben."*

As he ran upstairs to deposit his books, he wondered again how he could please both of them. Not long after that he had gotten his first winter coat.

Yesterday, as he'd done chores, he had paused, looking at the familiar fields, the creek, the grazing area, the house, barn and other outbuildings. He knew every inch of the place. After all, he had worked on this land for fifteen years. He was happy to be leaving it. But he was sad also because it was the only home he knew. Now, sitting in the kitchen, he smiled to himself. He would be on his own and not beholden to them anymore.

Chapter One
Two Different Worlds

John's father, who bore the same name, climbed the steps wearily and entered the kitchen to find it in chaos with his daughter crying and his two sons squabbling noisily. The Silver street neighborhood in 1880 South Boston swarmed with children – mostly Irish immigrants: O'Sullivan, Mullen, and Regan, some of whom spoke Irish or had an accent as he did. The three-story tenements in South Boston housed up to six families. He heard loud voices behind all the doors from his third floor apartment with its cramped quarters.

John stood for a minute and watched the boarder, Rose Ann, paring the potatoes, and ignoring the noise and the disarray. He looked around the room and then demanded of her, "And where is Annie?"

She looked up, giving him an aggrieved look. "She's in bed. I can't do anything for her." She raised her hands in frustration. "She's that sick, she is."

He put his lunch pail on the table and sat opposite her. He reached down to remove his boots. "I'll go in and see her," he mumbled. "I'll see if she needs anything." But he sat with his elbows on his knees and his head in his hands. Whimpering, the baby crawled over and pulled herself up to his knee. When he reached down and lifted her, she stopped crying. He said with disgust, "Ah, Rose Ann, can't you change the baby when she needs it?"

"I've changed her all day. Look around." She pointed to the cloths hanging on lines that draped around the room. "I can't keep up with it."

"God, woman, you've got to train her to use the pot. She's surely old enough."

"Don't tell me what I have to do," she turned red with anger. "I'm not your wife."

The two boys, after stopping to watch the exchange, had quietly gone back to their game.

John rose wearily with the baby in his arms. "Where can I find a clean, dry nappy? I'll change her myself."

She pointed to the bureau in the corner. "In front of your face," she snapped with head down and tears in her eyes.

When he returned from the children's bedroom, Mary was now smiling. He set her down next to her brothers at their game. He patted the two boys on the head. "I'll see how your mother is."

When he entered their bedroom, he heard the racking cough so familiar to them all. It broke his heart to see his wife suffer so. She was half sitting, with tears in her eyes – tears of pain and frustration. He sat on the edge of the bed and took her by the hand. She asked weakly, "How's the baby? I hear her crying. And the boys?"

"They're fine," he squeezed her hand gently. "Rose Ann takes good care of them."

"What would we do without her?" she groaned.

"Indeed." They sat quietly for some minutes. "What have you eaten today? Let me get you something – perhaps gruel or chicken broth." He wanted her to be well – to be the healthy woman he'd married six years earlier.

"No. I can't eat. Just hold me." She clung to him, crying, "What will happen to my babies when I'm gone?"

"Hush, you're not going anywhere. You'll be well again." Suddenly he felt a hand on his knee and another on his back. The three children looked with wide eyes at their parents. "Look who's here," he said with forced joviality. They separated as the children one by one embraced their mother, beginning with the oldest Tom, followed by John, and finally by Mary. With tears wet upon her face, Annie took her daughter into her arms.

She asked Tom, "Are you being good? Are you taking care of your brother and sister?" The four-year-old nodded. "How is John? Are you doing what Rose Ann tells you?" He too nodded solemnly.

Tom asked, "Will you get better?"

"Yes," she assured him. "I'll get better soon."

The young John asked, "Can we go to the park?"

"Yes. We'll go to the park and have a picnic." She started to cough again. John picked up the little girl and said, "Come, boys. We'll let Mam rest." They followed him to the kitchen and returned to their game in the corner. The potatoes bubbled merrily on the fire, and Rose Ann had cleaned and set the table for the simple evening meal. Later John brought some gruel to Annie, trying to coax her to eat a little.

Annie lingered for almost a year, but when the body could take no more, she slipped away quietly one summer morning. The parish priest, Father O'Callaghan from the nearby St. Augustine church, anointed her a few days before she breathed her last. That night she slept peacefully. John awoke with high hopes that she would recover as she had after other bouts. But it was not to be. Annie Graves Donahue died on July 14, 1881, at the age of thirty-two.

One of the last things she had said to her husband was, "I'm sorry."

"Ah, and what are you sorry for?" he'd asked, his heart torn.

"For being sick and for dying like this and leaving you with the three children. What will become of you all?"

"Don't you think about it." He only held her hand; he could no longer embrace her. His heavy heart watched the breath of life leave her. Later Rose Ann washed the body, preparing her for burial. They placed her in a wood coffin and brought her to the Church for the funeral Mass with burial in the nearby cemetery. The children, five-year-old Tom, John, four and Mary, two watched their father and wondered where their mother had gone.

Some months later the two boys John and Tom lay huddled together in their bed in the room next to the kitchen; their sister Mary slept at the end of the bed. The boys listened to their father and Rose Ann talking.

"John, I can't do it any more," Rose Ann sighed. "I'm that wore out. Your children are beautiful. I love them, but I have to leave you. My cousin Hannah has an extra room. I'll move in with her." After a moment of silence when he said nothing, she added, "You know I'm almost seventy. Too old to be caring for children."

After a long pause John pleaded, "Ah, Rose Ann. What'll I do without you?" He turned baleful eyes to her, his hands gripping his teacup.

She looked away, speaking tonelessly. "My advice is to put the children in the Orphan Home where you put the boys after Annie died. The nuns'll take good care of them till you get back on your feet or get someone to help you."

He lowered his head, "I miss Annie so much." They sat in silence. He stared at his knuckles, seeing nothing. Finally he said, "I'll talk to Father O'Callaghan. I'll have to bring them to the Home again. He'll help me."

The two boys shifted closer under the coverlet. They'd already been in the Orphan Home, so they knew what faced them. They shivered in dread. Their father's voice continued in the next room. "I don't get work every day. There's never enough money. And if you leave me, how can I care for Mary? She's just a baby. And the boys ..." He stared into the fire. "Maybe I could give up this flat and find something smaller and cheaper or go back to New York and find steady work. There's nothing for me here in Boston. When I'm settled I can come back for them." In spite of their dread, the boys eventually fell asleep.

The next morning the rain beat against the house as the children ate their breakfast of porridge. As soon as they finished, their father wiped their faces and handed them their thin jackets. Mary Ann would stay with Rose Ann. They hurried out along Silver street and onto Dorchester through the wet streets to nearby St. Augustine's Church. The boys skipped and half ran to keep up with their father. Thankfully, the earlier heavy rain had given way to a light mist. John rang the doorbell of the priest's house and stepped back. Father O'Callaghan's face soon appeared. He welcomed them in, peered intently down at the boys and asked, "Are you good for your da?" Just then the housekeeper came by with an armload of linen, and he asked her to give the lads some milk. He led them to the kitchen table. "Sit here, boys." He pulled out the chairs and helped them to climb up. "You wait here. Mrs. Lynch will bring you a bite to eat."

The two men moved into a nearby office. The woman returned with scones and glasses of milk for the children. While eating and drinking, the boys listened intently to their father and the priest.

"I don't know what to do, Father," John began. "Rose Ann is leaving to move in with her cousin. I can't blame her. She's not even a relative of Annie or me. How can I take care of my children, run a house, and look for work at the same time?" He shook his head in dismay. "Impossible."

The priest reached out and touched John's arm. He spoke softly, and almost pleading, he suggested, "Perhaps it's time to put all the children in the Orphan Home. The nuns take good care of them, give them their meals, and their schooling."

"That's best, you think?" John looked at him hopefully. His hands crushed his hat, as he worried it back and forth on his lap.

"Just till you get back on your feet. And in the meantime, you can visit them Sundays."

"Then you don't think it's wrong of me to send them to the Orphan Home again. They're not orphans," he defended himself. "It's not like I'm abandoning them."

"No," the older man said. "You're doing the right thing. This is what their mother would want, her babies taken care of. You get yourself together. When things are better, you can bring them home again." The priest leaned forward to put a reassuring hand on John's shoulder.

John looked down to avoid meeting the priest's gaze. "Thank you, Father," he mumbled.

"Do you want to pray?"

"Aye," John said and he slid from the chair to his knees.

The priest slowly knelt beside him. "Father in heaven, look down on your children, care for those in sorrow, comfort them, give them hope for a better future. May John know your presence and support. May his children be protected against evils and grow strong in your love. Amen."

"Amen." The boys heard their father echo the priest. Though they could not see him from where they sat, they heard an unmistakable sob, and then muffled words of comfort. After a few minutes, Father O'Callaghan lifted John to his feet. "I'm ashamed of my tears, Father," John averted his face.

"It's all right. God has given you a heavy cross to bear." They moved slowly across the small office into the boys' view. "Can you have them ready for tomorrow? I can get a wagon to take you to Harrison avenue in the morning. There's no reason to delay."

"We'll be ready. Won't we, boys?" John spoke boisterously as he moved into the entry room and stood in the doorway. "You'll go to where there's lots of children to play with." He wiped his eyes with his handkerchief.

The boys looked at each other and put down their glasses. They started to follow their father toward the door. The priest stopped them, "Boys, before you go, I'll give you my blessing." They bowed their heads. "May God protect you and keep you safe." He made the sign of the Cross over them and then gently rested his hand on each head. Their father watched from the doorway. The gentle and kind priest walked to the door with his arms around the boys. "You'll be fine, boys," he said softly, but with an edge of sadness.

The next morning, Mr. Fitzpatrick tapped his cane on the kitchen door. They had heard the horse and cart pull up in the street below. The sun rising out of the east shone on his bald head as he doffed his cap. John held his youngest and the two boys were finishing up their oats. The visitor asked, "Do you need help getting them ready?"

"Nay, Rose Ann will do that," John said. "She's got their clothes laid out for them. She'll be right back; the water is heating for their wash." He gestured to the stove where the basin was waiting. Mr. Fitzpatrick, holding his cap in one hand, stepped back, folded his arms across his chest, and leaned against the chest of drawers in the corner.

They heard the stairs creak as the old woman climbed slowly up to the third floor flat. She called the boys over to her. "Come boys. Time to wash up. We don't want the nuns to see you looking this way with your breakfast on you." They looked to their father who gestured for them to obey; they stood and slowly walked across the floor to the stove. The old woman dipped the cloth into the steaming water and rubbed soap onto it.

Tom whined, "We don't want to go to the Orphan Home, Da. We want to stay with you."

Rose Ann pulled Tom toward her and washed his face and hands, then handed him the towel. Young John, standing close to his older brother took his cue, echoing him, "We want to stay here."

The old woman pulled John to her. "Let me get your breakfast off you. My goodness, you have it on your chin and your chest." She scrubbed him vigorously. "Take the towel and give yourself a good rubdown."

The boys looked back at their father, who was still holding Mary. She was sniffling and clinging to him, her face buried in his chest. "It's only for a time, boys. Don't worry. Your Da will come and get you soon. I came and got you the last time, didn't I? Go on with you. Put on your clothes. You're big enough to get dressed yourselves." They didn't move, but when John put Mary down, pushing her toward the woman, the boys started slightly as he stepped menacingly toward them. They went into the bedroom and as they dressed, listened to the conversation in the other room.

Mr. Fitzpatrick stepped forward to hand John an envelope. "Father O'Callaghan wrote a letter for you to give to the nuns. You'll have no trouble getting them in."

"Thanks, Mo." John took the paper and, without unfolding it, put it in his pocket.

"We all feel bad for you. You've not been able to find work?"

"Nay, and Rose Ann leaves today to live with her cousin. I can't do it alone. Everywhere I go I read *'No Irish need apply.'* I might go back to New York and see if I do better there. When I've got something, I'll send for ..." His voice broke, becoming almost a whisper before he trailed off. He bowed his head and gripped the chair back.

Rose Ann led Mary around the two men and into the bedroom to dress her and to check on the boys. When the child was ready, she sat John up next to her on the bed. "Let me tie your shoes." Tom, looking grim, stood squarely on the bare wood floor, one fist tight against his side. "All right boys," Rose Ann said in false levity. "Mr. Fitzpatrick is waiting." She drew the three children to her. "Be good, and do what the nuns tell you! You'll like it. Lots of children to play with and lots of games." When her voice broke they clung to her. All of them cried, the old woman and the three children. She smoothed their hair back, then led them into the kitchen where she placed Mary's hand into her father's.

He headed toward the door. "Come along, boys," he said gruffly. "We need to get going." Rose Ann pushed them gently toward the stairs, but did not follow. In tears, the boys stumbled behind their father. John lifted the children onto the back of the cart, and hopped up next to the driver. They carried no luggage, no clothes, no toys, nor a single souvenir of home.

The small family rode the two miles to Harrison avenue through the tree-lined streets – up West Broadway, across the bridge, south onto Dorchester, eventually reaching Harrison. Mr. Fitzpatrick pulled the cart in front of the dreaded familiar brick building with its huge doors and windows. Their father hopped down and lifted Mary to the ground. The boys sat, staring into the distance up the road, back from where they'd come.

When they made no move to leave the wagon, he lost patience with them and spoke sharply. "Come boys. No dawdling." They finally allowed him to take their hands, hopped down and with slow steps followed him up the long stairs to the huge, heavy front door of the three-story brick structure. Their father pulled at the doorbell. Almost immediately a Sister of Charity dressed in her black habit and veil answered the summons. She ushered them across the gleaming polished floor to the office. The boys listened as their father told the superintendent, Mr. Duggan, that he must leave his three children. He handed him the letter from the priest. "It's only temporary. I just need to get work, and I'll be back to collect them." He pulled the boys forward. "This is Thomas, and John. And this little beauty is Mary."

Suddenly young John felt himself and his siblings engulfed in their father's arms. Just as suddenly, the children were herded away by two nuns who had appeared in a swish of black habits, veils and dangling rosary beads. He couldn't know, standing in the dim foyer of the Home for Catholic Destitute Children, that it would be the last time he would see his father.

One Sister dragged John and Tom down the corridor, while another nun took Mary in another direction. She led the boys up the broad staircase where gloomy portraits of a bishop and several priests stared down from the walls. When they reached the third floor, the nun gave each of the boys a towel and a bar of soap and told them, "You're to take a bath. Scrub yourself good, even your hair." They undressed and stepped in the tub together; she soaped up their hair and scrubbed their backs. Finally, she led them, wrapped in towels to the sleeping quarters where she showed them their beds and gave them new clothing. Their cots were at opposite ends of the dormitory.

John, shivering, stood next to a cot with the morning light straining to come in through the small high windows. While the tears flowed, he dressed, and then sat down. Sister returned with a pair of shoes and said, not unkindly, but business-like, "Put these on. Then use the comb in the box there at the end of the bed. As soon as you're ready we'll go downstairs to the classroom." She disappeared again in a swirl of habit and veil and a clatter of beads.

John put on his stockings and shoes, but he struggled with the laces. The tears came again. *Mother is dead and Da can't take care of us.* Sister called to him from the door, "Come along, John. Time for lessons. The others are already started." When he didn't move or turn around, she said again, "We're ready and waiting for you."

"I can't," he said in a small voice without turning.

"What is the matter?" she asked, coming in to face him.

Tom followed her, saying, "He can't tie his shoes." He knelt in front of his brother. "Let me help, John. It's all right."

Sister handed him a handkerchief from the small crate used as a chest of drawers. "Use this to wipe your eyes and blow your nose." She took the comb and said, "I'll take care of your hair for you." As she combed his hair, she said cheerfully, "What a mop of red hair you boys have!"

John, frowning said to Tom. "Where did they take Mary?"

The Sister spoke before Tom could answer. "She's on the girls' side. The boys are on this side – the girls are on the other. Don't worry. You'll see her later."

When they were ready, she led them to the classroom where a scowling Sister Callista stood with her arms folded. She came toward them to give them their seats and assignments. Twenty or more boys of various ages and sizes sat, side by side, working on their arithmetic. John sat next to a thin, blonde boy named Joseph, who labored over his slate doing sums. John picked up his chalk and began the arithmetic exercises. He quickly completed his work and set it aside. He reached into his desk, took out the *McGuffey Reader,* and began to read.

Seated at her desk, Sister Callista called him forward. "John Donahue, bring your slate. I want to see your work." She pored over his figures, "Excellent. You've got all the right answers. Just try to be neater. When you go back to your seat, do the next page." He started to walk away. "But before you do that, I want you to read a story for me. Bring your *Reader* up here." When he returned with the book, she opened to a story in the middle of the book. "Read this one," she handed the book to him.

He read several sentences, slowly and deliberately. "Good," she said, looking into his face kindly. "You haven't forgotten anything since you were here last time. Read the next story after you finish your next arithmetic exercise." When he got back to his place, he smiled at his seatmate, who met his glance with a shy smile.

Just before the bell rang at noon, Sister Callista said, "Attention, boys. We'll be going to lunch in a few minutes. Close your books. Put your things away neatly."

John and Thomas followed the others into the toilets, then downstairs to the dining room. Sister Dominica met them at the door and led them to a table. "Here are two places." A group of boys at the table looked at them with stony faces. "Boys, welcome Thomas and John," she said firmly. The others nodded solemnly at the newcomers. She hurried off to stop a small scuffle at a nearby table.

The boys stood as Sister Dominica led the recitation of the *Angelus* and grace before meals. They pulled out their chairs with loud scraping and chatter. A boy sitting opposite John said, "You're new here. Eat everything they give you. It's a long time before supper."

"We're not new," John said. "We've been before." He reached for the plate of bread. He knew the routine that faced them. A bleak light struggled to come into the Orphan Home through the high, narrow windows. Almost a hundred boys from the ages of four to fifteen filled the dining room. The older boys worked as waiters, bringing food from the kitchen.

Very early the next morning, John awoke with a start to the loud clanging bell. He sat up, trembling in the cold. He watched the line of boys hurrying into the bathroom. *This life again.* A small dark-haired boy in the next bed said, "Hi, I'm Peter. We'd better get ready. Sister doesn't like it when we're late." John swung his legs out of bed and stood. He followed the boy into the bathroom where Sister Beatrice watched the boys at the row of sinks and hurried them along.

They went to chapel for Morning Prayer and Mass. Then on to breakfast. Another day just like yesterday with lessons and chores till bedtime. Another like it tomorrow. Weeks passed. John and Tom went through the motions of their days. Their father never came back to see them or take them home.

Weeks went by, then months, and even years. The Donahue children still lived at the Home. Boys had outdoor chores – shoveling snow, raking leaves, and working in the garden. In the summer they weeded the assigned plots early in the morning; later in the evening they carried buckets to water the plants. One day as they worked in the garden, Joseph and Robert, who worked several rows over from John called to him, "Come on, John. Time to go in for class."

"Be with you in a minute," he said, but didn't look up as he concentrated on his work. "I just have a little bit more to do." He tugged at a clump of stubborn ragweed.

Robert said, "We're going in. Don't be too long. You know Sister gets angry if we're late."

On his knees in the dirt, John stared down the row at the nasty weeds. They'd kill the tomato plants if he didn't uproot them. He knew it was important to finish a job once started. Suddenly a shadow fell on him. He turned to see standing behind him a Sister's black habit. He scrambled to his feet. "I'm coming, Sister. I just wanted to finish this row. I don't want the weeds to take over." He stood with his head down, expecting a scolding. Sister Stephen said, "Good job, John! You'll have the best plants of anyone because you take good care of them. Come with me. I want to show you something in the greenhouse."

He brushed the knees of his trousers as he trotted after her, his heart pounding. He wondered what she wanted. He also wondered how late he would be to class. He followed her into the warm, moist greenhouse, with its long rows of low tables. "Here we start plants as seedlings. I asked Sister Superior and she said you could help me in here." John looked around as she pointed to plants of every size and color, some reaching up toward the clear glass of the roof. She turned back to him. "I'll teach you all I know about gardening. Would you like that?"

"Yes, Sister."

"I work in here every day before lunch and supper. Join me when Sister sends you to do yard chores. I think you'll make a good gardener."

He turned to leave. "Wait a minute," she said. "Brush off your knickers and scrape your shoes. Sister Helen won't be happy if you track mud in her hall." He brushed himself vigorously. "Good. Off with you. And don't forget to wash your hands before you go to class." She called after him, "Tell Sister James that I delayed you."

John hurried into the back door, took the stairs two at a time and slipped into his place. Sister James called him forward before he had time to take out a book. "Let me see your hands, John." He remembered his dirty hands and wiped them on the back of his knickers. He lifted them up to her. "You haven't touched any books yet, have you?"

"No, Sister," he said, hanging his head.

"Disgraceful. Look at those fingernails. Go to the washroom and give yourself a good scrubbing." He turned to leave but she went on, "Who knows how long you'll be here. You don't want the next boy to find a book that's all caked with mud." He turned from her again. "What do you have to say?"

He gave her a quick look and mumbled, "Thank you, Sister." Then he added as an afterthought, "Sorry."

"Good, now go along. No dawdling. You're already late."

"Yes, Sister."

"You're one of the better students, but you need to learn respect for books. Treat them as treasures." He moved from foot to foot. "Off with you," she said finally, and relieved, he hurried to the washroom. He came back to face her stern gaze. She stood with arms folded, overseeing the class. He raised his hands to her. "Better. Now, John. Tell me why you were late to lessons. All the others came into class long before you did."

He gave his excuse. "Sister Stephen wants me to help her in the greenhouse."

"Well," she said, more kindly. "You can talk to Sister Stephen about gardening any time, but not when you're supposed to be here. Sister Stephen knows you cannot be late for lessons. You come with the others."

"Yes, Sister."

"Today, when the others are excused, I want you to stay and finish all your lessons." She waved him away in dismissal.

"Yes, Sister." John went to his place and began with his arithmetic problems. His seatmate whispered, "What was she saying? She talked to you forever."

"Joseph." Sister James' voice boomed a warning. "Let John do his work."

"Yes, Sister."

John whispered, "I'll tell you later."

"*John*," she warned.

Smiling, he bent his head more closely over his work.

Halfway across the country lay Dakota Territory in what is now called the Upper Plains. In the 1870s and 1880s Dakota country was prairie land – wide open. With no trees, the endless sea of tall, waving grass and small wild flowers (prairie clover, sunflowers, geraniums, wild roses) were all the eye could see. That and the sky. Always the sky. Farms scattered through the wide area, miles apart. Many people lived in sod shanties or unpainted shacks for years. Both people and crops were at the mercy of the weather. The climate was a study in extremes – drought, hail, blizzards, dust storms, leaf rust and grasshopper infestations. Buffalo roamed freely, coyotes lurked around and whined, and prairie dogs dashed in and out of their holes.

A wagon train pulled into the Ethan area in 1882. The southeast corner of Dakota territory looked promising to William and Sarah Craig, who with their nine children had come from Cameron, Missouri. (Dakota wasn't separated and designated as the states of North Dakota and South Dakota until 1889.) Katherine, their tenth and last child, would arrive two years later. The Craigs (Sarah was a Doyle) – both Irish immigrants, had met and married in 1860 in Wisconsin, moving on to Missouri after four years: in an area near Cameron most of their children were born, and some grew into young adulthood. They were among the number of those nineteenth century immigrants who moved four or five times before settling in their final home.

From the age of thirteen, William had worked at farming, logging, canal building, and freighting. Now he wanted to farm. Free land through the Homestead Act of 1862 offered immigrants like the Craigs an opportunity for prime acreage. They were especially pleased to find other Catholic families living in the area and in the nearby town of Ethan: Crampton, Schoenfelder, Schurz, Oster, and Hohn were among some of the prominent names. In the beginning, from their farm a mile south of town, they traveled another several miles south to Rome to worship in the Church of Saints Peter and Paul. Later, when Holy Trinity Church was built in Ethan, Will, his sons and his sons-in-law helped to erect the structure.

As did most settlers of the Plains, they quickly set up a sod house, a dwelling that stayed warm in winter and cool in summer. The three men, Will, his older son John, and son-in-law Phil, worked together, and they built a large structure to house the family. They had first built the wood barn, believing as Will's Irish ancestors had that one could live and eat if he had a barn, but not if he only had a house. The large two-story home was built only after the barn was ready.

The Craigs proved to be among the many hardy pioneer families who braved the severe weather of the northern Plains and survived. With the nearness of the railroad and the convenient grain elevators, the men set to the job of planting feed grains that would find easy markets. Will laid claim to his 160 acres after he surveyed the flat, fertile land.

He learned that here you could see the full sky and in that sky read the weather system days in advance; storms always gave advance warning. In the winter he watched the clouds heavy with snow. Even though the earth might be dull brown and the plants and bare trees resting for a season, he could envision the white snow blanketing the earth. It occurred to him often that winter was a time of hope, hope for the spring that brings life and fullness. Winter taught him to wait, to store his energies for the coming spring when the ice and snow would melt, and waters would flow in the nearby James river and in scattered ponds and creeks. All of nature would come alive.

In late fall of 1885 after the required three years of farming the land, William Craig made the two-day trip to Mitchell with his two sons to file his claim for ownership. He had to wait until July of 1888 to receive his land certificate, but receive it he did, and signed by President Grover Cleveland, attesting to his ownership of the 160 acres he had worked successfully for six years.

The Coyne family moved to the same region in 1882. Michael J. Coyne brought his bride, Rosa Freidel, from the Yankton area on the Missouri river to make a home east of Ethan in the area later called Worthen. The young couple, both twenty years old, found a large piece of land on which to stake their claim. When Mike first arrived, he'd stood on the rise, overlooking the small creek. *Good pasture land for cattle. That's what I want, a stock farm. Amazing no one has settled here yet.* He turned to look west at the flat, broad expanse. Good for crops: oats, wheat, corn, barley. Soft, gentle breezes blew across miles of luscious native grasses, sending waves of billowing ripples across the expanse.

For the first several months they lived in a sod house, theirs carved out of the hillside, almost a cave. That first spring and summer, Michael built the barn and then turned to the work of erecting a two-story house on the flat land at the northern border of his claim. With its firm foundation, it would stand long. At first, they had only one floor finished with four rooms in which they ate, slept, played, and prayed. Eventually, Mike completed the upstairs rooms, and they moved the beds upstairs. In winter, they kept bricks on the stove and slipped the hot stones into a folded towel to bring up to bed. Other pioneers lived in sod houses for years, but Michael and Rosa moved into their home after a relatively short time. The first child came in a year's time, and two more followed in successive years. Later they added three more children.

Michael Coyne planted trees to work as windbreaks to protect house, barn, and farm. He had learned much in Yankton while working in the logging industry and knew where to get wood, seedlings and saplings, a help both in the barn and house building and in the tree planting. Traveling to the nearest Catholic church for worship was a challenge because their farm was a good distance from Saints Peter and Paul Church in Rome. But both Mike and Rosa believed it important, so when time and weather permitted, they attended services as often as they could.

From: Home for Destitute Catholic Children
788 Harrison Avenue
Boston, Massachusetts
January 4, 1885

Dear Father Joseph Lamesch:

Father George Sheehan of Walshtown visited our Home recently and encouraged me to write to you with our request. We are a Catholic organization that serves needy families in the Boston area as a temporary shelter for children before we find permanent places for them. We have sent children to farm areas in Massachusetts, as well as nearby states. Father Sheehan has brought orphans to Dakota where he found homes with Catholics there. I'm sure you're aware of the benefits of growing up on a farm and of children learning to be productive citizens.

I am writing to ask if you can help us by finding families in your area willing to take a child and give him a home. On a separate page I am including a copy of the guidelines for indentured servants. Of course, if it is mutually agreed upon, the family may legally adopt the child. These children are orphans or have no family member willing or able to care for them. They are Catholics and we want to ensure that they find homes where the Faith is practiced.

Our administrator, Mr. John Duggan, will accompany the children on the train and, upon arrival, introduce them to the waiting families. Please advise me at your earliest convenience if you can help us in this good work.

I remain gratefully in Christ,
Sr. Mary Angelica

From: Rev. George Sheehan
Walshtown, Dakota Territory
January 27, 1885

Dear Joe:

Let me assure you that Sister Angelica and the cause she is doing is a noble work. I write to encourage you to do what you can to accommodate the Orphan Home by finding generous and good people in your area to house these children. Farmers here have been pleased with the children they have accepted. Many have even adopted them, taking them into their hearts as well as their homes. God will reward both you and the good people who open their hearts and homes to the "least and lost of His children."

God bless you in all you do for God's people.
Father George

Soon after that on a Sunday morning, the Coyne families, Michael C. with his wife, and their son, Michael J., with his wife and their two babies, sat in St. Peter and St. Paul church. After Mass, they listened as Father Lamesch appealed to the assembled farmers. "I have a letter from Boston. The Sisters are looking for homes for orphans – immigrants like most of you. These children are strong and healthy and can help you with your farm work. You remember that Jesus said 'Suffer the little children to come unto me.' God will bless you if you take one of these homeless."

The Coynes knew farmers in the Yankton area who had taken in orphans from the cities in the East and found them helpful. They looked at one another. "Now's the time," said Mike. The women nodded and stepped outside to wait near the wagons; the men would take care of the business. Together, the men joined the short line to approach the priest. When it was their turn, the elder Coyne asked, "Do you have any brothers on the list? We figure if we each take one of them we'd be keeping the family together. I could sure use help, and Mike's boys won't be ready to give him a hand any time soon." They all laughed.

The priest picked up a paper, listing the names of the boys. "Yes, I see two sets of brothers on the list, the O'Connells, aged six and seven, and the Donahues, eight and nine."

Father and son looked at one another. Mike rotated his hat thoughtfully in his hand. "We were hoping for boys a little older."

The priest looked at the list again. "There are some boys eleven and twelve, but they're not brothers."

"What do you think, Pa?" Mike asked. "We could take the second set of brothers?" When his father agreed, he turned to the priest. "The Donahues, you said? Age eight and nine?"

"I guess that'll work fine," the elder Coyne said. "I'll take the older one and you take the younger."

Father clapped the young man on the shoulder. "Oh, God bless you now! You are two good men. You'll be doing good work and the Lord will reward you. Other families have agreed to take boys too, so I'll be writing to Sister to tell her the ones who'll find homes here. She'll make the arrangements." He took up some papers and handed them each one. "You need to review the agreement: you must provide room, board, clothing, medical care, education and supervision; in addition, you must provide Catholic faith instruction – just as if they were your own children. I'm sure you'll have no problems." He handed them a second paper. "This financial agreement tells you how much you have to pay for their train fare from Boston, their food for their weeks of travel, and their clothes." He handed it to Mike. "You can get the money to me when you have it, and I'll send it on with the letter. Any questions?"

"Are they healthy lads?" the elder Coyne asked as his eyes fell on the numbers over Mike's shoulder.

"Sister assures me that they're good, hardy boys, ready to work."

Mike said, "We'll give you the money now." The two men took out their purses, each handing $15 to the priest.

He said, "Then that's it. We're all settled."

Mike asked, "Are the lads schooled?"

"Yes, the nuns made sure they had their lessons in the Home." He put their money into a purse, slipping it into the breast pocket under his cassock.

The elder Coyne said in parting, "You let us know when we can pick up the boys and we'll be at the depot."

They shook hands, and the Coyne men headed out. Mike turned back and said, "What are their names again?"

Father looked at the list. "Donahue. Thomas and John."

Mr. Coyne said, "Good enough. We'll be waiting to hear when they'll be coming. I hope they're here in time to help us with the plowing."

"Ah yes. God bless you both." He raised a hand in blessing. "I'll let you know."

Several weeks later in Boston, one evening after supper, Sister Angelica called a group of twenty boys into the classroom. John and his brother Tom were among the group, all wondering why she had assembled them. "Boys," she said. "I have wonderful news for you. You're going to farms to help with the work. You'll have lots of good food, fresh air, sunshine and exercise. You'll be able to drive horses and oxen and perhaps even have a pet. Families have agreed to take you in and let you live with them. What I want you to do is to pack your things. Take anything that belongs to you from your desk here, anything you have in chapel, and in the dormitory. You'll find a new satchel on your bed to put everything into, and a set of new clothes."

The puzzled boys looked at her, then at each other. What did it mean? "Let's kneel and say a prayer of thanksgiving for the good people who are so generously opening their homes to you, and for the good people who supported you while you've been here with us." They knelt and folded their hands. They recited with her the *Our Father*, the *Hail Mary*, and the *Glory Be*.

She led them in the prayer for benefactors that they prayed daily after Mass. "Vouchsafe we beseech thee, thy grace to the benefactors of the poor, most tender Jesus who hast promised a hundred fold and a heavenly kingdom to those that do works of mercy in thy name. Amen. Eternal rest grant to our departed benefactors, Lord, and let perpetual light shine upon them."

When they stood an older boy asked, "Where are we going?" Before she had a chance to answer, another piped up, "How far is it?" Voices began to overlap each other with innocent but urgent questions. "Will we come back here when we're finished?" "What if my father comes looking for me, how is he going to find me?" "Can me and my brother stay together?" "How long will we be gone?" "What about school?"

Sister held up her hand. "We'll answer all your questions later. Go, gather your things and pack. When you finish, those of you who have sisters are to report to the reception room to say goodbye." She looked at their confused and worried faces and went on. "Remember, take only what belongs to you personally. Don't take things that belong to the Orphan Home. Above all, don't take any school books."

John went to his desk taking out pencils and an exercise book. He also had a book. It was not a textbook, but a storybook that belonged to him. He also found a few small seashells. He headed to the door where Tom waited for him. They walked toward the chapel together. John said, "What do you have?" He showed his few items. "This is all I have." Boys moved all around them.

Tom had a slingshot, a rubber ball, pencils and exercise book. In chapel they collected their rosary beads and prayer book. As they climbed the stairs, Tom pointed to the things in his brother's hands and asked, "Where did you get the book?"

"It's mine." John said defensively. "*Tom Sawyer.* Remember the ladies that came? They gave it to me and told me to put my name in it. Didn't you get one?"

Tom shrugged, "I guess. But I must've lost it."

"I've read it already, but who knows if we'll have books where we're going. Besides, it's mine. They gave it to me." When they reached the third floor, John said, "Help me, then I'll help you." Tom followed him to his section in the dormitory. John reached into the crate for his few belongings. "Is there anything worth taking?" he spoke almost to himself. "I have nothing from home. Nothing." He found some pictures he had drawn and a few prayer cards. He put them on the cot with the rest. *So few things. And this is all I have.* He added his comb and handkerchief. He picked up the new clothes and started stuffing them into the satchel. He stopped when he noticed a tag. "Look," he said, "the bag has my name on it."

Sister Beatrice descended on him. "Here, let me help you with that, John. You don't want your things to get all wrinkled." She separated one set of clothing, placing it carefully into the bag. She laid aside the second set. "This is what you'll wear tomorrow," she said. "See, you have everything here you need for underclothes and your knickers, hose and shirt. And you have a new pair of shoes. Everything is brand new. The people who said they wanted you sent money for all this. Isn't that wonderful?" While she talked, she added the personal items he had gathered. "All done, John," she smiled at him, and then turned to his brother. "Thomas, have you packed yet?"

"No Sister." He kept his head down. "I was going to help John. Then he was going to help me."

"Come along. I'll help you." While she packed Tom's things, she prattled on how lucky they were to go to a farm. "Who knows? The family may very well adopt you and you'll have a new family. Won't that be wonderful?" They did not agree with her, but said nothing.

We have a family. Da had said "a temporary setback." We'll be together again soon. I'm not going to let anyone adopt me.

Sister straightened up and looked at them kindly, "Go along to the parlor and see your sister." She gave them a little push toward the stairwell. "Go now." Off she went to help another boy pack his things.

In the formal parlor on the first floor, several groups of brothers and sisters gathered to say good-bye. The Donahues, who had been at the Orphan Home for several years, hadn't been in this room with its stiff furniture and thick carpet in all that time. What could they tell their little sister, Mary? They were going to help on the farms, and then they'd be back.

In too short a time, the girls were called to return to their side of the Home. Mary turned back, looking small and unprotected. (It was the last time they ever saw her.) The boys were led upstairs and told to take a bath and go to bed. John lay awake for a long time, shivering under the thin blanket, more with fear of the unknown than with cold. Through the high window, he stared up at the stars, colder and more distant than ever.

John walked along a narrow, dark path where huge trees loomed over him. His clothes caught on the branches on both sides. A hand propelled him. He turned to see what followed close on his heels – a beast-like figure with frightening green eyes. His heart raced, shocking him awake. He opened his eyes. Before him only darkness. Sister Beatrice was leaning over him, saying softly, "Get up, John. Time to get ready." A dream.

Reality hit him as he looked around and saw the sleeping figures of the others. He didn't like this place, yet he didn't want to leave it. He got up quickly and dressed, still shivering. His fingers fumbled with buttons, his teeth chattered. When he returned from the bathroom, he found his satchel closed and several other boys waiting at the door with the nun.

John found Tom and they walked downstairs together. He moved as if sleepwalking. After being rushed through breakfast, they were brought to the front hall where the Sisters gave them their jackets and a small blanket. "Put the jacket on and hold on to your blanket," Sister Beatrice told them. "You'll need it."

They didn't see the identity tags sewn in the jackets until later when they were on the train. Ushered out the door and onto the waiting wagon, they clutched their bags and blankets to their chests for comfort, as well as for warmth. The early March morning in Boston was gray and damp. One boy pointed to a second wagon at the other end of the building.

John turned to Tom who was jammed next to him. He whispered. "Are the girls going to do farm work?"

"Probably not," Tom said. "They work as servants in a hotel or somebody's house. I heard the nuns talking – Sister Beatrice and Sister James. I couldn't get to sleep. If the ride is long enough, maybe I can rest on the wagon."

They rode through the streets of Boston, not seeing anything but the hunched figures of the other boys crowded together on the wagon and the bare trees overhead. The rhythmical clip clop of the horses echoed on the dark, almost empty streets. *Where are the farms? Where are they taking us?*

When they pulled into the railroad station, they jumped down, glad to move their arms and legs. Mr. John Duggan and another man whom he introduced as Mr. James O'Connor led them to the platform where all was noise, confusion, and people milling around. Suddenly they heard a loud roar and harsh squealing. John grabbed Tom's arm in terror when he heard and saw the black beast belching smoke heading straight for them. Tom assured him that it was only the train.

In a few minutes Mr. Duggan led them to a car down the track. When directed, the children climbed up into a car. John clung to his brother. They piled their bags in a corner and found places to sit on the benches along the outside wall and down the middle of the car. Mr. Duggan said Mr. O'Connor would go with them to "help make sure you find the farmer who asked for you."

The brothers sat together with their backs resting on the side of the car. After awhile Tom slipped off his jacket, looking idly at the label, uncomprehending for some minutes, but finally realized what he was reading. The neatly sewn tag was on the lining near the collar. He could see, in careful printing, his name, the place name, Dakota and two more names. He poked John. "Look at this. Do you have one?"

John took off his jacket so they could compare the labels. Identical. *Donahue, Dakota, Lamesch, Coyne.* They looked at one another in amazement.

Tom whispered, "You don't think we're going to the same place, do you?"

"It looks like we are." John grinned at his brother. They hugged one another. Better than anything they could hope for. They'd be even closer than they had been at the Orphan Home.

Suddenly they heard squeaks, the gasping of the steam engine, a loud whistle. The car jolted, and some of the children fell off the bench onto the floor of the car. The boys laughed with abandon and relief. The journey began.

𝕭𝖔𝖘𝖙𝖔𝖓 𝕸𝖔𝖗𝖓𝖎𝖓𝖌 𝕹𝖊𝖜𝖘

March 24, 1885

Orphans Begin Cross Country Journey to New Homes

On Tuesday morning groups of children from several orphan asylums in the city gathered in South Station, brought there by agencies dedicated to helping destitute children find a better life. They boarded railway cars for a trip that will take them to rural areas in the Midwest and West.

The waifs, ages six to twelve, all dressed in new clothes, arrived in horse-drawn wagons. They carried bags or bundles with a change of clothes and a blanket for the trip that could take several days or even weeks. Some carried personal belongings, photos, mementos or envelopes with addresses of family members.

The scene on the platform was one of confusion with orphan groups trying to find the right car for their group. James Higgenbotham, agent of the New England Home for Little Wanderers, explained that the children would become healthy in a new environment. "These children of immigrants did not find a welcome in the city. Most will find a good home with farm folk where they will have plenty of food to eat, opportunity for exercise, fresh air and a loving family to care for them."

Josiah Jacobson of the same orphan home said, "We want what is best for these abandoned ones. We have been sending children to the West and South for many years and have had great success. Children have prospered, and some have even been adopted. We can only pray that this group will do as well." Adults will travel with them to see them safely to their destination and introduce them to the families taking them in.

John Duggan, the superintendent of the Home for Destitute Catholic Children, said the children in his group are orphans with no family to provide for them. "Families who have agreed to take the children will meet them at the railway stations in Iowa and Dakota Territory," he said. These children had tags sewn onto their jackets listing their name and destination. Duggan said, "We have brought several groups now to the West and our children find a better life away from the city and in more healthful environments. Because our goal is to save souls, we have contacted priests who have found families to take the children."

Duggan explained that the Catholic organization program is different from the practice of other organizations. "Others send handbills ahead to the depots announcing the arrival with invitations for farmers to choose one of the children. Our children have a destination and a home awaiting them."

As the train chugged along, John held on to the hope that indeed he and his brother were going to the same farm. What else could he think? He fingered the bit of cloth. They heard a shout and looking up, saw some boys standing at the window while others pushed and said, "Give way. We want to see, too." The groups jostled one another and there followed a scuffle. Mr. Duggan stepped forward. "Now boys," he said with authority. "You have to take turns. There's plenty of time for everyone to see out the window. Line up."

John and Tom joined the line behind the others. When it was their turn, they looked out at the trees, fields, hills and valleys. They looked to the front of the train, seeing the black smoke belching from the engine. John wondered if this was like the fire-breathing dragons he read about. At the Worcester Depot the train slowed down and eventually stopped. The boys asked, "Is this our stop?" "Are we getting off here?" "Are the families here to meet us?"

Mr. Duggan, making his way to the door of the car laughed and said, "No, to all your questions. We'll just stop here for a few minutes while some people get off and others board. You can get off to stretch, but don't go far. This is a short stop. Stay near the car."

Several stops later when they reached New York, they felt travel-weary and sore. The benches had no cushions, and the ones in the middle had no back support. Mr. O'Connor made the children rotate seats every couple of hours, so they all had a chance to sit where they could rest their backs. Only a few of the boys had anything with them to occupy their time in the weeks of travel.

They traveled farther west for days, and the stops became routine. Each time they stopped, the adults insisted that the children stay within sight. Mr. Duggan said on the second day, "On another trip one of the boys wandered too far. And since the train had to keep to its schedule we had to leave without him. That meant the family who paid his fare were disappointed and lost their money. We don't even know what happened to him. Stay where we can see you at all times. If you can't see us we can't see you."

They saw more rural areas and fewer towns. Occasionally they saw a solitary cabin or house, separated by wide stretches of endless fields and forests. They had an increasing sense that the country was a large and lonely place. Most of the depots were nothing more than a rude shelter in the middle of a wilderness. On the last several days they saw nothing but flat land with its stretches of rolling prairie, smooth and bare. For meals the adults passed out jam sandwiches, an apple and a cup of water, sometimes on the train and sometimes in the depot. The children ate their meager meals hungrily.

The first night, when the shadows got longer and longer, the adults told the boys, "Lie down with your blankets. You can use the bench or lie on the floor. Time to get some sleep. Another long day tomorrow."

John and Tom lay huddled together. John whispered to his brother, "How is Da going to find us if we're so far away? We just keep going. It seems like we're going to the end of the world."

Tom patted him on the arm. "The trains go both ways. When we finish the work, they'll send us back. You heard Sister. She said we're just going to help with the farm work and then go back." John smoothed his tag in his jacket. Tom added, "To Dakota and back. Don't worry." John felt that they would travel for the rest of their life on the train. Eventually the rhythm of the train lulled them both to sleep.

United States Senate
April 1885

Congressional Record – Proposed Bill #304450
For the Abolition of the Practice of Sending Orphan Children to Farms as Indentured Servants

Massachusetts Senator Abbott: Mister President, honored and revered colleagues, I propose the adoption of Bill #304450 to stop the practice of taking children from orphan homes in our eastern cities and sending them to farms of the West and Midwest of this country and forcing them to work as indentured servants until they reach maturity. The children taken from homes are wards of the state and innocent victims of circumstances over which they have no control: they have neither asked for, nor wanted their situation. For us as a nation to continue taking these babies (and I am talking of boys and girls as young as age five) and shipping them off in trains, to work on farms for strangers, no kinfolk of theirs, is no less than a national disgrace.

Kansas Senator Barnes: May I ask a question, Senator?

Abbott: Please ask your question. I yield my time to the Senator from Kansas.

Barnes: Is it not a fact that the children have definite advantages by being removed from our already over-crowded cities? And isn't it a fact that the boys working on farms have a more nurturing environment, a situation that is more conducive to health and well-being? They will have the opportunity to enjoy the fresh air, have good meals – in fact grow and develop strong bodies, where they may become part of a family and learn to become productive adults.

A second question: Is it not a fact that that many young people upon being released from such institutions find themselves on the streets of our large cities at age sixteen, homeless again, unable to find work, and where they turn to thievery to take on the wicked ways of their fathers in bars and mothers in brothels? Senators, which future do we want for these young immigrants? I have facts and figures of problems with young hooligans in the cities. I can tell stories of boys and girls once in a Home and how negative the outcomes have been both for them and for society.

Abbott: Are you finished, sir? May I answer your questions?

Barnes: Please, I will be interested in your answers.

Abbott: Sir, the boys and girls are children; they are not their parents, nor do they have to fall into the paths of wickedness. I recommend that we develop programs for them in the cities, establish agencies to work with young people when they reach the end of their time as wards of the state. Let us look to equip the orphan homes with better educational opportunities so the children may take a productive role in society. But for us to countenance the shameful practice of treating American citizens as little more than slaves is abominable. May I remind the floor and especially my esteemed colleague from Kansas that in 1863 Abraham Lincoln freed the slaves and that in his Emancipation Proclamation he declared that "all persons held as slaves within any state or designated part of a state ... shall henceforward and forever free." If we accept this for the black man of America, should we not say the same of our children? For children who are least able to protect themselves? For orphans who have been left to the care of the state? Is this how we care for our children?

Barnes: May I make one more point?

Abbott: Be my guest, sir.

Barnes: Let me remind you of the great opportunity that the West affords, the West that is rapidly becoming the breadbasket of our country. The area cries for the increased productivity that young workers offer to farms in rural areas, where numbers of the work force are few and help is sorely needed, where more hands can produce the crops to feed the people of our nation. Do we want to stand in the way of getting the most out of our rich land and what it can give us?

Abbott: Mister President, fellow Senators, I believe that the Senator is confusing the issue. Let us, by all means, encourage adults to choose to become farm workers, and let us offer them a salary commensurate with their contributions to the work they do. Let us invite strong fully developed males the opportunity to contribute to the feeding of America and its people.

But I have stories (I invite you to read these yourself) of

indentured servants who live in most deplorable conditions, who are deprived of the very food that you say is so plentiful, who are considered little better than "workhorses" by their host families. They even consider themselves the owners of the children. Often these children are offered only a meager education at best. Are we preparing them for a better future? For becoming productive adults? Are we not rather planting the seeds of bitterness and hatred? Are we not sowing a crop of malcontents? Do we not see this as a breeding ground for ugliness and crime following on despair and hopelessness?

I ask my distinguished colleagues. How would we feel if one of the children were a relative? The child of a friend or neighbor? Would we so glibly write them off as so much chattel? Are not all children worthy of equal opportunities? We are talking of children – many of them immigrants. They are innocent victims of poverty and loss.

Mister President: I ask that we take a vote on the proposal.

The measure did not pass.

Chapter Two
Indentured Servitude

Pursued by a big, black monster, with its wailing in his ears and feeling the hot breath of the creature on him, John stumbled as he tried to escape. His body ached, his heart raced. Suddenly awake, he knew he was in a real bed. But where? He sat bolt upright, shivering. He opened his eyes. Blackness. The beast might have swallowed him. He was buried in black wool. He could see nothing. He listened. He heard not a sound. *Where am I?* Then he remembered the strange guttural voice of the woman he had heard earlier in the day. He saw in his mind's eye the big man who drove him in the wagon to this distant place. The man who smelled of animals and earth. A wave of sadness washed over him. He was in the farmhouse.

Suddenly he heard a baby crying followed by the creak of bedsprings. He heard the woman, crooning low. Gradually the infant ceased his crying. *The baby. What was his name? Robbie. No, that was the older one. William? No, what was it?* John lay down again, but he remained awake for some time, finally crying himself back to sleep. The dream of the black monster that brought him here came often over the next several months and always filled him with terror and a profound sense of loss.

Late in the afternoon of that day, John had sat in the wagon next to the man for whom he would work on the farm. When he'd been taken off the train, Mr. Duggan and the priest, Father Lamesch, brought him to Mr. Coyne. They'd told him this man was his foster father. *I have a father. I don't need a father. This man is a stranger.* Before he even had time to think, he was pushed into the road and lifted up to sit on the wagon next to the man named Coyne. As they rode, he found he could lean against the barrels behind him.

Some time earlier, when they had pulled into Yankton, the first stop in Dakota, a small group of boys, Tom among them, was called to the door of the car. Others had left the train in Sioux City, Iowa. "No," Mr. O'Connor had stopped John, trying to follow his brother. "You stay here."

John had given an anguished cry, "My brother." Tom had turned ashen as he looked back into the car. Mr. Duggan held Tom firmly by the arm as he led him away.

Mr. O'Connor had led John struggling back to the bench, sitting next to him and holding his head into his chest as the child cried. In a few minutes, Mr. Duggan had returned without his brother and the others;

the train continued on its way. John's stop was about fifteen miles south of Mitchell at a small town called Ethan.

Later as they rode along on the buggy, filled with barrels and large sacks, the farmer asked, "How're you doing, young fellow?"

"All right, I guess." He was so tired. He looked around at the fields. "Where are we going?"

"Home, Boy," Mr. Coyne laughed expansively. "We're going to your new home on the farm."

This man is confused. Home is on the other side of the world, back in Boston. How could this be home? He was just going to Dakota and back. Tom said it on the train. The Sister promised he wasn't going to stay here forever – just help with the farm work. But they lied. Tom and he had the same tags on their jackets, and Tom was gone. Where did they take him?

The man interrupted his thoughts, "And you'll have two little brothers," he said proudly. "We have two boys."

He didn't want two brothers; he already had a brother and sister. He said nothing. Later he asked, "Where are all the houses? Doesn't any one live here?" All he saw was grass.

The driver laughed. "Well, this is wide open country, and people are just beginning to move here. Pioneer land. We've only been here for about three years ourselves, the Missus and me. We staked our claim, built our house and barns, and have planted wheat, soybeans, and sorghum. Yield was small the first two years, but we'll expand this year and hopefully do better." He peered down trying to see the child's face. "You ever milk a cow?"

"No," John said in a small voice. He had only seen cows at a distance, not even up close.

"Well, you'll learn tonight. That'll be one of your regular chores. I got your jobs all lined up for you." The wagon turned a corner. "There's our farm!" Mr. Coyne exclaimed, pointing proudly to a cluster of buildings, hugging one another.

Already late in the day, the sun hung low in the sky, bathing everything in a red tint. John saw several unpainted buildings: the house, the barn, and other small outbuildings. Smoke curled out of the house. He could hear the clucking of the chickens in the hen house. Mr. Coyne hopped down and, after helping John down, handed him his bag. "Go ahead in. Mrs. Coyne is waiting for you. I'll be along in a minute." He pointed to the door of the house, where a dog looked menacingly at him. The child hesitated. Mr. Coyne assured him, "The dog won't hurt you. Go right along on in."

John walked up the few stairs, opened the door and stepped into the kitchen, small and cramped with a table and chairs, sideboards, butter churn, and cradle. The woman with her back to him was busy at work at the hearth. After a few moments of standing awkwardly, first on one foot and then the other, he said in as loud a voice as he could muster, "Hello, I'm John."

She turned and eyed him. *"Johann, welkommen."* He didn't understand her, she didn't sound welcoming, and he saw no welcome in her eyes. Her harsh voice seemed to come from deep within her. *Didn't she speak English?* The baby howled in his cradle. A second child, a two-year-old, waddled toward him. Mrs. Coyne picked up the infant, soothed him and said, "Charles," gesturing to the baby. Then, "Robert," pointing to the toddler. Robert stopped a few feet from him and looked at him with interest.

Mr. Coyne entered the kitchen. "I see you met the boys." He lifted the older child into his arms and stood beside Mrs. Coyne. They all looked at him. "This is our new boy. What do you think?"

The woman answered in her guttural tongue. They talked in German while John shifted uncomfortably because he knew they talked about him. She pointed, *"Zu klein. Warum? Ve vant gros."* Eventually he learned that to her he was always too small; she wanted someone older and bigger.

The man shrugged and said to him, "Come. I'll show you where you'll sleep. Follow me." He headed into the next room, still carrying his son. "Can you manage your satchel?"

John nodded and followed him, not into a room, but up narrow stairs just inside the door to the second floor. As he climbed, he felt like he was being sucked into a hollow tube. What further terrors awaited him? He could hardly move his leaden feet on the narrow, steep stairs.

"Come on, Boy." The child felt himself being pushed into a room on the left. "There it is. Your new room. What do you think?" He looked at the room, not at John. "We haven't hung the doors yet," he said almost apologetically. "Eventually."

John stumbled in, dropped his bag, and sat on the bed. He put his hand down on the quilt – not a drab brown like in the home but a myriad of bright colors – not stiff either, but soft and almost inviting. Opposite the bed, he saw a box on which sat a towel, pitcher, and basin. Mr. Coyne said, "Under the bed is a chamber pot if you need to use it in the night. I'll show you the privy after we eat." He paused looking around the room. "Supper is almost ready." He pointed across the hall to the other rooms. "Ma and me are in here. And over here is Robbie – this fellow here. There's another room beyond ours. Still empty for now. How does everything suit you?"

"Fine, sir."

"Sorry we don't have a chest of drawers for you yet. I hope to make you one this winter. You'll have to make do with putting your things in the crate for now. See how it's turned on its side so you have an opening there." Next he showed where he put nails to hang up his clothes. He shifted the child in his arms and said, "Wash your hands and face and come on down. Mrs. Coyne left water, a bar of soap and a towel for you there. You can unpack later. All right?"

John nodded. Mr. Coyne disappeared down the stairs. The child looked around, trying to piece together what was happening to him, but he was too tired to think. He let himself slide down onto the bed and put his head on the pillow. He must've dozed off, because suddenly he heard a voice call, "John? Are you coming? Supper's on the table."

He rose. "Coming," he said sleepily. He splashed water on his face, rubbed it dry, and went downstairs.

They had not waited. The farmer pointed, "Here, John. Here's a place for you."

John ate hungrily, and when the bowl of stew was empty and Mr. Coyne asked if he wanted more, he nodded and finished the second helping as well. He ate the homemade bread and downed the glass of milk – his first hot meal since he left the Orphan Home over a week ago.

The farmer and his wife talked with one another in German. Finally, the man turned to him and said, "Mrs. Coyne doesn't speak much English yet, but you'll learn the German. I did. Now if you're done, we'll take a little look around." He headed to the door. "Come along."

John rose and stumbled along behind him. *Just to rest. I need to sleep.*

After they took turns using the privy, Mr. Coyne said, "Now we'll take a short tour. You'll see more of the farm in the daylight."

He pointed off to a distant point. "There to the west are the fields. We'll start the plowing soon." He glanced down at him. "Ever walk behind a plow?"

John looked at the flat bare ground and shook his head. Everything was so big.

His guide pointed in another direction. "And here to the south is the grazing area for the cattle. That's what this farm is really about – raising cattle." He spread his arms, "See down the gully. We have a creek and farther along a small pond. Perfect. Never have to worry about bringing them to the water."

John nodded again. He just saw a lot of grass. Darkness wanted to swallow him.

"Now it's on to the evening chores. I'll show you the cattle in the daylight." He headed toward the barn. "Come with me."

John found it hard to move. Half asleep, his legs felt leaden.

Mr. Coyne turned to see where he was. "What's the matter?" When he saw John's sleepy eyes, he said, "You need to go to bed. Go back to the house," he said annoyed, "I'll show you your chores tomorrow." John stood, not moving. "Never mind," he spoke more gently. "Come on. You need a bath. Then you can go to bed." He took John by the arm and led him to the house. "When was the last time you changed your clothes?"

John mumbled, "I don't know. When we left the Home."

He stopped, looking at him incredulously, "You've been wearing the same things since last week?" He pushed him into the kitchen. "Rosa, *wasser,*" he called. "Set up the tub. This boy needs a good scrubbing."

John stood while Mr. Coyne poured cold water from one bucket into a huge tub, adding hot water from another bucket on the stove. He helped him undress; then he started to bathe him. Mrs. Coyne took John's clothes in a pile, holding her nose in the air. When she returned, the man left, and she washed his hair; when he was finished she helped him out, handing him a towel. Suddenly he remembered how Sister Beatrice had scrubbed him and Tom at the Orphan Home. Where was Tom? Tears sprang to his eyes. Maybe the man would know. He couldn't ask *her*. He couldn't understand anything she said. She handed him a nightshirt and walked him upstairs, putting him to bed.

John felt his arm being shaken by the farmer. "Come along, Boy. Time to do the morning chores. Get your clothes on and meet me downstairs."

John wiped the sleep from his eyes. The room was pitch black. From the lamplight in the hall he found the chamber pot. He washed his hands and face, took his clean clothes out of his bag, dressed, pulled on his shoes and his jacket.

When he entered the kitchen, Mrs. Coyne grunted, *"Guten morgen."*

Mr. Coyne stood at the door waiting, "Don't dawdle, Boy."

John had to skip along to keep up with the farmer. He felt like he was sleepwalking still. Last night he had a fitful sleep filled with nightmares in a strange house where he lived with strangers. Mr. Coyne opened the barn door and he followed him inside. His nostrils were assailed with the smells of the animals, and when his stomach rebelled, he retched.

The man said, not unkindly, "You'll get used to the smells. Relax.

Today, watch me. Tomorrow I'll let you help." He set to work, demonstrating how to milk a cow.

How will I ever learn? The animal is so large. He tried to listen to the instructions, but he couldn't concentrate. On the way back to the house, they stopped at the pump where Mr. Coyne showed him how to fill the water bucket. They washed their hands and brought the two buckets into the house — one of milk and the other of water. "This will be another of your regular jobs," he said, "making sure Mrs. Coyne always has enough water in the kitchen." John knew he could barely carry one bucket, never mind two pails. Too heavy. He'd have to make two trips.

The kitchen felt warm after the cool outdoors and barn. Robert sat at the table, eating his cereal while Mrs. Coyne cradled the infant Charles in the crook of one arm. Without putting the baby down, she ladled out oats for her husband and John. She said, *"Setzen sie auch,"* and pointed to the same chair he had sat in last evening.

John ate his breakfast hungrily as he listened to the babbling of the two-year-old, and the husband and wife in their half German-half English exchange. Mr. Coyne leaned over to John. "Ma says to hang up your towel. Don't throw it on the floor. There's a nail on the wall." He laughed. "She'll call you '*Dummkopf*' if you do something stupid like that."

"What's that?" John asked meekly.

"It means 'stupid.' There's your first German lesson. *Dummkopf.*" He looked at his wife and they both laughed again. Then he turned back to John. "All right?"

John winced but said, "All right." Mrs. Coyne smirked. No smile in her eyes. He lowered his head. He didn't want the man to see his tears.

Mr. Coyne said again, "I put several nails up on the wall for you. Hang your jacket on one, your towel on another."

"Yes, sir." He felt like his mouth was full of cotton batting. He found it hard to hold up his head and keep his eyes open. The man shook him gently and said, "Go back to bed, John. I'll start you on your work later." He turned to Mrs. Coyne and laughing said, "Looks like the train travel just tuckered this boy out."

Stumbling, John left the kitchen, climbed the stairs slowly, removed his jacket and shoes and tumbled into bed, pulling the quilt up. Instantly, he fell into a deep sleep, this one undisturbed, in contrast to last night's with the big, black monster. Physically exhausted from the long journey of several days, he also felt the pain of loss. Ripped from all he knew in the city and at the Orphan Home, he felt exiled in a foreign world. His mother died; his father disappeared; Mary stayed in Boston. Now Tom was gone, too. He had no one.

He awoke several hours later to find the woman standing in the doorway. She said, *"Comme zu mitt,"* and disappeared again down the stairs. The sun shone brightly through the uncurtained, narrow windows. He rose, splashed his face with water, making sure he hung the towel on the nail just above the pitcher. Now he saw the nails all in a row. He put on his shoes and jacket and joined the others for lunch.

When he entered the kitchen, another stranger was sitting at the table. Mr. Coyne said "George, this is John Donahue – all the way from Boston to learn how to be a farmer. John, this is George, my farmhand."

The man grabbed John's hand and said, "Welcome to Dakota, young fellow," giving him a toothy grin. "We'll make a farmer of you in jig time." His hands were rough and callused, but his eyes were bright and welcoming. George peered closely and, without taking his eyes off John, said, "Mike, he looks a might puny. You're gonna have to fatten him up a bit, I reckon."

"Oh, I'm not worried," Mr. Coyne said. "He's been living in the city in an orphan home. Give him a few weeks of fresh air, good exercise, and a few home cooked meals and he'll be strong enough." He turned to John and asked, "Well, how you are feeling? Get enough sleep finally?"

"Yes, sir. I'm better now." John started to eat, finding that he was hungry.

"Good, after lunch I'll show you around the place and get you started on your chores." He poked George on the arm and said, "This child slept all night and all morning. I hope that's going to be enough for awhile." As he ate his lunch he ignored the two men talking about the work. *George is like me, a worker. And he's the only one to make me feel welcome.*

Later the farmer took John around the farm. The boy couldn't take it all in – so much land. Land that went up and down small hills. Mr. Coyne asked, "What do you think of my land?"

He didn't know. He mumbled, "Good." He thought the man would like to hear that.

"Good? Is that all you can say?" he exclaimed. "This is prime country. You know what Pa says?" He laughed easily, "Reminds him of the old country." They walked south along the ridge of the hill. "'Course I never saw the old country because I was born in England, God forgive me. But he says that this is what Ireland looks like. I guess I have my piece of Heaven here." They headed toward a large herd of cattle feeding in the pasture. "What do you think of my stock?"

"I don't know what you mean." *What does he want me to say?*

"The cattle, the cows," the farmer said impatiently as he swept a wide arc with his arm.

"They're good." He looked at the huge animals, then up at the farmer. "What do you do with them?"

Mr. Coyne's voice took on an edge of irritation. "We fatten them up, sell them to market."

"Why?"

"So we have money, Boy. That's what it's all about."

John faced the east. "What was that?" he asked excitedly.

The farmer turned to where John pointed. "Nothing," he said. "I didn't see anything."

John pointed, insisting, "I saw an animal come out of the ground." They both strained to see if it would reappear. "There it is." John shouted.

Mr. Coyne exploded. "Oh, blast it all! Just when you think you're rid of them, they come back. That means a whole family of prairie dogs. And they're a nuisance. They destroy crops." He started walking back to the barn. "If you see one, you know there's a family. We'll have to get rid of them."

John had stayed rooted to the spot, fascinated by the small creature. Suddenly he lunged at the man's retreating back and pounded on him with his fists. "Where's my brother?" Tears of anger and frustration sprang to his eyes. "What have they done with my brother?"

Mr. Coyne turned back, took John's hands in his, and laughing said, "Is that what's bothering you, young fellow?"

John slipped to the ground with his head in his hands. The farmer crouched down next to him. "You're worried about your brother?" he asked. He laid his hands on John's shoulder.

"Where is he? When will I see him again?" the child moaned.

Mr. Coyne soothed him, "It's all right."

"I'll never see him again," he sniffled. "I lost my mother, my father, my sister. Now they took my brother away from me."

"No, your brother is not far. You'll see him again."

"When?" With tear-stained face, he looked doubtfully at the man. "They told us we were going to the same farm," he insisted. "They lied."

"No," Mr. Coyne said again. "They didn't lie. Your brother is on my father and mother's farm – twenty miles south of here. You'll see him. When we visit them. When they visit us. And in church."

"Really?" John looked at him hopefully through his tears.

"Really," Mr. Coyne assured him. "Do you have a handkerchief in your pocket?" When John shook his head, he reached into his back pocket and handed him his. "Wipe your face and your eyes. Then come along. We have work to do."

When they got back to the farmyard, he showed him the pigsty and the hen house, introduced him to the dog Dusty who helped with the cattle, told him the names of the horses and cows and cats. Each animal had a job to do on the farm. John was overwhelmed with all he had to learn.

Several weeks later Mr. Coyne called up the stairs. "John, come down here."

The child descended the stairs with a questioning look. "Yes, Mr. Coyne?"

"Where were you?" the man demanded.

He put his head down and said quietly, "In my room."

"What were you doing?" The farmer spoke sharply.

"I was reading my book, sir."

"But you have work to do."

John said, "I did my chores, sir."

"Don't you 'sir' me." Mr. Coyne mimicked John with biting sarcasm. "I did my chores, sir." John put his head down. "Do you think I paid all that money for you to come here and then let you sit in a room and read?" He shouted angrily.

"No, sir." John kept his head down and spoke almost in a whisper. His heart sank. *Is this it? My life is not my own. It was bad enough in the Orphan Home, but it's worse here. Why is this happening to me?*

Mr. Coyne turned away, "I sent for you because I need help. It looks like I'm not getting what I paid for. Maybe I should just send you back." John remained silent. The farmer turned back to him. "Come along. We have fences to mend, rocks to move out of the fields, and a dozen other things to do around the farm today." He headed toward the door.

"Yes, sir."

"One more thing." He whirled around to face the child squarely and pointed a finger at him. "Don't you let me see you sneak off to read again. This is a big farm, with lots of jobs to do all the time, and I don't expect you to be reading when there's work to be done." He glared at him. "And If I can't use you, you're to work for Mrs. Coyne in the house. God knows she has enough to do." He made a sweeping gesture around the kitchen taking in her myriad tasks. "You just march yourself in here and she'll give you something to do."

John hung his head even lower. "Yes, sir."

He went on, "When we finish the chores in the morning, I want you to ask me what the jobs are for the day, and I promise you there'll be work everyday." When the child didn't answer, the farmer added bitterly, "I don't know what kind of a bargain I thought I was getting from Boston. I thought I'd get a worker, not a slacker. Come along. We'll go to the barn and get the tools we need to mend the fence. This is a two-person job." They headed to the barn.

Later that afternoon, when they come in from the fields and were cleaning up at the pump, they heard a team and wagon pulling into the yard. John's brother Tom and an old man got down.

Mr. Coyne greeted the man, "Hello, Pa. What brings you to this neck of the woods?" Father and son walked to the stoop where they sat side by side.

Grandpa Coyne said, "Hello, son. Let me rest my weary bones."

The two brothers could hardly contain themselves, so excited were they to see one another. They embraced awkwardly, then wandered to the edge of the yard where they sat on the ground.

"We went into town to get supplies, and your Ma said I should stop to see how you're getting on," the old man said.

Mr. Coyne smiled, "We're doing okay." The two watched the two redheaded children sitting across the yard. He waved in the direction of the Donahues. "Well, that one. Sometimes I wonder if taking in an orphan was the best thing. Sometimes he's more bother than he's worth. You have to tell him everything. And he'd rather be reading than working."

Grandpa Coyne placed a hand on his son's arm. "Give him a chance, Mike. All this is new to them. Hell, I remember when you were that age and how you hated work." He paused, watching the boys. "You'd never miss the fact that they're brothers," he mused almost to himself.

"Shoot. That was different," his son exploded. "We were crawling around in a coal mine. It was cold and dark and smelly. Here he's out in this good clear air. We've had such good sunny days lately. I don't get it. You'd think he'd want to be outside."

"You know," he nodded in sympathy, "young Tom's okay. They've had a tough time of it. Their Ma died when they were real little and their Pa put them in that Orphan Home and disappeared. We've gotta give them time to get used to us and our ways. They didn't have to work much before they came here – just mainly went to school." He paused. "Wait a minute. You were twelve years old when you worked in the mine. John's a lot younger than that, isn't he?" They sat quietly for a few minutes. Then he added, "Tom is smart as a whip."

The younger Coyne said, "John is smart enough. And when I show him how to do something, I don't have to show him a second time. It's just he wants to be reading all the time."

"Nothing wrong with that. Better'n mooning over some filly, which he'll be doing some years down the road." They sat quietly for some minutes. "How's Rosa? And the babies?"

"Fine." He stood and extended his hand to his father. "Come on in and say hello. Rosa's cooking supper." He helped his father up, and they stepped into the house.

Meanwhile, the brothers were having their own conversation once they got over their initial awkwardness. John said, "He was angry at me this morning because I was reading after I finished my chores. He told me I had to ask every day about the jobs for the day. I read yesterday and there was no problem."

His brother assured him, "Don't worry. That's what farm work is, I reckon. Some days you gotta work and some days you have time to yourself."

"That's it," he complained. "I just want time to myself. Every minute, it's 'Do this. Come here. Fetch that.' He's nice enough – most of the time. He shows me how to do things and teaches me stuff. It's hard with her, though, because she mostly speaks German. And he told me today I've gotta help her with the house work too." He shook his head as if in disbelief, adding, "When he doesn't have work for me to do."

Tom laughed, "Maybe you want to learn some German."

"I already learned one word," he sounded chagrined.

"What's that?"

John spat out the word, "*Dummkopf.*"

"What does that mean?"

"Stupid. She called me stupid the first day because I didn't hang up my towel on the nail on the wall. I didn't even know there were nails to hang up things."

Tom exhaled with an "Oh." They sat quietly for a few minutes, each of them pulling on a blade of grass.

John looked at his brother and asked quietly, "Do you think they'll let us go to school?"

"They have to. It's the law. Grandpa Coyne showed me the papers about indentured servants where it says it. That's what they call us – indentured servants. But right now things are too busy. Grandma Coyne says we'll go as soon as the busy time is finished." Since Tom faced the house, he saw the men step inside. "They're going in the house. Grandpa Coyne wants to see the babies. Grandma Coyne told him she wants a full report on her grandchildren."

John screwed up his face and asked quietly, "Why do you call them

Grandpa and Grandma? They're no kin to us."

"They asked me to, and it's just as easy as saying Mr. and Mrs. Coyne."

"I'm never going to call these people mother and father because they don't want me to. Besides they're not my parents." John spoke earnestly, "Tom, we have a mother and father and no one can take their place. I don't care if they're dead or if they abandoned us. We've got to remember who we are. These people are all right but they're strangers. It's like when we were in the Orphan Home. That wasn't our home either."

When the two men came out of the house Tom and John jumped up. Tom said, "It looks like we'll be going now. We've got to get back before it gets dark." They walked slowly to the men, who stood by the wagon.

Grandpa Coyne smiled at John, "Looks like we'll see you again real soon, young fellow. We're all getting together in two weeks." The younger man helped his father up onto the wagon. The two boys embraced. Mr. Coyne went back into the house, but John watched the wagon as long as he could see it moving down the road. He was alone, and in spite of his own resolutions to be brave, felt tears on his cheeks.

On a cool morning, not too many days later, John stood stock-still with a dumb-struck look on his face. Mr. Coyne turned and saw John covered with a real mess. "What happened to you, Boy?" he exploded.

Tears sprang to John's eyes. "I don't know," he wailed. "I was just going to the next stall and the cow …" He was splattered in cow manure.

"Come with me," Mr. Coyne ordered.

He took him to the well, where he filled a bucket. "Now stand still and I'll pour water over you a couple of times to get rid of most of the mess. Then …"

"Ow, it's cold," John jumped when the water hit him.

"You know the water's going to be cold." Mr. Coyne spoke sharply, "Don't be such a baby. Stand still. We've got to get rid of this mess."

John stood dripping and shivering.

After several dousings, Mr. Coyne said, "Take off your clothes and put them in the bucket there. And go, get dry clothes." He pointed to the house. "And remember after this not to go behind the cattle."

John sniffled. "I tried to, but the cow hit me with her tail and I slipped."

"Leave your shoes outside the door." He stopped him. "No … Wait. I think you need to take a good wash in the tub. I'll go in and fill it. Stay here until I call you." He turned to look at John again. "The stuff's even in your hair. You are a sight."

John disrobed and waited outside the door. He shivered in the early morning chill. Soon Mr. Coyne called, "Come on. The water is still cool but the tub is next to the stove."

He entered and stepped into the tub. Robbie slid down from his chair and toddled over, but his mother scooped him up just before he got wet and said, "*Nein, bleiben.*" She handed him to her husband who sat eating his breakfast. She picked up the yellow lye soap and washcloth, knelt beside the tub and washed his hair. "*Ach, mein Gott in Himmel. Das ist schade.*" She wrinkled her nose. "Phew. *Wondervoll.*"

Mr. Coyne said, "Did you hear that? Ma says you're wonderful." The adults erupted in laughter, Robbie squealed in delight. John saw the humor, too and joined in the laughter. Mrs. Coyne scrubbed his hair, neck, ears, and back. Finally, she heaved herself up and left him to finish. He stepped out of the tub and wrapped himself in the towel she had laid out for him. He winked at Robbie and headed upstairs to get dressed. Robbie squirmed out of his father's arms and followed him, crawling on the bed to watch. "Can we play?" he asked.

"When I finish my chores, we'll play." He was buttoning his shirt when the farmer called impatiently, "John, let's go. We've got work to do."

"Coming." He descended the stairs into the kitchen with Robbie trailing behind. Mr. Coyne waited at the door. "I haven't had breakfast yet," he pleaded, looking at the food on the table.

"Oh, all right," Mr. Coyne grumbled. "Sit down and eat. I'll be in the field. Join me there." He turned back, "No, wait a minute. Before you sit down, help me empty the tub. We can't leave that for Mrs. Coyne. Bad enough she'll have to wash your clothes." They lifted the tub and carried it to the door where they dumped it away from the house. After his morning oats John joined the farmer. He walked barefoot because his shoes were wet.

He promised himself it wouldn't happen again.

John, whose chin barely reached above the pew, knelt in church next to Mr. Coyne. Mrs. Coyne sat on the other side of her husband holding the baby with Robbie by her side. John watched the priest at the altar say Mass. He remembered church in Boston. *In the Orphan Home we had Mass every day and visited the chapel for prayers several times a day. Now we only go to church when it rains. Things are sure different here.* What wasn't different was the Mass or Latin or the people around him all fingering the beads. *I'll bring my rosary next time.*

Earlier that morning when they had finished their chores, Mr. Coyne had surprised him by announcing, "Wash up and get ready. We're going to church."

John looked up quickly. After living on the farm for almost a month, he had forgotten all about church. He really didn't know one day from another. Every day was the same – work and chores and always being tired and dirty. Work in the barn, work in the fields, work around the house. He asked, "Is it Sunday?"

"No," Mr. Coyne chuckled. "It's Wednesday, but we haven't been able to go on Sundays because the days were too good to lose in the fields. But since it's raining, we'll go. They have Mass one day a week in Rome besides Sunday." He handed the towel to John.

"Will my brother be there?" he looked hopefully up at the farmer.

"Probably." They hitched up the team to the wagon. Then he said, "Go, tell Mrs. Coyne we're ready to leave. Come on. Get a move on." He reached down and smoothed John's hair in a rare gesture of gentleness. "Get your jacket and hat."

When John hurried into the house, he almost knocked down Mrs. Coyne who was coming out with the two boys. She told him to hurry, *"Gehen sie schnell."*

A minute later when he returned, Mr. Coyne pointed, reminding him, "Close the door, Boy." He turned back to pull the door closed. He jumped up in the back of the wagon and asked again, "Will my brother be there?"

"I don't know. Probably." Irritated, Mr. Coyne turned slightly in the seat to look at him. "They might be there. Who knows?"

After they rode for a few miles, John asked, "How can we go to Rome? Isn't that where the pope lives?"

"You silly goose," Mr. Coyne laughed. "We're not going to Rome, Italy. We're going to Rome, Dakota. It's a town just south of here." The Coynes laughed, and he heard that word *dummkopf* again. *I'm not stupid. Just confused.*

During Mass his thoughts wandered. He found it difficult to understand why they didn't go to church on Sunday and yet they prayed daily. On John's first full day at the farm, just before bedtime the farmer had said, "We'll say the beads now. Do you have a Rosary?"

"Yes, they're in my bag upstairs. Should I get them?"

"Yes, go," Mr. Coyne said pointing upstairs. "You can find them quickly?" John nodded. He hurried upstairs. After waiting some minutes,

Mr. Coyne called up the stairs. "Where are you, Boy? I'm waiting."

Tears of frustration clouded John's eyes. He had so few things, yet he couldn't find his beads. He cried, "I can't find them."

"Never mind. Come down and use your fingers."

John entered the kitchen, sniffling; he wiped his nose on his sleeve.

Mr. Coyne scolded, "Don't be such a baby." He got up from his chair by the hearth and knelt behind it. "We'll pray every evening before we go to bed. Sometimes Ma's not able to join us when she has to tend to the children." The child knelt and saw for the first time the crucifix over the cabinet in the corner. He wanted God to send him back home. *Perhaps it's all been a mistake and I'm not supposed to be here.* Every night for months, he prayed the same prayer. In church he prayed for release from the life he now had – living with strangers, always working.

As the years went on, John came to love the excursions to church because indeed Tom was often there with the elder Coynes, and they usually had a chance to talk, even if just for a few minutes. He also liked to look at the altar and the statues and the stained glass windows. He liked the smell of wax candles and the incense. He liked hearing the rhythm of the Latin and the hymns. He liked the peace and quiet of the church. He liked being with people and knowing that others existed besides the Coyne family. He felt isolated on the farm, seeing no one else for weeks.

On the way back from church, John asked, "Mr. Coyne, what's the difference between a chapel and a church? You called it church today, and in the Orphan Home we called it a chapel. They look the same to me."

"Oh, John. You are full of questions." He thought for a minute. "Well, I don't rightly know, but I guess that a church is for regular people and a chapel is for nuns. The place you lived in had nuns? Right?"

"Yes," he said, settling back to watch the scenery. It was his first trip off the farm, and he marveled at the wide expanse of land and sky. The rain had stopped, and he saw fields and meadows in every direction. He mused aloud, "Everything is so different here. No trees, no houses, just fields." No one answered. *It's like we live on an island at the farm.*

John stood on the rung of the fence behind the house gazing toward the east horizon. As far as the eye could see, he looked at waving grasses – tall and undulating, bending and lifting again and again.

What is this? It seems to be some kind of sea – an odd sea, yes, but still some kind of sea. He listened, hearing a *whish, whish.* Yes, it was the same sound he heard at the beach. He fingered the seashells in his trouser pocket. Sometimes he carried them to connect to the past.

He thought of the day they spent at the beach when he lived at the Orphan Home in Boston. Some women prepared lunch and took the children on the train. He stood on the edge, looking at the rolling surf. Most of the others ran into the water immediately, but he stayed motionless, watching the water moving forward and retreating repeatedly. He did not run to the water. He looked on it with a kind of awe. This moving water could bring danger. It could swallow him up. Since his mother died, he'd been tossed back and forth. His father put them in the Orphan Home; then he came for them and tried to raise the children with Rose Ann's help. But when she left, he brought them back to the Orphan Home and disappeared.

Now John seemed to be looking at the same kind of scene. The light breeze moved the grasses to and fro. The colors varied from yellow to tan to green, whereas the seawater had shades of gray blue, green, tan and white.

At the beach he had wondered what it would be like to take a boat ride. And if he did, would he be set adrift? Lost forever? Swallowed up by the sea? His body gave an involuntary shudder because he knew he was on the boat that carried him so far that he was set adrift. No one would find and rescue him; he would wander out here endlessly. His father and mother were dead, so they couldn't help him. He would never see his sister again, and his brother seemed happy with his new family. These people were not family. Isolated, lost, alone. He turned his eyes full of tears to the house. It stared at him with empty eyes. It gave him no warmth, no welcome, no feeling of home or sense of belonging.

The summer storm rocked the house; the wind and rain rattled the windows and chimney; lightning flashes lit up the kitchen, followed by the booming thunder. In the kitchen Mr. Coyne and John sat at the table, while Mrs. Coyne busied herself at the stove.

Mr. Coyne lifted his head at a loud thunder crash. "Ah, a storm like this reminds me of the stories of the fairy folk that my father used to tell. Stories of the wee folk in Ireland and the mischief they do."

With a pang John remembered his father telling stories from Ireland. "My Da told us about the fairies." His voice sounded louder than he wanted it to be. He felt his face get hot.

"Did he now?" Mr. Coyne looked up at him from the accounts. "Do you remember your father, then?"

John retreated. "Not much," he mumbled.

"But you remember about the banshees?" He didn't wait for an answer, but put his pencil down and launched into stories of the Irish spirits. The child barely listened; instead he thought of how his father told of the banshees wailing when his mother died. For years afterwards, he would hear these tales from their common heritage. John went back to his work of cutting carrots for Mrs. Coyne, but his mind flew to the other side of the world where he started. *Had one of the fairies that Mr. Coyne talked about carried him away from his family? Is this why his life was spent among strangers?*

"*Nein, es ist zu gros.* Like so. *Klein.*" He shrank when Mrs. Coyne's large figure loomed over him. She showed him how small she wanted the pieces of carrots. Just as suddenly, she returned to her work at the stove.

Gradually, the wind and rain calmed down. The worst of the storm had passed. The farmer went to look out the door. "I'm afraid we've lost the crops. But I don't think we can blame the fairies for this mischief." He stood, looking out for several minutes in silence.

The following morning the sun shone down hot, though still early in the day. After breakfast, Mr. Coyne said to no one in particular, "It's going to be a scorcher." He turned to his farmhand, "George, I want you and John to go to the south field and check it out." He put his hat on and turned with a final comment, "I'm afraid the plants didn't survive yesterday's rains. I'll check on the cattle."

"Sure. Mike," George said, getting up and heading to the door. He gestured for John to follow him.

As they walked across the field, John fell behind. George turned to him and said, "What's the problem?"

"My feet hurt," John complained.

George came back. "Show me your shoes." He put his left hand down to steady him and with the other hand lifted John's foot to look at the bottom. "Look at those holes. You gotta get another pair of shoes. Tell Mr. Coyne you need shoes."

"I need boots." John said. Even he knew the shoes the Orphan Home gave him were too flimsy for work in the fields.

George looked down at him. "How long have you had these?"

"They were new when I came from Boston."

"And you've been here several months. Right?"

"I guess." He shrugged. "Mr. Coyne said he'd take these to the cobbler."

"Well, we're almost there. Just keep walking." He spoke even more kindly. "And watch where you're walking. Don't step on the stubble.

And, I'll slow down for your little legs."

"What are we looking for?" John asked. "I don't even know what we're supposed to look for. All he said was to check on the plants." He walked along slowly, watching his steps.

"You'll know when we get there. The heavy rains we had yesterday probably destroyed the crop. We'll have to plow it under and plant a new crop."

"But why? It was rain. I thought rain helped plants to grow."

George stopped walking, put his hands on his hips and looked into his face. "Are you daft? That rain was heavy and with our sandy soil here, it just washes everything away." He shook his head and walked on. When they arrived at the field George said, "See the plants – all ruined. They didn't have a chance as new growth. If they were more mature, they'd've been able to hold on." He reached down and came up with a handful of dust and dried leaves. As far as the eye could see the field looked devastated. Some plants drooped while others had washed away down between the rows. "So now you know what to look for when we have another storm. Right? We'll have to plow it under and start all over again."

"Oh, I see." *I helped to plow and plant this field, and it's all for nothing.*

They headed back to the barn. The sun shone, high and hot, the sky a ball of fire. The one break in the heat had been the heavy rainstorm of yesterday. John felt like his whole body burned, his face, his arms. He wondered if he would shrivel up like those young plants.

George interrupted his thoughts. "When we get back, you go right in and tend to those feet. Ask Mrs. Coyne for some ointment. I'll talk to Mr. Coyne about getting those shoes taken care of right away. Maybe he'll buy you a pair of boots. Those shoes they gave you in Boston don't look like farmer's shoes."

"Thanks, George." John smiled gratefully at the man who was always so kind to him, so easy to talk to.

Another long, tiring day. No time to think. Groom the horses, clean out the stalls, feed the chickens, the hogs, the dogs, collect the eggs, bring in wood and water, grab the cobs from the pigsty for fuel in the stove. *It doesn't end. To the fields to push the plow up and down rows that lasted forever. Too much to do.* He hated the smells of animals and manure and dirt.

He worked with Mr. Coyne and often George and another man called Uncle Al. Farm work was hard – almost unbearable. Because he was small, he could only groom the horse by standing on an old chair. He lifted the water bucket or the milk pail or a bale of hay by using all his strength. He walked the long rows in the fields feeling great tedium. The summer sun, relentless and strong, had burned his fair skin several times. He burned, and then blistered again and again. His feet hurt. His hands blistered. He developed calluses. If he complained Mrs. Coyne said, "*Aller anfang ist schwer.*" And Mr. Coyne told him that meant, "All beginnings are hard." Neither of them gave him any sympathy.

He didn't understand why he had to come here where the only people he saw were the Coynes, the two babies, and the farm help. He didn't understand why he had to do so much work. Life at the Orphan Home was different. He went to school, he worked a little in the yard or garden, and he played games. *I'm just a workhorse here with no time for myself. I want to go to school. I want to read and learn. Mr. Coyne told me I'd go to school. Soon enough, he said. When I get the chance, I'll learn. I will not spend my whole life working on a farm.*

In early September, on a Sunday evening, after chores and prayers, just before he went up to bed, Mr. Coyne put his hand on his shoulder, "John, you're going to school tomorrow. Now that the harvest's in, I can spare you for a bit. We'll get an early start. Right after breakfast. That all right with you?"

"Yes, Mr. Coyne." John had mixed feelings: dread because it was a new school and he didn't know any of the other children, but also delight because he wanted to go to school. He knew, also he might spend time with other boys his age and perhaps play some games. "Will Tom be there?"

"No," Mr. Coyne laughed. "He goes to a school south of here."

In the morning, Mr. Coyne roused him early. "Get up, Boy. You've got to do your chores before we leave. Get dressed and get out to the barn."

"Coming," John said. He splashed water on his face and dressed. After doing his chores, he ate his bowl of morning oats and jumped up as soon as Mr. Coyne called to him from the door, "Come, John, you don't want to be late for your first day of school, do you?"

Mrs. Coyne stopped him, handed him a pail and said, "Der lunch. *Auf wiedersehen.*"

"Thank you," he said grabbing his hat and heading out the door.

Mr. Coyne hollered, "Jump up, Boy." He signaled to the horse. They rode along listening to the morning sounds. "What a long time it took you to do your chores," Mr. Coyne teased. "I don't think you want to go to school."

John bit his lip. It wasn't that at all. He tried to hurry, but milking the cows was never easy for him. And because he was nervous, he found himself more awkward than usual. He said in a small voice, "I want to go to school. I've missed a lot." He picked at a loose thread on his jacket sleeve. "I want to go to school," he repeated with more conviction.

When they pulled up to the schoolhouse, he hopped down. Mr. Coyne said, "Go on in. I'll be back to pick you up at the end of the day. Your teacher knows you're coming. I signed you up one day last week on the way back from town."

What Mr. Coyne didn't tell John was that when he went into town recently, he had met Father Lamesch who asked how the boy was doing in school. After talking to the priest, he knew he had to get John to school as soon as possible. Father reminded him that the law was clear. "You can have him do farm work, but you must see that the child is educated. School's already been in session for several weeks, so get over there and give the teacher his name and age. Mr. Duggan and Sister Angelica from the Orphan Home expect you to do right by these children. Remember, the law on indentured servitude says they have to go to school until they're sixteen."

"Yes, Father. I'll do that today." Mr. Coyne had doffed his hat. He turned it around, looking at it, instead of the priest. "It's just that we've been busy with the harvesting."

Father said earnestly, "Just do what's right for the boy, Mike."

John opened the door and stepped inside. The students were bent over their slates doing sums. The teacher, Miss Bracha, a tall thin woman, motioned him forward. "You must be John. Come here." She stood, smiling to welcome him. "Mr. Coyne said you'd be coming today. I'll have you sit here in front so I can watch to see how well you can read and cipher." She pointed to an empty place with the smallest children.

He heard giggles from the older boys in the back of the room.

"All right, class. That's enough. John Donahue is our new pupil. We welcome you, John, and hope you like it here." She smiled at him. Then she turned back to the others. "Get back to work. I'll be around to check on your exercises in a few minutes, starting with the oldest." The room became very quiet.

A few minutes later the teacher asked him to read for her. Then she watched as he did some exercises. "Very good. Sit here with Rudolph." She spoke kindly. "He'll show you what to do." She led him to a place about half way down the aisle where the boys were about his age. The girls sat on the opposite side of the room.

When his seatmate smiled shyly at him, John returned the smile. *It will be good. I'll be learning again. I'll prove that I'm not a* dummkopf.

At noon, the children took their lunch pails and sat outside on the grass. The early fall day, mild and pleasant offered them welcome. John sat at the fringes of the group who for the most part ignored him. After they ate, the boys lined up to choose teams. John hovered, hoping that one of the sides would choose him. When all the boys had been picked except him, Jacob said, "I'll take the new boy."

His teammate Adolph added, "We'll take you, Red." He pointed at John and laughed. The boys all laughed.

"My name is John," he protested. Now they howled in laughter. He ignored the hooting and stood his ground. "Come on, let's play."

At the end of the day, Mr. Coyne waited in the wagon. "How was the day?" he asked as they headed back home.

"It was good," John said. "It's different because all the children are in one room. In the Home, the girls and the older boys had their own rooms."

When they got back to the farm, Mr. Coyne told him, "Most days you'll have to walk to school. You see how close it is. I won't be able to drive you all the time."

"I know the way," John said. "I can walk."

Mr. Coyne laughed. "Well, lazy bones. You'll have to get up earlier."

John hugged the book under his arm. He had a new book to read. *Let him laugh all he wants.*

Early one November morning Mr. Coyne roused him. "No school today. We've got ourselves a big storm. Come along quickly. We've got to get to the barn to tend to the animals."

Even with the warning, John found himself unprepared for the storm that raged outside. They had snow before this, but now he faced his first prairie blizzard. In the kitchen they donned boots, coats, hats, and mittens. Mr. Coyne warned him to stay close to him because often the drifting snow blinded people and they lost their way within yards of their doorway. John walked in his footsteps holding on to his coattail. The snow bit his cheeks, clouded his eyes and gathered quickly on his coat and hat. When they reached the barn, Mr. Coyne said, "We'll put out double rations for the stock in case we can't get back tonight. If the storm keeps up, it will be dangerous for us to come out again."

When they headed back to the house, the snow flew straight into their faces. Mr. Coyne almost had to drag John. Before entering, they filled several buckets with snow and brought it into the kitchen. "Can't get water from the well," he explained.

They took off their wet coats, hats and boots, shaking them near the door. They were glad for the warmth of the kitchen and for their hot morning oats. The family spent the day in the kitchen near the stove. The light of the kerosene lamp cast eerie shadows on the wall. Mr. Coyne pored over seed catalogs, worked on his accounts and mended equipment, Mrs. Coyne did her regular work of baking and sewing. John was put to work doing dishes and other kitchen duties. The children played with blocks and small, carved figures. Several times John was sent to collect more snow in the buckets. In the afternoon when the children napped, John thought he could read. But Mrs. Coyne set him to work cracking nuts with a hammer. Mr. Coyne saw him struggling and took over, but had John extract the meat from the shell. During other storms closer to Christmas, or on Sunday afternoons, Mrs. Coyne showed him how to string dried apples that would go onto the branches of what they used in place of the Christmas tree. She said, *"Äpfel, nüsse, mandeln."* The treats of the holiday included: apples, nuts, and almonds. They listened as the wind howled, rattling the windows while the snow scraped the sides of the house. When they retired for the night – earlier than usual, they continued to hear the storm buffet the house.

The next morning John awakened to an immense silence. Seeing and hearing nothing, he burrowed deeper under the quilt. He dozed off for a bit until Mr. Coyne called him, "John, get up. The storm is over, and we've got lots to do."

He dressed and hurried downstairs. Mr. Coyne was ready in coat and boots, attaching a long rope around his waist with the other end tied to the back of the door handle. "Get your coat and boots on." He turned to John. "You watch this rope. This makes sure I get back safely. When I get to the barn, I'll yank it like this. You hold onto the rope and join me. Walk in my footsteps." They stepped outside the door. John stood with his hand on the rope waiting. After a few minutes he felt the rope twitch and set out following in Mr. Coyne's footsteps. The snow filled his boots.

In the barn they shook off the snow, clapped their hands and stomped their feet to warm up before tending to the animals. The horses neighed and snorted, the cattle moaned in their stalls. John followed Mr. Coyne, moving down the line, soothing and coaxing. They milked the cows and fed the stock. After breakfast they shoveled a path to the barn and then to the other outbuildings where the snow banks towered over John.

Often on Sundays after lunch, Mrs. Coyne went upstairs and napped with her children. Mr. Coyne sat at the kitchen table settling his accounts, while the eight-year-old John sat on the opposite side working on school lessons. When John tore out a clean piece of paper from the back of his exercise book and wrote, Dear Da, Mr. Coyne looked up and asked with amusement, "What are you doing, Boy?"

"I'm writing a letter to my father in Boston. I'm telling him that he can send for me now because the work is finished." He knew he had to do this. "I want to go home. They told us we were coming to help with the work." He looked up to see Mr. Coyne's mocking smile.

"You're not going anywhere," he sputtered. "And you're certainly not sending any letter."

John repeated doggedly, "I'm writing a letter to my father. I've been here long enough." He swallowed hard, choking on the words, "I want to go home." He watched Mr. Coyne's face get red and the amused expression change to one of anger. He jumped when the man exploded.

"You're not going anywhere, and you're not sending a letter to Boston. This is your home. I paid for you." He added, "Furthermore, the work is not finished. Farm work is never finished. Get that into your head."

John's lips trembled. Tears sprang to his eyes. He gripped his pencil. "But my father ..."

Mr. Coyne yelled, "Your father is dead. I'm the only father you'll ever know." John watched as the farmer reached across the table, snatched the paper and crumpled it. He tossed it across the room into the fire. As John watched the paper burst into flame and disappear, he felt a loss of hope, the hope that he had held with this plan to write a letter to his father. *I'll write to my father and he will send for me. And we can go home. It's too hard living here; it's cold and dark, and I'm always tired.* He grabbed his books and stood, facing Mr. Coyne. "You're not my father. My father is in Boston. He wouldn't make me work the way you do. I hate Dakota. I hate the farm." He paused, and then with a choke he added, "I hate you." And he ran upstairs to throw himself on the bed where he sobbed into the pillow. Mr. Coyne did not follow him.

He woke to feel Robbie's little hand, shaking him gently. "John. Come to supper." He sat up and rubbed his eyes. "I'm coming." He splashed water on his face and followed the toddler down the stairs into the kitchen. Mr. and Mrs. Coyne stood talking at the stove. He slipped into his place, waiting with his eyes on his plate. What would Mr. Coyne say? The couple came to the table, he with the meat platter, she with the plates of vegetables and potatoes. They took their places. After Mr. Coyne said grace and while Mrs. Coyne plated the food, he asked John,

"How are you? Get some sleep?"

He mumbled, "Yes, Sir."

"Good." He carved the meat and talked to Mrs. Coyne in their half German-half English way. John wondered if that was it. *Am I stuck here and he doesn't care?* That night when they knelt to pray the Rosary, Mr. Coyne said, "John, I'm sorry I yelled at you today. I lost my temper." He looked him full in the face. "But, you have to understand this is your home now. Your father will not send for you. He's dead. I'm the only father you'll know from now on."

John mumbled, "I'm sorry too." *My father is not dead. I know he'll send for us.*

On a warm spring afternoon John looked around the schoolroom at his classmates. He listened to the buzz of the voices quietly doing their lessons. Most sat hunched over their books or slates. The second level children sat with the teacher in the front of the room with their *Reader*. Behind him the older children worked on their arithmetic problems. John, who was helping Rupert on his arithmetic problems, looked approvingly at the boy's slate. He felt good that he had learned so much at the Home. He made the most of school, only in session here three months of the fall and spring when they had little farm work.

Rupert nudged him. "Is that right?"

John nodded. "Yes, do you understand it now?"

"Yes. Thanks." His seatmate grinned.

"All right," John said. "Why don't you try these problems?" He turned to the next page.

His partner groaned.

"It's all right," he reassured him. "You can do them. Just do the same thing you did on the last ones."

John turned to his own work, confident in his coaching. He had started to help him several weeks ago. Their teacher had asked him, "See what you can do to help Rupert with his arithmetic when I'm working with the others. He's having trouble." In the beginning the boy had resented his help, but gradually he had warmed to John's gentle prodding.

No longer did the others tease him as they had when he had first come. For months the boys taunted, "Where is your mother? You haven't got a father. You talk funny. You wear funny clothes." No matter that most of them spoke with foreign accents because many were the children of German immigrants. About a month ago he could take the teasing no more. At recess one day, when he heard the familiar chant, he flew at the two most vocal of the boys and punched them. Since he had done nothing before about the taunts, but walked away, he took the tormentors by surprise. The others crowded around to chant, "Fight. Fight." One of the older girls ran into the building to get the teacher who rang the bell for the end of recess.

The onlookers reluctantly ceased their cheers and jeers and looked up. Miss Bracha spoke sternly, "Go into class and continue your work. Clara is in charge. Wilhelm, Adolph, John, come with me." She took them to the bucket of water and said, "Wash your hands and face and then let me look at you to see how badly hurt you are." After they washed their hands and faces, and she saw that they had only bruises and minor cuts, she made them shake hands and apologize – even John. Each mumbled, "Sorry." She said, "John, go into the schoolroom. You two stay," she stopped Wilhelm and Adolph with a look. "I want to talk to you."

John tried to listen, but she spoke very softly. Besides, Clara saw him at the door and told him to take his place and do his work. Maybe it was what the teacher said to the boys or maybe it was because he decided to defend himself, but whatever the reason, the teasing stopped and they gave him a grudging acceptance.

Chapter Three
Growing Years

Early one morning, before they headed to the fields to work, Mr. Coyne stood up from the breakfast table, cleared his throat, and said nervously, "John, Ma and I want to talk to you. We have something we want to ask you. Come along." He waved his hand and headed toward the next room as Mrs. Coyne, wiping her hands on her apron, followed him. The eleven-year-old child trailed after them. *What could they want with him in the parlor?*

"You sit there." The burly man pointed to an overstuffed chair opposite the couch. "Ma and I'll sit on the davenport." Mr. Coyne took his place and shuffled through papers from a large envelope. Finally, he looked at him with what John saw as a forced smile. Mrs. Coyne wore her familiar stern expression, avoiding John's eyes. The child sat uneasily on the chair, the horsehair scratching his arms and legs. He realized his feet didn't touch the floor. Mrs. Coyne pursed her lips and folded her arms across her chest.

"Ma and I've talked. We think it's time we adopted you." Mr. Coyne sounded irritated, even almost angry. "You've lived with us now for a couple of years. We think of you as family. You're another one of our children." Though the man looked at him intently, John saw no warmth or kindness in his eyes. "Robbie and Charley would be your real brothers and Anna Marie your real sister." He added boisterously, "You can even have our name."

"Adopt?" John whispered. His heart pounded and when his leg jumped, he put his hand down to stop it.

"Adopt you," the man repeated. "Make you part of the family." He made a wide sweeping gesture as if taking in everything – the family, the house, the farm.

"Family?" John's voice was still almost inaudible. He shifted in the chair; he couldn't look at them. Instead he fixed his eyes on a patch of wallpaper where he saw a strange kind of pattern. *Why were they doing this?*

Mr. Coyne's voice rose. "Family! Ma and I'd be *your* Ma and Pa."

John's body jumped again involuntarily. "But ..." The words stuck in his throat. *How could I be a part of their family? A family that never shows love – nothing but coldness. Made to work. Made to feel different.* He glanced at Mrs. Coyne, the woman who said so often, "Johann vill eat in kitchen. Johann does not like potatoes. Johann vill clean up." *What about Da? What about*

Boston? He looked back to the farmer and spoke slowly, "I better talk to my brother. I … I don't know." He swallowed hard. Is this what he should do? *Should I say yes?*

"Well John, I'll tell you Grandpa wants to adopt Tom," he reasoned with him. "So you would still both have the same name." He shook the papers at him. "It would just be Coyne, not Donahue." He looked to his wife, and then turned back to John. "We're going to church Sunday. Talk to your brother if you need to. Don't disappoint us, Boy." He paused, shuffling the papers again. "Ma and I are counting on you becoming a member of the family." He turned to her for agreement.

"Ya, das ist richtig." For the first time since he lived with them, John thought he saw a flicker of warmth in her eyes.

Mr. Coyne folded the documents and put them back into the envelope. "Well," he said, standing and towering over John, "We'll talk again." The couple left the room. John sat on, confused and worried. *What was happening? What did it mean? How could he change who he was?*

On Sunday after Mass, Tom and John walked down the road away from the others. Tom took his brother by the arm and whispered, "Did Mr. Coyne ask if they could adopt you?" John nodded. "Grandpa Coyne said they want to have me change my name." The boys looked back across the yard toward where they saw the Coyne family gathered by the wagons.

They walked even farther before John spoke. "They said I'd be a part of the family, but they don't treat me like family," he complained. "They treat me like a slave. Sometimes, they act like they don't even like me. Especially *her!* I've told you how it is with them."

Tom said, "Did you see the papers?" John shook his head. "If we let them adopt us, they can take us out of school when we're twelve. I'm already twelve. I don't want to leave school. If we stay the way we are, they have to let us go to school till we're sixteen." He emphasized the last word. "Besides, Da is still alive and when he gets better he'll send for us."

John, squinting against the morning sun, looked back toward the Coynes. "You're right. We can't let them adopt us." He frowned, "I want to stay who I am. I'm not a Coyne, and I don't want to be a Coyne."

"Grandpa Coyne will be angry. He wants me in the fields or barn all the time." They looked again at the families. "If I don't go to school, he'll make me work even more."

John stood up taller with his head held high. "Besides, we're the Donahues from Boston. Just because we've lost everything else, we don't have to lose our name." He touched Tom's hand lightly. They looked into one another's eyes as if sealing a pact. "We have to remember who we are." Mr. Coyne called them, and they began walking back slowly. "What do I tell them?" John said, under his breath. "What if they make us?"

"Tell them you want to stay who you are," Tom said. "That's all."

"They won't like it."

"You can do it, John," he patted his arm. "I'll do it, too."

The Coyne children were calling for John to come. "Gotta go." John said. "See you next week at the picnic." He squeezed Tom's hand quickly and ran the last few yards, jumping onto the back of the wagon. Irritated, Mr. Coyne signaled to the horses immediately.

Later that night, after the children went to bed, John came back down and stood in the doorway of the kitchen where the Coynes sat drinking their tea. John gripped the back of a chair for support and looked at the table. He was afraid to look at them. "Mr. Coyne, Tom and I talked today, and we agreed we don't want to be adopted." His voice trembled, "I'm much obliged for the offer, but I have to say no."

Husband and wife looked at one another. Mr. Coyne's face darkened. "Goldarn it, John," he exploded, slamming his fist down on the table. He pushed his chair back and stood, his body rigid. He glared down at the boy. "We're offering to make this your home."

John looked up at him finally, and though he quaked inwardly, he spoke strongly. "I'm sorry, Mr. Coyne, but I just want to work out my time and then be free." He paused to gather his strength. "I want to go back to Boston and find my father. I know he's alive."

"Hell, if your Da is alive, he's not able to take care of you. Besides, you'd be as good as free as soon as we adopted you." The man angrily paced the kitchen. "I don't understand you, Boy. We offer to make this your home. And you say no. Look at what Ma and I have done for you." He gestured toward her. "We've given you a home, fed you, clothed you, treated you like one of our own – for years. We don't understand." He stopped at the end of the table and faced his wife who sat stone-faced, "Do we, Ma?"

"Nein," she said gently, looking at John, "Ve vant you be son."

John had shifted from one foot to the other during this tirade. Mentally he forced himself to stop shaking. "Sorry," he mumbled, and turning, left the kitchen and climbed the stairs. Once in bed he heard them talking for a long time.

A few weeks later John stood in the kitchen doorway, watching the

Coyne family seated on the wagon as it pulled out onto the main road. Even though it was early, the day promised to be hot and sunny like the ones they'd been having these September days. The Coynes were on their way to the family reunion, but John would stay on the farm. Before now, he had always gone with them. The night before Mr. Coyne had said to him, "Tomorrow we're going to Grandpa Coyne's, but you'll stay here and watch things. You're in charge of the animals. See that they're fed and their stalls cleaned out." He had spoken brusquely. "Do the regular chores. You know what needs to be done."

Tears had sprung to John's eyes, but he'd said simply, "Yes, Mr. Coyne." He had turned away to wipe his face on his sleeve. He knew they were treating him more harshly since he refused their offer of adoption. Mr. Coyne found fault with everything, and Mrs. Coyne was more abrupt, if possible, than ever. He frequently held back tears. He didn't want them to see his hurt.

When he could no longer see the wagon, he headed to the barn for the morning chores. He tended to the animals and then returned to the kitchen where he saw that he was meant to do the washing up. He set to work. He'd gotten used to doing household chores.

John washed the dishes and put them away. He glanced at the clock and saw that it was still early. What would he do for the rest of the day? He wandered through the house examining the familiar furniture and knickknacks. He walked into the parlor, a place he seldom entered. When his eye fell on the family Bible, he walked over and opened to the first page where he saw the family names: Michael J. Coyne, Rosa Freidel Coyne, Robert Emmett Coyne, Charles Thomas Coyne, Anna Marie Coyne – each with the date of birth. He flipped the pages, stopping at a random page. He read, *It is God who sees justice done for the orphan and the widow, who loves the stranger and gives him food and clothing.* He shivered and closed the book. *I'm an orphan. I don't know anything about justice.* He thought he spoke aloud and looked around as if someone could be listening.

Disheartened, he turned and headed up the stairs. It felt odd not to hear the children at their play or Mrs. Coyne working in the kitchen. He thought of the children's chatter at breakfast when they realized that he was not going with them. "Why isn't John coming?" Robbie had asked petulantly. "We want John." His father stopped him with a glare.

John went into his room and sat on the bed. He wouldn't be able to stay upstairs because once the sun rose high in the sky, it would be stifling hot. He picked up his exercise book and pencil. He skimmed through the pages looking at the few entries. On the next blank page he wrote the date and then sat chewing the end of the pencil. Finally he wrote *I've been here for years. I still don't like it.* He chewed some more, staring off into space. After awhile, he shook himself and carried his pencil, exercise pad, as well as his book downstairs. He would read and write in the kitchen.

At the table he tried to concentrate. Instead he listened to the ticking of the clock. He couldn't write, nor could he read. He left his things on the table and stepped out the back door into the yard. He looked up at the huge Dakota sky. Surrounded by sky. He looked around in all four directions. Nothing but all this emptiness in all directions. No trees but a few scrawny ones that Mr. Coyne planted. Cottonwood. He was suddenly struck. *How could they be cottonwood?* Clothes were made of cotton. He learned about trees in Boston: maple, oak, elm. They grew bigger than houses, but these trees were not much taller than he. He listened but heard no birdsongs. He wandered around aimlessly, picking up a stick. He turned over a bucket and sat tracing designs in the dirt. He looked up at the spinning windmill, which reminded him of the slow progression of the clock marking time. He got up to walk to the creek and watched the flow of water, occasionally swirling his stick. Somehow he didn't feel soothed.

He watched a family of prairie dogs pop up out of the ground. Mr. Coyne maintained they should be trapped and killed because they were the enemy. They just wanted to live and keep their homes. He looked up suddenly when he heard the swish of a bird's wings. A hawk wheeled overhead. As John watched, it made its lonely path south. Suddenly, it dropped from the sky and into one of the gullies. Though he stood and watched for a long time, it never reappeared. Lost and alone. Like him.

Later, when he saw the sun high in the sky, he returned to the kitchen for lunch. Yesterday, he had smelled sweet cake baking. "Mmm, good," he'd said to Mrs. Coyne.

She had scowled at him, *"Das ist der kuchen. Sehr gut. Ja."* Now he knew she meant there was no cake for him. They'd eat it today, and he would have to be satisfied with bread. He took the loaf and sliced himself a thick slab, spreading on strawberry preserves. He took a piece of cheese and a pear and sat outside the door in the shade. The dog Dusty, looking at him with soulful eyes came and lay at his feet.

Late that afternoon, as he stood in the doorway looking out onto the yard, he watched the shadows of the barn grow longer with the fading light. He felt chilled though the day was warm. He heard occasional odd animal noises in the barn and across the fields, as well as creaking in the house. He turned his face to the doorjamb and wept. After a few minutes, he shook himself and headed to the barn for evening chores. When he returned to the house, he watched night descend on the farm and listened to the distant coyote crying under the rising moon. *Where are they? Why don't they come?* The tears flowed in spite of his resolve not to let his loneliness and the Coynes' cold treatment bother him.

The next several times they had family gatherings, they left him on the farm alone "to care for the animals." Eventually, they softened and took him again on some of their outings.

One evening John sat playing with Robbie and Charley on the floor. When the two boys left to go to bed, he picked up a toy they had tossed aside. Why couldn't he have it? Robbie and Charley had the new toy soldiers. He had nothing. They'd never miss it. He slipped the tiny wood figure into his trouser pocket. When he went upstairs after night prayers, he sat on the edge of his bed where he tried to examine it by the light of the kerosene lamp in the hall. He thought it the most wonderful thing. Very small and delicate. And yet so clearly you could see that it was the figure of a man – a pleasant man – a fisherman. With the hat and boots he looked like the fisherman he'd seen years ago in Boston.

Suddenly he heard footsteps on the stairs. He stuffed the figure under his pillow and began to undress. Mr. Coyne appeared in the doorway, his solid form blocking the lamplight.

"Why aren't you in bed, Boy?" he spoke sharply. "Time you were asleep."

"Yes, sir," John fumbled as he pulled off his trousers.

"I suppose you were reading. Don't dawdle. Get to sleep. We have a big day tomorrow."

"I'll be ready." John put the nightshirt over his head and crawled under the covers. *Every day is a "big day" with thousands of things to do.* Mr. Coyne turned off the lamp and stepped into his own bedroom.

John reached under the pillow and caressed the toy figure. He'd have to hide it in his box under his clothes during the day in case Mrs. Coyne went in to make the bed before he came back from early morning chores. Most days, he pulled up his own bedclothes like they'd taught him in the Orphan Home.

He had no toys, no mementoes. When he came from Boston he'd brought with him a few seashells, but they were gone. One day he'd left them in his trouser pocket, and after Mrs. Coyne had washed his clothes, he'd found only fragments. He'd cried at the loss. Now he would be more careful; this one small thing, this smiling figure was something to hold onto.

A few days later while doing morning chores, he realized that he had left the carved figure under his pillow and hadn't made his bed. He'd woken late and had to hurry to his chores. When he remembered, he panicked, realizing that if Mrs. Coyne discovered the toy, she'd accuse him of stealing it. As soon as he returned to the house, he ran upstairs to rescue and hide it. He pulled up the bedclothes and vowed to himself not to forget again. Downstairs at the kitchen table, Mr. Coyne asked what was wrong.

"Nothing," John mumbled as he ate his oats.

"You look like you've seen a ghost," the farmer said, giving him a suspicious look.

"No, I'm fine," he said, smiling up at him.

Another evening, John sat on the floor playing with the two boys. When Mrs. Coyne took her children to bed, he stayed where he was on the multicolored rag rug and stared into the fire. Watching the flickering lights in the fireplace, he put his head down on the chair cushion. He fell asleep and later found himself in bed. He wondered fleetingly, *how did I get here?* But he was too sick to wonder much.

The next morning, when Mr. Coyne shone the lamplight in, calling him for morning chores, he tried to get up. He couldn't move. His head and body ached. After a few minutes he heard the farmer's impatient voice, "Come on, Boy. I'm waiting."

He tried to sit up but he felt so weak. The farmer stood in the doorway. "What is it? Are you coming?"

"I can't," he moaned. "I'm sick."

Mr. Coyne came to the bed and put his hand on his forehead. "Oh, my. No chores for you today." He eased him back down into the bed. "Stay under the covers. Mrs. Coyne will tend to you." His voice was uncharacteristically gentle and sympathetic.

When he awoke again, Mrs. Coyne sat beside him, bathing him with alcohol. Still later, she appeared with a bowl of chicken broth, which she fed him as he lay propped against the pillows. He lay in a sweat, sleeping most of the day. His body burned, but he kept the covers on because she told him to. For three days the woman, who was ordinarily so remote, ministered to him with baths and food. She rolled him gently from side to side to change the bedclothes. She spoke little, but her touch was surprisingly gentle. She seemed someone other than the familiar figure with her cold, abrupt ways.

Years later, when he looked back to his time on the farm, he thought that only during times of illness did the name Rosa fit her. Yes, she was gentle and loving with her husband and children, but most often, unless he were ill, she showed him only the thorns. Not the soft velvety flower.

On the fourth day of his illness, he began to feel his strength returning and, though not called for chores, when he heard the breakfast clatter, he dressed and slowly made his way downstairs. When he walked into the kitchen, Mr. Coyne said heartily, "Look who's here, Ma. *Resurrect sicut dixi!*"

"*Gut,*" she said in her own language. "*Setchen sie auch.*" She dished out a bowl of hot oats and set it in front of him.

"How are you feeling?" Mr. Coyne asked.

"Better," he said.

"Good. Today we do some weeding. I'll show you the difference between the weeds and the plants." They ate in silence. "I'll be glad to have another pair of hands."

Later, after working a few hours, John went across the rows to where Mr. Coyne was working. "I don't feel good," he told him.

Mr. Coyne lifted himself up from his knees. "Oh, for Christ's sake," he exploded. He didn't look at him, but at the rows still to be done. "Four day's rest isn't enough for you!"

John turned away, and with head down, headed back to where he'd been working.

Mr. Coyne stopped him. "Show me how far you've gotten." The child pointed. "Oh, go take a nap. You're no good to me if you're going to droop like that."

John walked back to the house, climbed the stairs, and crawled into bed. When he came down for supper, he knew he was back to normal.

This May morning at Mass was a special one for John because he made his First Communion. He knelt in his place after receiving Communion. The priest had said he would now belong fully to the Church. What did that mean? He didn't feel any different. He gazed at the image of Christ Crucified above the altar. *Jesus suffered unjustly at the hands of others. And why? That he might save me. And if he saved me, why am I here and not with my own family? Jesus died for me.* Perhaps someday he could pray as Jesus did, "Father, forgive them for they know not what they do."

About a month ago, Father Lamesch had stopped him as he left church and asked, "John, tell me. How old are you? Are you ready to receive your Communion?"

"I'll be twelve this summer." John stood as tall as he could and squared his shoulders.

The priest asked him, "Do you know what Communion is?"

"It's the Body of Christ in the form of bread and wine."

"Exactly," he beamed. "Who taught you that?"

"You did, Father." The child returned the smile.

"Good for you!" The priest looked toward the adults, standing nearby. "That means at least one person listens to me when I preach." He turned back to John. "So, do you want to receive the Sacraments? Are you ready?"

"Yes, Father."

"I don't see why we have to wait until next year." He called Mr. Coyne over. "Mike, this child is obviously ready for the Sacraments. I'll have him join the group that receives next month." He placed a warm hand on John's shoulder. "The first thing you need to do, John, is to make your confession. You can do that in two weeks. Do you know how?"

"It tells how to make confession in here," he showed Father his prayer book. "It doesn't look hard."

"Right. Look it over, and I'll help you if you need it." He gave his shoulder a gentle squeeze, "Don't be afraid to ask questions."

Two weeks later he waited in the back of the church near the confessional with a few others. When it was his turn, he rose from the kneeler and entered the dark space. He heard the grille slide open and by a small light saw the shadowy figure of Father Lamesch, who put his hand up to his face while leaning toward the grille. John opened his book and in the dim light read, "Bless me, Father, for I have sinned. This is my first confession, and these are my sins." He recited his childhood misdeeds: anger, neglect of duties, disobedience. He stopped. He couldn't think of anything else as sins. *Was it a sin to take food from the larder without permission when he was hungry? Was it a sin to miss Mass because he lived far from the church, and they didn't go because of field work? Was it a sin not to say prayers at night when he was so tired? Was it a sin to resent the Coynes who made him work?* He kept these questions to himself.

After a few moments of silence, Father prodded him, "Is that all?"

"Yes, Father," he answered in a small voice. *Maybe the priest can see I kept some sins back.*

"And are you sorry for your sins?" Father asked gently.

"Yes, Father," he said closing the book.

"And will you try to sin no more?"

"Yes, Father."

"For your penance say an Our Father and three Hail Marys. Now I want you to say an Act of Contrition before I absolve you."

John hurriedly opened the book for the closing formula. He began, "Bless me, Father ..." He faltered.

"No," the priest said gently. "O my God, I am heartily sorry."

He flipped a few pages and found the right formula. "O my God, I am heartily sorry for having offended thee ..." When he finished the Act of Contrition, the priest said the words of absolution, concluding with, "Go and sin no more." He closed the grille. The small space was plunged into darkness. As he left, John's foot got caught up in the heavy curtain. He almost wanted to laugh with relief. He went back to the pew and knelt to say his penance slowly. He thought of the recent reading when Jesus said, "I will not leave you orphans. I will come to you." *No earthly father, but I have a heavenly Father.* He remembered the other saying in the Gospel, "In my Father's house there are many mansions. I go to prepare a place for you." *Not a mansion but his own home. Perhaps God had a place for him. Some day.*

One early autumn day, a day when the work could wait, Mr. Coyne took his two sons and John fishing. A rare day off the farm and away from work. He brought the wagon as close to the water as he could and stopped. "Here we are, boys. The James river. Hop down and let's go. The fish are waiting." His two sons, Robbie, age six, and Charley, age four, jumped down and ran to the water's edge looking for frogs or toads; their father followed behind them. After going a few steps, he turned to the twelve-year-old John, who remained standing by the wagon. "John, secure the horses." He added as an afterthought, "Join us." He called his sons, "Over here, boys – a good spot for some fishing. Robbie, Charley. Over here."

In a few minutes John joined them by the riverbank, exclaiming in awe, "Wow, the water is beautiful."

"You like it here?" Mr. Coyne turned and smiled.

"Look, you can see the trees in the water, but upside down." The beauty mesmerized him. A rare close-up look at water, trees, and lush growth. He stood gazing with open mouth.

"Well, we're here to do some fishing." Mr. Coyne rubbed his hands together. "Where are the worms and the poles?" He poked him. "Go get them. From the back of the wagon."

Later he sent him to get the lunch pail. The cloudy, dull day gave way by late morning to a bright, sunny one. Much of the morning they sat in silence, watching their poles. Most of the chatter came from the two small boys.

"I saw the ocean once." John ducked his head down. He didn't mean to speak out loud.

"The ocean?" Mr. Coyne asked. "When was that?" He dismissed him with a wave of his hand. "Oh, before you came to us." The child, embarrassed, didn't answer, but turned away. Mr. Coyne went on, "I came across the ocean from England," he said. "Two weeks on the water. When I was twelve years old. I guess you can't tell me about the ocean." He chuckled. John stared into the water, lost in his own thoughts.

Robbie implored, "Tell us about the ship." Charley moved closer to listen.

Mr. Coyne told the familiar story of his migration to America, a story which his children never tired of hearing. John fixed his eyes on a lone oarsman as he made his slow progress north. He watched until the boat disappeared around a bend of the river. He brooded, barely listening.

Perhaps it was best to forget about the ocean. He really didn't remember much anyway. Perhaps it was best to forget his early life. Perhaps life began when he came to this place so far from the ocean, this place with little water, where he thirsted for something and his thirst was not slaked. *Water is essential for life. What about love? People caring? Paying attention?* He moved away from them and when he turned back and looked again at the water, he saw that their images were reflected - the father and his two sons. He saw himself as if looking through a window at a scene from which he was removed. He had no father to care for him the way this man cared for his children.

Michael Coyne
Worthen, South Dakota
September 15, 1889

Dear Tom,

Our harvesting is pretty much done. In fact, the other day when we had some time I took the boys fishing in the James river. Robbie and Charley loved it. Our boys bring Rosa and me much joy. I wish you could've been along. Remember the happy days we had at the Missouri to swim and explore? I took John along. He's the orphan boy we took in. Good thing. He helped one of the boys while I worked with the other. We got a fine mess of fish, let me tell you, and Rosa cooked it up for supper. I even taught them how to swim. They loved it and did all right for the first time. John surprised us. Sure, and you'd think he'd been swimming for years, taking to the water like a duck. That child amazes me sometimes because he learns everything quickly.

Rosa and Anna stayed home. We thank God we've had no serious illness or accident this year and pray that we stay healthy. Ma and Pa are fine. I saw them the other day when we went into town. The boy they took in has worked well for them and proves to be a real help. Pa would have had to give up farming without help. His name is Tom, and he's the brother of the boy we have from the Home.

Write and let us know how you and the family are.
We miss you.
Your brother Mike

John lay in bed, listening to the parents soothing Robbie in the room across the hall. *Well, they should.* He hugged himself. After all, Robbie was hurt today with that nasty cut on his leg. But his physical hurt would heal in time, and the pain would go away. But they had no idea of what John suffered. He had no mark on his body, no scar. What he longed for, they never gave – attention or affection. They housed, fed, and clothed him, as required by law. But they gave him no more attention than they gave the animals. Taking in a child seemed to indicate the intention of opening their hearts to someone outside their own family. Perhaps if he agreed to be adopted, things might be different. He moved restlessly in bed. *No, I made the right decision.*

The accident had happened earlier that day. The farmer had gone to town, and John had to do the chores, as well as watch the two boys. Anna Marie stayed with her mother in the kitchen. While he was pitching hay, Robbie suddenly darted in front of him ran into the pitchfork. The child clutched his leg, yelped in pain and fell to the ground. John dropped the pitchfork, leaned down, and saw the tear in Robbie's trousers and a lot of blood. He felt the color drain from his face. *It will be my fault. They'll blame me.* He turned to Charley, "Go, tell Mama, Robbie is hurt." The child stood frozen. "Go," he said, and he pushed him in the direction of the house. Charley ran, crying, "Mama."

John stooped down, "Can you walk? How bad is it?"

"No, I can't walk," Robbie wailed. "Look." Tears were streaking his face.

"You'll be all right," John patted him on the arm. "What happened?"

Before he could answer, Mrs. Coyne ran out of the house with Ann Marie toddling along behind her. She pushed John aside and knelt beside her son. "Vat happen, my baby?" As she examined his leg, Robbie howled in pain. "Shush," she soothed him, then turned to John with an anguished look, "Help, *bitte, im haus.*"

Between them they managed to carry Robbie into the kitchen with Charley and Ann Marie following. They set him down on the rocker. "*Basin mit wasser. Warmes wasser.*" She snarled at John. "*Schnell.*" She knelt in front of the chair. The injured child's sobs gradually lessened as she bathed his cuts, soothing him. John was relieved to see that the injury was not terribly severe. She told John, "You let my boy be hurt."

John stood tall to defend himself. "It wasn't my fault. He got in the way." He added, "He knew I was using the pitchfork. I told them to stay away." He wouldn't hurt these children for anything.

"*Gehen sie.* Cloth. In basket. *Und* scissors." She stepped to the cabinet for iodine. Robbie howled again as she painted the wound. John came back with the cloth that he helped to cut into strips for the bandage. When she finished wrapping the leg, she lifted her son in her arms and sat down, cradling him, soothing and saying, "My baby."

John stood feeling helpless. *Robbie is not a baby. He's six years old.*

Mrs. Coyne suddenly looked in his direction and gestured to the door. "*Gehen sie.*" Relieved to be dismissed, he left the kitchen. "Anna Marie and Charley, stay *mit mir.*" He heard her talking to her children. He calmed himself with the physical activity of pitching the hay.

Later, Mr. Coyne told him, "Farm accidents happen." At supper when John told Robbie he was sorry, the younger boy said, "It wasn't your fault." For days, Robbie, proud of his bandage limped around the house and the yard.

"Today we take the cattle to the stockyard," Mr. Coyne announced at breakfast. "Get your hat, John. I want you at the end of the line so we keep them together." He put his hand out to stop the child who had jumped up immediately. "I'll lead, riding the nag. You bring her back to the farm. Do you think you can handle it?"

"Yes, Mr. Coyne." John jumped up. He could barely contain his excitement. Riding the mare from town was a rare treat. He grinned as he headed to the door.

"Walter will come along. He'll guide the middle of the herd." Mr. Coyne reached for his hat from the hook inside the door, "You bring up the rear."

"Yes, sir." The three of them, Mr. Coyne, Walter and John rounded up the herd with Dusty's help. John ran alongside the animals, shooing them into a line toward the gate.

When they were ready, Mr. Coyne mounted the mare. Walter and John would walk. The farmer called to his workers, "All right. I'll go ahead. Be careful to keep them in line." He started out, then turned back to add in John's direction, "I'll go slow enough. Make sure there are no stragglers. I'm relying on you, John."

"Yes, sir." John held a switch, ready to prod a wayward cow. All he saw were rumps and tails. Two miles north. Five miles west. To the railroad depot in Ethan. About half way they stopped for a water break. The sun high in the sky beat down on them. When they stopped, the cattle grazed on grass along the roadside.

By the time he finally joined the men, they were almost ready to move on. Walter looked at John's dusty feet and asked as he handed him the water jug, "Where are your shoes, John?" Before John could answer, he turned and asked, "Mike, this boy has no shoes?"

"His shoes just plumb wore out, and we haven't had time to get him a new pair." Mr. Coyne gave a wry laugh. "Next week. When I get back from Chicago." He wiped his face with his neckerchief and took the water jug for another drink. "It's hard keeping children in shoes. They grow fast. Just like weeds." He turned to John, "You're all right, aren't you?"

"I'm fine." He held his hand up to his eyes, squinting at him through the sunlight. "I don't mind walking barefoot." He took another drink of water.

When they arrived at the stockyard, they drove the herd bawling through the gate and into pens. Walter disappeared. John stood by the fence listening to Mr. Coyne talk business with Mr. Drake, the cattle yard owner. They talked of fair market value, profit and loss. He watched Drake's men weigh, measure, evaluate and tag the animals. The creatures bellowed. He watched them attach the tag on the ear, and he thought with a start of the tag with his name, the name of the family, and the word "Dakota" sewn in the jacket that the Home had given him.

He let his gaze wander beyond the animals to the open cattle cars waiting to take them to the slaughterhouse. *Just like me. Put on a train and shipped away. How different things would be if I'd stayed in Boston. I'd be in school learning lessons. I wonder what kind of fair market value I am.* He put his head down. *Cheap labor, that's all.* His foot idly traced a circle in the dusty Dakota earth.

Mr. Coyne startled him when he put his hand on his shoulder, "John, go back to the farm. Take the horse. I'll be home in a few days." After he dismissed him he started to walk away, but he turned back to chide him, "Do the regular chores. You know what to do."

"Yes, Mr. Coyne." John headed toward the horse tethered to the fence post at the entrance to the cattle yard. He would enjoy the ride back to the farm mounted on the horse. He would pretend he was free and this was his horse.

The harvesting always seemed endless. Some days they had extra help – neighbor farmers – but often it was just the three of them. And when they weren't working the Coyne farm, they often traveled to help other farmers bring in the crops. For days, they had been working in the fields. John stood on the bottom of the haymow where he saw yellow and variations of yellow with tan and green grasses intermixed – even when he closed his eyes for a second. Mostly yellow. Unrelieved. How could he look up and see the brilliant blue of the sky, with its happy clouds scudding across the wide expanse? At night too when he closed his eyes, he'd see these wisps of massed color.

He felt confined even within the huge open expanse of Dakota. Only when they stopped for lunch could he take a moment to see what was before him and what seemed like miles more of the same. The skin of his callused hands cracked and his back ached mercilessly. Leaning back in exhaustion, he studied the mournful postures of the draft horses with their heads lowered to the ground. They labored without protest, not knowing how beautiful the world was around them.

Of all his jobs on the farm, the only one John truly enjoyed was garden work. Though the Coynes' vegetable plot was fairly large, the fields were simply endless – 160 acres of open, straight rows. Working the fields was monotonous. Plowing long rows, planting long rows, weeding long rows, harvesting long rows. Up and down endless long rows.

But the garden was manageable in size and variety of tasks. They'd start the garden in the early spring by turning over the soil. By the time he turned twelve he'd taken on the job alone. "You know what to do in the garden," Mr. Coyne had said to him one morning. "After you turn the soil over, go to Mrs. Coyne and she'll give you the seeds and plants you need to put in. Do you remember what we did last year?"

"Yes, Mr. Coyne." He'd been pleased to be allowed to work on his own and be responsible for the garden that fed the family year-round.

By summer, when the plants grew and ripened, he loved to stand looking at the colors of the vegetables: green beans and cucumbers, orange pumpkins, yellow beans and squash, red tomatoes. Beneath the soil was the promise of potatoes, orange carrots, purple rutabaga and red beets. He also learned which flowers were best to plant for the bees to pollinate the plants.

He didn't mind weeding the garden because the rows came to an end. He didn't mind picking the vegetables because they fed him and the family. During canning season, when released from fieldwork, he'd wash mason jars or cut up vegetables or stir the pot. Later he'd carry pickled beets, cucumbers, beans, and stewed tomatoes to the root cellar where he arranged them on shelves. In the winter he'd fetch the jars at Mrs. Coyne's bidding. Years later when he moved into town, married, and had his own place, he would always have a garden. It would be something he and his wife would work at together. Someday he'd bring to his own garden all the love for the gardens he'd tended at the Orphan Home and here at the farm.

One day Mr. Coyne returned from his few days away, and as he washed up at the outdoor pump, John stood quietly near him. "I helped a cow with calf today," he said as he watched the farmer rub his neck with the rough towel.

"You did?" Mr. Coyne looked at him skeptically. "She was ready?" John nodded. "I thought she'd need a few more days," the farmer said in surprise. Then he added incredulously, "You knew what to do?"

"Yes, sir. I've helped you often enough," he rubbed his hands on the back of his trousers.

"You have indeed," he agreed. "Well, let's go see how she's faring, and about her calf." They crossed over the farmyard and headed to the pasture. "Where did this calving take place?" he turned to John, who walked a pace behind him.

"Down near the pond." he tried to catch up with the long legs of the farmer. "I was scared, but I remembered what to do." He looked up at him to see if he was pleased.

"I thought she wouldn't be ready until next week," Mr. Coyne said again. "This is a surprise." After they went another twenty yards, he asked, "Did she have a lot of trouble?"

"Not really. I helped her – I mean, you know – getting the mother to do her thing in cleaning the newborn," he spoke hesitantly. "That's all I ... I had to do," he added lamely.

They walked down the hill and headed to the small pond where most of the cattle gathered at the water's edge. They found the cow and her calf set apart from the others. Mr. Coyne examined the animals. "Everything seems to be all right. I guess you did a fine job, Boy." He ran his hand over the calf. "Seems we have a fine animal here. Don't seem to be any problems." He stood and passed his eyes over the other animals as they grazed. He looked back at the newborn. "Yep, a fine bull calf."

John winced. He hated to think about it. This animal would be castrated. That was one job he hated to be a part of. The fierce bawling just tore at his heart. Mr. Coyne frowned and asked, "How's the salt lick?"

John hesitated, "I – I think it's all right."

"When was the last time you checked?" Mr. Coyne spoke sharply.

"I ... don't ... I don't remember." He bit his lip and started to back away. "I'll go now."

"John, you know that's got to be checked once a week," his voice took on even a sharper tone. He pointed in the direction of the salt lick, "Go, do it. And let me know what it looks like."

"Yes, sir." John took another few steps.

"You know what you're supposed to do." He heard the exasperation in his voice. "Just do your job. I don't want to have to remind you of everything." He put his hands on his hips and scowled. "And another thing. You did a poor job of mucking out the stalls today. I expect you to do as good a job as if I watched you."

He walked away with tears stinging his eyes. How *can I remember everything? Why does he expect me to be perfect?* He tried, but he couldn't satisfy the farmer. The sense of pride he experienced in helping the calving evaporated before he even had a chance to enjoy it. Why did it always happen this way? Why couldn't he do anything right? He wiped the tears away with his sleeve. When he came to the salt lick, he saw it was fine. *At least the cattle didn't suffer from any neglect.* He breathed a sigh of relief. He didn't have to tell him that it should've been replaced.

He flopped down on a nearby hillock, remembering the first time he'd seen a calving. He'd only been on the farm a week or so. He and the farmer, still strangers to each other, had stood in the pasture, gazing at the newborn calf. Not an easy birth for the cow, but as John watched, he saw that Mr. Coyne had known what to do. It had been in the middle of the night, and his job was to hold the lantern. "Steady, hold it steady, Boy," he'd said sternly.

He'd almost dropped the lantern when he saw the farmer's hand and arm disappear into the animal. He was astounded even more several minutes later at the sight of the newborn. He'd watched as the mother washed her calf. Since that night, every calving seemed a miracle. At the farmer's side, he learned when to intervene and when to let nature take its course. Suddenly he heard Mr. Coyne call. He jumped up and ran after him to return to the farmhouse for supper.

After the meal and dishes the family sat around outside in the fading light. The night creatures echoed around them – crickets in the grass, coyotes in the distance, the lowing of a few restless cattle. Darkness came on slowly, but they'd be asleep before the stars or the moon showed in the wide sky. The elder Coynes sat on kitchen chairs, John and the children on the steps. He tried to listen to the talk of the adults, but he found his head nodding. Mr. Coyne announced, "All right. Time for bed." He put out his arms to his children for a goodnight hug. As John followed them in behind their mother, who had gone first, Mr. Coyne said, "We've got to clear that field in the west, John. We'll get an early start." He didn't even look in his direction. *No hug for me. Business as usual.*

Upstairs he wondered again why he couldn't please this man. Though he'd been drowsy downstairs, sleep came slowly. Whenever he did something right, Mr. Coyne found fault with something else. Would it be so with his own father? No, his father loved him.

That night he dreamed the old dream of the train – the black monster that had brought him here. He felt again the hot breath of the belching smoke and heard the lonesome wail of the whistle. He awoke in terror as he had in his dreams so many years earlier. He pulled the quilt closer and shivered. He wanted home. The farmhouse remained cold and dark. No warmth, no light, no welcome. *This was just a dream, and he wouldn't let it frighten him any more. Some day he'd have a family and home of his own. He would love and be loved.*

He tried to imagine his family and home in Boston. He tried to see the kitchen on the third floor, warm and cozy and welcoming. He tried to picture his mother, kneading dough. He tried to see his father, reading by the fire. He tried to see his brother and sister. Try as he might, he only saw Tom's face. He couldn't bring the others into focus. Too long ago since he'd seen any of them except his brother.

By age fourteen John plowed the fields, working alongside Mr. Coyne almost like a man, even though he was still small. One morning, as they stood on the edge of the field, Mr. Coyne said. "Today, you'll work on the south field. I'll start here. We should meet in the middle." As an afterthought, he added, "There're fewer acres on the south side." As always he talked business without looking at him. *As if he were talking to the cattle or his horse.*

"Yes, sir." John didn't mind working on his own. In fact, he preferred it.

They hitched up the team together. "I think we'll have a good year with the early thaw we had."

John walked behind the team, pushing the plow up and down the rows, trying to make them as straight as he could. In less than a half-hour he had built up a sweat. He took off his jacket and hung it onto a fence post. He rolled up his shirtsleeves and wiped his face and neck with his kerchief. Later, when he felt the unrelenting sun high in the sky, he scanned the horizon, looking for his lunch. When he saw Robbie and Charley with the lunch pails, he stopped, tethered the horse, and wiped his brow. He watched them trudging along, each carrying a bucket with food and drink for both him and the horse. Even though he loved these boys dearly, he felt pangs of jealousy and resentment – jealous of the freedom they had and the obvious love their parents had for them, and resentment that they didn't have to work like he did. Robbie was about the age he was when he first came to the farm, and though he had some chores, they were nowhere near what he'd been doing all these years.

Still he greeted them warmly. "I'm glad to see you fellows," he said as they deposited the buckets near the fence. He gave the horses their water and oats before he sat on the ground to eat his own lunch. The boys sat with him by the side of the pasture.

"Daddy wants to know how much you got done," the six-year-old Charley asked. He sat up straight and looked at his older brother.

"Well, let's see." John stood to survey the field as he chewed on his bread and cheese. "I think I'm about half done. I should be able to finish before supper." He sat back down. He teased them, "You don't want a story, do you?"

"Yes," they said together with a happy look of anticipation. "Tell us a story."

"It'll have to be just the very beginning," he said. "I have to get back to work as soon as I finish lunch." He laughed at their look of disappointment. "I'll finish it before you go to bed tonight." He began the story of Rip Van Winkle.

When he finished his apple, he stood and said, "Off you go. I've gotta get back to work." He stretched and headed toward the horses. "Tell your mother thanks for lunch. That'll keep me going for the afternoon."

They grabbed the empty buckets and headed back to the house, chorusing, "Bye, John."

When he'd stopped, he'd felt the chill of the early spring day, but once he got back to work, he'd heat up fast. He liked to keep his mind busy with the stories he read in school. Farm work was so monotonous and backbreaking, he needed to focus on something else. He knew he would fall into bed that night numb and aching with exhaustion. But no matter how tired, he often told the children a story. *Oh, how wonderful it would be to have a long sleep like Rip Van Winkle's.*

A rare day away from the farm – away from chores. Sure there were the regular morning chores, and they'd have work tonight, but the harvesting was done. It was a grand day. The two Donahue boys took their plates from Mrs. Coyne, and as always at one of the Coyne and Freidel family gatherings, went to sit away from the others with their backs against the side of the barn. The adults sat at long tables on chairs and stools outside the farmhouse. Some of the children sat on the steps going into the house or on the grass.

When he finished his meal, John set his empty plate on the ground in front of him and asked, "What happens when you turn seventeen? That's in four months? Right?" He spoke quietly and looked toward the Coynes, making sure they couldn't hear him.

Tom nodded and smiled. "Grandpa Coyne starts paying me same as a farm hand right after my birthday in January." He lowered his voice almost whispering. "It's the law."

"Did he say he'd pay you?" John asked.

Tom nodded. He put his plate on top of his brother's. He sat hugging his knees.

"Then what?"

"Well, when I'm twenty-one, I can do what I want. I can stay and hire on as a farm worker, or I can leave." He looked off in the distance as if looking into the future. "I can find my own place to live. I'll be free."

"Where will you go?" John asked. "Will you go back to Boston?" He looked at him sideways, afraid almost to hear his brother's answer.

"I don't know," Tom shrugged. "I don't know yet."

John leaned his head back against the barn, "That means I've got over two years without pay. But Mr. Coyne never shows me any of the papers or says anything about what's going to happen. I'm not staying any longer on the farm than I have to." He spoke with quiet conviction.

"You don't like farm work?"

"I hate it." He spoke with venom and then turned to look toward Mr. Coyne laughing at some story Uncle Al was telling.

"I don't mind." Tom said gently, "I like to work with my hands. And the Coynes are good to me."

"Mr. and Mrs. Coyne never got over the fact that I wouldn't let them adopt me. It's like they want me to suffer."

They fell silent. John leaned his head back against the barn and closed his eyes. *Why?*

Tom interrupted his thoughts, "What do you think? Will you go back to Massachusetts?"

"No," he lifted his head and said sadly. "That dream is over. I guess I'll just live here in South Dakota." He cast his eyes over the landscape near and far.

Chapter Four
Reaching Maturity

Several years later, John, intent on mending a saddle, sat in the warm sunshine outside the barn. "Johnnie's got a beard, Johnnie's got a beard," Robbie and Charley chanted as they ran circles around him.

"My name is *John*," he snapped. "Call me John." They stopped in their tracks and shrank from him. John moved his hand over his jaw, feeling the scratchy hairs. *They're right. I'll have to learn how to shave.* He looked at the contrite faces of the two young brothers. "Sorry I snapped at you," he said. "Find some other game besides tormenting me." The boys didn't move. "Off with you," he said gruffly. He smiled as he watched them run off to the creek. Lately he felt out of sorts – not like himself.

After breakfast the following morning John followed Mr. Coyne to the corner of the kitchen where a small mirror hung near the door with a razor strop beside it. A small shelf held his shaving supplies. As the farmer prepared the lather for his daily ritual, John said, "Excuse me, Mr. Coyne."

The farmer turned slightly to look at him, "What is it?"

"I think it's time I learned to shave," he raised his hand to his jaw. "Will you show me?"

Mr. Coyne put the brush into the cup and ran the back of his hand across John's face. "Surely you're not old enough to shave?"

"Yes, sir." John stood taller, trying to see himself in the mirror.

"I'll be jiggered. Sure enough." Mr. Coyne picked up the razor, saying, "Watch how I do it and then I'll help you. Maybe at the beginning you won't have to do it every day – but eventually you will. So, first you make some lather with the soap. Then you brush it onto your face. Like so. Then you take the razor and drag it along your cheek and chin." He used the razor with deft even strokes. When he finished one half of his face he stopped, peered at John, and asked, "What about a beard? Wouldn't you want to grow a beard?"

"No, sir."

"Not even a mustache?" He tried to look in the mirror to see the expression on John's face. "I hear the girls are partial to men with facial hair." He continued to shave the other side, occasionally peering at the young man in the mirror.

"No, sir," John said again. "I want to be clean-shaven."

"So, you did some thinking about this? Well, I'm not surprised. You think about everything." He paused, and then added, "You'll have to figure out the space under your nose on your own. Since I wear a mustache I can't rightly tell you how to handle that. 'Course that's where you have most of your peach fuzz right now." He finished his own shaving, wiped his face, and cleaned his brush and razor. "Always take care of your razor and brush. Keep them clean."

Mr. Coyne proceeded to guide John through the steps, showing him how to sharpen the razor with the strop. "You want a good sharp edge," he said. "Just like I always tell you with farm tools. Like the scythe." He laughed, and John saw a rare glimpse of warmth. "A man's hair is tough as hay." He suddenly looked at John with an odd expression.

"What's the matter?" John asked.

"Nothing." His gaze swept from the boy's feet to his face, "It just dawned on me you're growing up."

"I'm almost sixteen."

"I know. Almost a man. It just surprises me. Seems like yesterday when you arrived – just a wee lad."

It should be my father who teaches me how to shave and how to be a man. He said aloud, "I don't want to use your things, Mr. Coyne. Could I … I mean …" He hesitated. "Could we … get my own …?" He trailed off. He hated to ask for things.

"Don't see why not. Next time I go into town I'll get you a razor. Good idea."

John finished and turned for inspection. "Did I do all right, Mr. Coyne?"

"Good job! Only a few nicks. It'll be easier each time. And as I said, you won't have to do it every day. Maybe just two or three times a week." He looked him over again, as if seeing him for the first time. He shook himself and said brusquely, "Now come on. We have work to do."

When John finished his work in the haymow, he knew he needed to rest. His body ached, and he found it hard to keep his eyes open. He sat down, put his head on the bale of hay, and almost immediately fell asleep. Suddenly, loud voices jerked him awake – it was the farmer and another man. Mr. Coyne had just shouted, "Changes need to be made in that school."

"You have a problem with the school board?" John heard the other man ask mildly.

"Damn right, I do," Mr. Coyne asserted. John sat up, opened his eyes fully to listen.

The man said, "Only one way to solve that. Get on the board and have some say in what goes on over there."

"I might just do that," he replied, somewhat placated. "I have three children now, and we'll probably have more. They've got to get the best education, which they can only get in a good school."

"Shoot. What about John?" The listener sat up straighter. "He's been here all his school years, hasn't he? Don't he count?"

Mr. Magnason. That's who it is. He finally figured out the voice.

"Well … he's not really ours." Mr. Coyne sounded dismissive. "An orphan boy, you know, we took in. Can't educate him too much. We can't let him rise above his station now, can we?"

John's eyes seared with sudden tears. After all he had done on the farm, this is what they thought about him. He wanted to drown out their voices, but he was trapped. It wouldn't do to descend the ladder now and make his presence known. They would think he'd been eavesdropping. He closed his eyes.

"You should count yourself lucky with the orphan you got," Mr. Magnason said. "My wife's cousin took one in. They live up in Vermillion. Had a terrible time with him – a real rotten apple."

Mr. Coyne rejoined, "I have to keep after this fellow. He'd rather be reading than working."

"I'm talking bad. Thieving and cussing and fighting with everyone. Real surly. It got so bad they decided to send him back to the Orphan Home."

"What happened?" Mr. Coyne's voice took on a tone of curiosity.

"He just ran off one day. Saved 'em the trouble. Seems like you got a good one. I hear tell of other boys …" Their voices faded as they stepped out of the barn.

I'll show them how I can rise above my station. I'll make the most of my last few months of school. He put his head in his hands. *Why do I have to be in this place?* He wiped his eyes on his sleeve with the resolution that no one would define who he was or what he could become in life. *Rise above his station indeed! What did that mean?*

He descended the ladder, stepped out of the barn, and strode toward the men. They turned at his approach. John extended his hand to their neighbor. "How are you, Mr. Magnason?" he asked, brightly, able to mask the hurt he had experienced a few minutes ago.

"Good, good. My, how you've grown," Mr. Magnason answered, giving John a warm smile and a strong, warm grip.

Mr. Coyne laughed. "He's shaving now. Had to give him his first lesson last week." He clapped John on the shoulder and continued, "Just peach fuzz is all he has, but he insists he wants to be clean shaven. He does it every day."

John said firmly, "Every other day, for now."

"Well, Mike. Looks like you've got a man on your hands."

"Don't I know it!" Mr. Coyne laughed again. "And don't I say about time!"

"I finished the work in the barn and in the fields," John said. "Do you want me to check on the cattle?"

"No, they're fine." He stroked his chin and looked toward the barn. "Why don't you straighten out the haymow?"

"I did that."

"Fine." Mr. Coyne looked around the farm as if trying to find a job for him. At last, he shrugged. "See what you can do to help Mrs. Coyne."

"All right." John reached out again for their neighbor's hand. "Good to see you again. Say hello to Mrs. Magnason for me." He walked away from them, knowing they were studying him as he headed to the house.

After the usual morning chores and their breakfast Mr. Coyne and John moved a table into the yard. Then John brought out the pots, bowls, and knives they would use for the hog slaughter. Mr. Coyne had said to him, "Come on, John. Today we'll slaughter the hog." He gave a sweeping gesture around the kitchen. "Ma's ready to salt the meat for the winter."

As he headed to the pigsty, John picked up a switch. Mr. Coyne called his sons, who would help by carrying the meat into the house. The two boys appeared from behind the barn. "Come on, boys. We're slaughtering the hog." The boys walked on either side of their father. John, following them, remembered how when he was their age, he'd first helped with this job and had felt overwhelmed at the animal's panic and anguish.

The two small boys peered through the lower bars of the fence while Mr. Coyne and John looked over the top bar at the sow and her brood. "We'll take that one over there." The farmer pointed to the largest of the two-year-olds, wandering away from the others. "That's the one we want. Climb the fence over there behind him." He pointed to the far corner. "Chase him over here, and I'll grab him." As John made his way to the far side, Mr. Coyne gave directions to his sons. "Charley, climb up here on the fence, and don't get down for anything. Robbie, stand by the gate, and as soon as we're out with the pig, close and lock the gate."

John climbed over the fence, let himself down into the yard, and approached from behind the animal. Meanwhile Mr. Coyne slipped through the gate and faced him. John struck the pig's flank with the switch, all the while shouting. The creature bolted toward the farmer who grabbed him by the front legs. "Grab his hind legs!" he hollered. The pen erupted in anxious squeals. They moved quickly out of the sty with the animal squirming furiously between them. Robbie pulled the gate closed and secured the latch. The sow howled. The piglets squealed. All done in less than a minute.

They carried the animal to the table, and while John held the animal on its back, Mr. Coyne slashed its throat with a quick deft movement. Brilliant red blood gushed into a waiting bowl held by Robbie while the animal continued to bawl for several more minutes. "Your Ma uses the blood for the sausages," he told his wide-eyed sons, who made faces of disgust.

Robbie said, "You mean we eat that?"

Mrs. Coyne came out of the house carrying a bucket of hot water to clean the carcass. Mr. Coyne opened the hog with his knife and drew out the entrails, tossing them into another large bowl. By now the beast had ceased moving. Mr. Coyne and John washed it before proceeding to divide the flesh into several parts, so that they could both work in cutting the meat into pieces.

Mr. Coyne glanced idly across at John. "Do you remember the first time I had you go into the pen to chase out a pig?"

"I remember." He gestured to Robbie and Charley. "I was about Robbie's age."

"No, you were older," Mr. Coyne contradicted him. "You must've been about ten."

"I was Robbie's age," John repeated.

"Oh, well," he made a dismissive gesture. "Anyway, the sow we had at the time got up from where she was." He worked quickly and efficiently as he talked. "Remember we thought she was asleep and she charged you. I never saw anyone move so fast."

Robbie asked, "Who moved fast? The hog? Or John?" They all laughed.

"I guess John moved faster because he's still here." They concentrated on their task. "How did we close the gate?" Mr. Coyne suddenly asked.

"Mrs. Coyne," John reminded him.

Robbie moved closer to John and asked, "How long have you been with us?"

John didn't look up. "I came when you were two and Charley was a baby."

"I'm not a baby," Charley declared. They laughed again.

"And have you been cutting up pigs since you came?" Robbie asked John.

"No," Mr. Coyne said defensively, "at first he only milked the cows and brought in water for Ma."

John added, "And collected the eggs and groomed the horses and a dozen other chores. I helped with the slaughter of the hogs, although I didn't cut them up like I do now." His brow was furrowed in concentration, but also pain at the memory.

"You didn't do all that." Mr. Coyne attacked the carcass. "At their age?"

"Yes."

"You always were a good worker," he said grudgingly. He turned to his sons. "Now boys, watch what we're doing here. We use every bit of the animal. We saved the blood and entrails for the sausage. In that pail there. Your Ma makes the best German sausage. This bit here is for the bacon. And John has the rump we'll use for ham." He directed John, "Use the cleaver and cut that piece in half." He turned back to the boys, fascinated with the work. "Ma salts some of it, and we'll put some in the smokehouse." He pointed to the meat. "We've got a lot of good meals here – meat for the whole winter." As the pieces were ready, Robbie and Charley carried them to their mother in the kitchen for the next step in the process – smoking or salting or sausage-making.

An air of excitement pervaded the house because Mrs. Coyne's old friend, Helga, with her family, was coming to visit. Mrs. Coyne had spent days baking special desserts and breads, and early that day she had put the meats to roast on the fire. She had dressed herself and her children in their best clothes. *Perhaps this time will be different. Perhaps Mrs. Coyne will say 'John will eat with us in the dining room.'* It seemed they'd become warmer toward him lately. He asked, "You want me to set twelve places?"

"*Yah, das ist richtig,*" she replied curtly.

So it is like every time they have visitors and I eat in the kitchen. Why did I think this time was any different?

"Johann vill eat in kitchen," she said to no one in particular. "I put food on table." She looked him full in the face and asked him, "*Verstein sie?*"

He nodded. *Yes, I understand that I will never belong to this family – just a servant – always a servant.* When the company came, he saw them as they went through on their way into the parlor to join the family. Later they moved into the dining room. Mrs. Coyne came into the kitchen to put the meal onto serving dishes, leaving John to wash the pots and pans. As he worked, he listened to the happy commotion of talking, laughing, and clinking of dishes and glasses. About ten minutes later, Robbie brought him a plate of food. "Mama sent your dinner," he said.

John sat down to eat. Not enough, never enough. And as often happened, Mrs. Coyne did not give him potatoes. He remembered the first time Mrs. Coyne skipped over him as she plated the food. "Johan does not like potatoes," she had said.

He had started to protest, but was stopped by her glare and Mr. Coyne's sharp rebuke. "Don't you dare speak to Mrs. Coyne like that, Boy. You eat what's put before you. We'll hear no complaints from you."

He remembered the nuns at the Orphan Home promising him plenty of food on the farm. How little they knew! He'd just finished his meal when Mrs. Coyne and Robbie brought in the empty plates, platters and serving dishes. She left without so much as a "*Danke.*" Inwardly, he rebelled. Outwardly, he did the work expected of him.

Later, the children ran through the kitchen to play in the yard, and Robbie took him by the arm, saying, "Come on, John, we're going to play 'crack the whip.' We need you on our side."

"Go ahead. I'll be with you in a minute." He stared at the wall. *When I have children, they will have what I have not had. Time to be a child.*

When John stepped outside the door, he found the children sitting on the grass panting. "Are you finished already?" he asked.

"Yes," said Robbie. "We're resting." They sat quietly for a few minutes. "Tell us a story, John." He turned to the visiting children. "John tells the best stories."

Charley and Anna Marie said together, "Yes, tell us a story."

John sat down, and they formed a circle around him. "What do you want to hear?" Charley said expectantly, "Tell us a new one."

"You always say the same thing – a new one." John looked at the familiar expectant Coyne faces and at the Altermann children, who appeared skeptical. As soon as he launched into the story, they too listened intently.

Olga Reinhart
Worthen, South Dakota
March 20, 1894

Dear Rudolph,

Dearly beloved. I may call you that, may I not?

It's amazing to me that after just two years I have found that school teaching suits me so well. Perhaps it is because these children in Worthen are so wonderful. Do all teachers fall in love with their pupils? Do you remember when you told me not to be afraid to try new and challenging assignments? Well, I had the older ones conduct a debate on – of all things – the Populist Movement. I can only do this because I have some very intelligent children.

One older student in particular, John, led the others and helped them to get the arguments ready. My heart goes out to him – an orphan living with a farm family. It's my understanding that when he turns seventeen this summer, the family will pay him as a farm laborer, and he must work until he's twenty-one. He's already worked for them since he was about eight. I'm ashamed to think that we as Christians allow this.

Please forgive me for going on about this, but if you could but see him – rather small with red hair and bright blue eyes, reflecting such intelligence, you would know why I feel the way I do. He should become a doctor or lawyer, and yet he is trapped in farm work. Everyone likes him and looks to him for guidance. It is because of pupils like John that I want to stay in teaching. Tell me you understand.

I read your last letter again and again. I'm so happy that things are going so well for you in your work. Write again soon. I count the days till our wedding.

Your own
Olga with love

The storm over, John left the house to tend to the chores. Mr. Coyne was away for a few days, and he did all the work alone. The black clouds lay heavy on the eastern horizon, but when he looked to the west, he saw the brilliant blue sky and the sun shining high above. When he looked back, he stopped suddenly in his tracks, his heart lifted at the sudden beauty of a rainbow. A sign of hope – hope for him, perhaps. One day he would leave the farm and make something of himself – something brighter, something softer.

He remembered the recent day when he had stood before the teacher, who had asked to see him after class. The last day of the term and the end of school for him.

She had said, "John, I have a proposition for you."

"Yes, Miss Reinhart."

"I think you'd make a fine teacher, and I want you to consider taking the test for a teaching certificate." She smiled in encouragement and added, "You know we have nothing more to offer you here in this school, and you will not be returning in the fall. With your ability and interest in reading and studies, I think you'd be quite successful, and I know you'd enjoy the work."

John felt his face grow hot. Yes, *perhaps after all I might escape the lifelong drudgery of farm work.*

She continued, "To take the test you have to go to Mitchell and pay a small fee. That's not a problem, is it?"

"No," he said tentatively. "I can ask Mr. Coyne for the money."

"Good. Here are the guidelines along with the dates to register and take the test." She handed him some papers. "You might find it helpful to do some extra reading. Use these books to get ready," she pointed to a stack on the corner of her desk. "The test is not terribly difficult. They just want to know if you can read and write." She paused, looking at him earnestly. "John, you're an extremely bright young man. You have been such a help to me with the younger children." She looked at him for a long moment, and then asked, "Have you ever thought of becoming a teacher?"

"No, I haven't." He was both surprised and pleased at her suggestion.

"Please think about it. After the test you can look at the school districts. You'll make a fine teacher."

"Thank you, Miss Reinhart."

"If you have any questions, I'll be happy to help you. I'll be here for another week cleaning and putting away supplies. Or you can find me at Tobey's home." She pulled a piece of paper in front of her. "Here, I'll write down my home address, so you can send the books to me when you finish with them." She handed him the paper, stood, and shook his hand. "Good luck, John. I wish you the best."

John left the schoolroom with a lighter step, thinking of the possibilities before him. On the way to the farm, however, he realized how impossible it would be. He couldn't leave. Mr. Coyne would never let him go. He'd have to work until he was twenty-one. He hugged the books to his chest. *Well, at least, I can read these books. And some day …*

Olga Reinhart
Worthen, South Dakota
July 30, 1894

Dear Theresa,

Dear friend, it is so good to hear from you, and to hear all your news. I'm happy that things have worked well for you. …

Do you remember the bright young man I told you about in my school? I thought I could encourage him to do something other than farm work, so I gave him the application for the teacher certificate test. I thought if he passed the test, he might win the approval of his foster family to take a teaching position. After all, he could still work on the farm when school was not in session.

But I was wrong. I saw him once more before I left the area, and he asked me not to talk to the farmer. He said he wanted to finish his time of indenture, and when he was twenty-one, he would take the teacher test. I cannot tell you how frustrated I am.

Enough. I can't do anything about it. I love to read about your happy life. We'll have much to share when you come to the wedding. Mama and Papa look forward to seeing you again also.

Your friend, Olga

Several months later, after breakfast, Mr. Coyne said, "John, Mrs. Coyne and I want to talk with you. Let's go into the parlor." Mrs. Coyne wiped her hands on her apron – a familiar gesture – and followed her husband. John, who had been drying the dishes, followed them, and when he entered the room, found them sitting side by side on the davenport. John sat opposite them uneasily. He remembered the day years ago when he'd sat in the same chair and they'd told him they wanted to adopt him. He remembered how his feet didn't touch the floor, and how lost and alone he'd felt.

Mr. Coyne began, "John, you've had your seventeenth birthday, so we'll begin to pay you a farmhand's wages." He shuffled through some papers he had in his lap. "According to the indenture agreement, you'll have to work for us till you're twenty-one, and then you're free."

John lowered his head and squeezed his hands. He'd been expecting this. After all, Grandpa Coyne had been paying Tom for two years now with the same promise of freedom. He looked at the man. *He doesn't even know when my birthday is. The only reason he knows I'm seventeen is because his own son Robbie had his eleventh birthday. Did Grandpa Coyne tell him he had to do this? or Father Lamesch?*

Mr. Coyne reached into his pocket, took out a small wad of bills, and handed it to John. "I'll pay you what I pay my workers." He paused, adding almost as an apology, "I took out your room and board." John pocketed the money without counting it or even looking at it. They sat in silence, John listening to the clock on the mantelpiece – a measure of the time he owed the Coynes. Four more years. What could he say?

"You might not remember," Mr. Coyne said, "but Ma and I offered to adopt you years ago. If you had agreed, things might be different now." He turned to his wife, sitting stone-faced with her gaze on John. He turned back to John. "Our offer still stands. We could still adopt you if you wanted."

"Thank you, but I have to say no." His heart was heavy in refusing them, but he could not agree to be their son. He thought of the years he lived with them, and how they'd never shown him any love. Besides, if he agreed to be adopted now, they wouldn't have to pay him as a farmhand. He'd be worse off than ever. When he had his twenty-first birthday, he'd leave the farm. *The money won't be much, but I can do some things for myself and not have to ask for everything.*

Mr. Coyne interrupted his thoughts. "We like you, John. You're a good worker, dependable and strong. This is your home as long as you want. When you're ready to move on, we'll be sad to see you leave. Isn't that right, Ma?"

"Ja. Ve like you, Johann," she said giving him one of her rare smiles, "und vant you should stay."

The Coynes stood. "Is that satisfactory?" Mr. Coyne asked, pointing in the direction of John's pocket. "I noticed you didn't count it." He gave a rueful laugh.

John remained silent with his head down. After they left the parlor, he rose slowly and followed them into the kitchen where he went back to the dishes. "John, when you're done here I need you in the barn," Mr. Coyne said from the kitchen door in his ordinary businesslike tone.

"Yes, sir," John turned slightly to answer him. "I'll be right along."

Anna Marie sat on the hearthrug, playing with her rag doll; the baby, Willie, played with some blocks nearby. Robbie and Charley ran into the kitchen pleading, "John, we need you."

"John has his chores," Mr. Coyne, who still stood in the doorway, spoke curtly. "Off with you." The boys turned away disappointed. "And no whining," he warned as he stepped out the door.

John knew that when he left, he'd miss these two oldest children — no one or nothing else. He watched Mrs. Coyne knead her bread-dough. She had almost a gentle expression as she worked, almost the way she looked at her children or her husband. Toward him, she always seemed indifferent or remote. He could never be a son to them, no matter what any paper said. He was a servant. He finished the dishes and headed to the barn.

John went to bed, tired but content. He had spent the day on his own in town — a rare free day. He had no farm work, or demands from Mr. Coyne, or children hanging on him. As he looked to the future, he knew he must be patient, patient like the animals and the plants. They grew and developed and came to fruition in due time.

On the other hand, he knew no one triumphed over nature here. He saw what the biting cold, the relentless winds, the scorching sun, and the drenching rains did to everything. He knew he had had enough of milking and plowing and harvesting and tending to animals. But, he wouldn't leave Dakota. This was his home now. Boston did not call him back. He had read somewhere that the word Dakota meant friends, and in this place he had made friends. He remembered the beauties of the day: the red geraniums in such abundance and the sweet, happy call of the meadowlark. He fell asleep, content with the vague sense that autumn was indeed a time of promise. A time of abundance before the long months of winter.

When he'd headed into town earlier in the day, his heart sang. He was on his own; he had money in his pocket. In the year since Mr. Coyne started paying him, this little bit of money gave him a sense of freedom. He also sensed a shift in how the farmer treated him — more like the hired hands.

He headed toward the crowded square where buyers and sellers gathered on market day. As he looked about his eyes fell on a lovely young figure among all that throng. His heart skipped a beat. He looked at her golden hair piled on the top of her head, her mustard yellow blouse and brown skirt, so neat and attractive. John drank in her delicate features as she stood in profile. Young and lovely. Her skin pure and her cheeks rosy. Yes, promise for the future, promise of delights.

He straightened his tie and ran his fingers through his hair. He glanced down to check his jacket and trousers. Perhaps he could speak to her. And though he didn't know what he would say to her, he resolved that he stand in the background of life no more. He took a step toward her, coming within speaking distance when he saw a young man join her. He stepped back.

"What are you doing here, John?" He jumped when he felt a hand on his shoulder. He turned to face his friend.

"Just looking," he said.

Oscar laughed. "Oh, yes, and that lassie's not for you."

"It doesn't hurt to look, Oscar." He gazed again at her. "When you see beauty like that, what's the harm in looking?"

"Only that her intended might not take it lightly that you gaze at her that way," his companion rejoined affectionately.

John blushed. "He's a lucky man. Look how pleased they are to be together."

"Forget her, John." Oscar put his arm around his shoulder and led him away. He said, "Come on." He gestured to a group of young men. 'We're getting up a ball game."

As they walked toward the group of young men, John said, "Count me in."

One evening, as John did his work on the farm, he felt euphoric. Attending Mass always gave him a lift, but today was even more special because the bishop had come to confirm the young people in the area, and he was among those receiving the sacrament.

He'd worn his best suit, the one he had bought with his own money. He'd felt proud because for the first time in his life the trouser legs touched the top of his shoes; his sleeves reached his wrists and were not frayed, nor did the elbows shine. He had starched his collars and cuffs and used the flatiron to make them look as good as new. He knelt with the others, some like Robbie as young as fourteen and others like Tom who were twenty-one. John was twenty. He watched the bishop and priests in their gold vestments. He listened to the swell of the organ with its triumphal music. He watched the incense rising up above the altar. His heart sang.

John walked down the aisle in the long line with the young men on the left with the young women opposite them. He thought of how Father Lamesch had explained in his sermons about the oils placed on their foreheads that would strengthen them in the faith. He wanted a strong faith. Sometimes he was angry with God. In discouraging times, when tired or overworked or overwhelmed with loneliness, he asked himself why. *Why did this happen? Why couldn't I stay where I was born? Why was I sent to this desolate place?*

Today he didn't feel that way. In just over a year he would be free of his indentured servant status. Then he could leave the farm. He didn't know where he'd go or what he'd do, but he knew that he wasn't cut out for farm work. When it was his turn, John stood before Bishop Thomas O'Gorman, who anointed him with the holy oil with the sign of the cross, intoning the Latin formula. Then John felt the light blow on his cheek. He thought of how his faith had been assailed by more strenuous means than this light tap. He walked back to his place and knelt, praying in thanksgiving.

He looked up just as Tom walked down the side aisle. The brothers grinned at one another. Tom was the only piece of his early life he still had. He saw how much they looked alike, the strong family resemblance. These were Donahue faces now signed and sealed as adult Christians.

After church, as they stood around in small groups, he looked toward a gathering of young women. He nodded at Agnes Bowar and Christina Schroeder. He caught the eye of Bessie Craig and smiled at her. All lovely girls. *Maybe I could marry one of these young women. Not yet, though! I can't think about settling down until I'm free and established.* He turned back to talk to his brother, Tom.

Since young Robbie was also confirmed, Mrs. Coyne made a special dinner. And as always on special occasions, the family ate in the dining room and John in the kitchen. Even on this important occasion, they wouldn't welcome him into their circle. *On the day of my First Communion the Coynes didn't pay attention to me either.* Afterwards in the barn John slapped the horse's flank and let the animal muzzle him as he held out a handful of oats. *Yes! One day I will leave here and make my own way.*

When John left the house to check on the cattle, he stopped on the doorstep, looking south. He was alone on the farm for the day. He thought of those days when as a child they had left him behind, how lonesome he had felt, how long the days had seemed, how frightened he had been of the long shadows and the strange noises as night came on. Not anymore. The sky was heavy with rain. He shivered. Before him he could see the creek nestled in the small ravine, and beyond that the cattle huddled together, a sure sign of an impending storm. He looked up. Gloomy and dark, like his mood. But then amazingly, he saw on the far horizon a tiny glimpse of blue. A hint of something brighter.

Yes. He shook himself. *Life will be better when I turn twenty-one.* The blue sky in the far distance, as well as the miles of green land in front of him, told him of life beyond the farm. He often pondered the questions. Was it his destiny to be a farmer? Did he have to bow to the inevitable? What kind of farmer could he be? One who worked for other farmers? With the paltry salary paid to farm workers, he'd never be able to save enough to have his own farm. Besides, this kind of daily grind was not for him. He wanted to use his mind. *No! Now's the time to take the teacher test Miss Reinhart encouraged. Impossible then, not now. If I pass, I'll live away from the farm and its work for six months of the year. And who knows what other bright future may open for me? I must move on, find another path in life.*

He heard the low moan of the cattle and strode forward to tend to them. *Yes, I will do it!* Suddenly his decision became apparent and the sky, far off in the distance, even looked brighter.

Chapter Five
On His Own

At age twenty-one when John won his freedom, he took the teacher test, passed with high grades, and easily found a position in a rural school fifty miles east of Ethan. He would live away from the farm for the three months of the school session in the fall and again in the spring.

At the end of the first session, before he headed back to the Coyne farm, he sat in the little room where he had boarded with Mr. and Mrs. Rasmussen. *How hard to settle down when it's almost time to leave. All packed and ready to go but at loose ends.* He didn't understand why he was anxious to return to the farm. But after all, it was all he knew. There was nowhere else to go. He told himself he had to be patient, save his money, and wait for something to come. He could be patient. That was a lesson he'd learned on the farm. Patience. And living away from the Coyne farm gave him a new perspective. No daily farm chores. Not too long and he'd be back to teach in the spring. He thought of the little boy who came from Boston, the child who loved to read and who loved every minute of school. He knew the farmer had jobs lined up for the winter. He could hear him saying as he had when he first arrived so many years before, "I've got your jobs all lined up, John." But the difference was that now he would pay him farm hand wages, and even a little more than he had paid him as an indentured servant for the last four years.

A knock interrupted his thoughts. He opened the door to find his landlady Mrs. Rasmussen. "Do you want a cup of tea before you go?" she asked solicitously. "You have time, yes?"

Glad of the distraction, he said, "That would be good, thank you." He followed her to the kitchen, where tea was already steeping in the pot. She had biscuits and jam for him on the table. "You'll be needing to eat a little something. We don't want you fainting on the way." She poured his tea and placed a plate in front of him. "Take a biscuit and eat up." She poured herself a cup of tea and sat opposite him. "We'll miss you, John," she said watching him she stirred the sugar into her tea.

He smiled and looked at her warmly. "It's kind of you to say that. Don't worry," he said as he spread the jam on a warm biscuit. "I'll be back for the spring session, so I can enjoy more of your good cooking." He smiled across at her and gestured with the biscuit before he bit into it.

"John, I mean it. We'll miss you. Everyone will. Everyone loves you here – the children, the parents. Elmer and I've loved having you stay with us. We've loved hearing your stories of school and of the children. You've brought light and, if not joy, contentment back to this house. You've brought life into our bleak existence. We're grateful."

"I haven't done much. Sometimes I think I must be boring you with all the stories of school. But I love the children. They're so much fun."

"You've done so much. Just think of all the work you've done around the house. Elmer couldn't have done all that without your help. But most of all you've helped us to deal with our grief. Since our Mary died last year, life has been gloomy. You've brought sunshine back into our lives."

He watched her face as he listened to her telling again the story of her youngest daughter's death. On the threshold of adulthood, she'd suddenly taken ill and had died within a matter of days. He heard the story often in the short time he boarded with them, but knew how much good it was for her to tell it again. "Who knows? If she lived and you two met, perhaps you might have married. Lovely and gentle girl. I think you have much in common with her." She sighed.

He finished up his tea and rose. "Thank you for all your kindness while I've been here. Now I must be on my way. And I'll let you know when I'll be back for classes in the spring." He brought his dish, cup, and saucer to the washbasin. She jumped up to shoo him away, lest he stop to do the washing up as he most often did.

About a month after the spring school session John stepped off the train in Ethan. He was glad to be back and looked for a familiar face – someone who could give him a lift back to the farm. The last month or so, he had spent in the military, offering his services in the trouble in the Caribbean. When he spotted Tom with his red hair and serious expression, his smile broke into a wide grin. He hurried to meet him, put down his valise, and embraced him. "You're a sight for sore eyes."

"Why's the train so late?" Tom asked. "They said it was due an hour ago. I asked the ticket agent what happened, but you might as well talk to the wall for all the information you get from him."

"Some hold up in Sioux Falls. A problem with the track." They walked together to Tom's wagon outside the depot. John handed his luggage to his brother, who tossed it lightly into the back with the sacks and barrels of supplies for the farm.

"You must be tired," Tom said, giving him a sympathetic look.

"Not too bad. I was able to rest on the train. I'll be glad to be back in my own bed, though."

Tom turned the horse east out of Ethan. The brothers waved at the folks they passed along the way. Some shouted, "Glad to have you back, John."

Tom asked, "So how was it? Military life?"

"Fairly bad." he shook his head with a rueful laugh. "The conditions at the camp left much to be desired. Every day I thought they'd get better. They just seemed to deteriorate even more. Then I got a fever. Pretty sick for two weeks. We got word the trouble in Cuba was over about the time I got better. They told us we could go home as soon as we wrapped up things." They rode in silence for some minutes. John broke the silence by asking, "How are the Coynes, and how's work?"

"They're the same. They don't change at all. Work's slow right now. It's good to get away for a change, even if for a few hours." Tom poked him. "You sure are thin."

"I'll fatten up soon," John said, chagrined as he thought of the meager meals awaiting him at the Coynes. "Let me tell you, the army has to serve the worst food in the world."

They rode along in companionable silence for some minutes. Tom gazed at John sideways as he guided the team. "Did you have to go through training?"

"Did we have to go through training?" John echoed his brother. "You bet. We had training and drills and courses in military strategy. I knew I was in the wrong place right away. Why did I think I had to help out in that dispute with Cuba? Why did I listen to Michael J. Coyne?"

"When you headed out, I said to Grandpa Coyne, 'My fool brother's headed out to fight that war.' And before I even had the words out of my mouth, he said, 'What in tarnation? John?' And I said, 'Well, I only have the one brother.' And he said, 'John Donahue wouldn't hurt a fly. He's the kindest, gentlest, most mild-mannered man in the world. That's the wrong place for him to be.'" He gestured to the fields along the road, "How's the land out there?"

"Pretty much the same. We weren't far into Minnesota. Just over the border. Farms in the area look like these." He interrupted himself, "Mild-mannered? Grandpa Coyne never saw me with the cow when she didn't want to give up her milk, or when I got to the end of the last row after plowing or haying all day. I've had my moments." In the near distance a small herd of cows lumbered toward the fence. As he watched them, he thought of the work facing him and sighed.

"Mr. Coyne will be glad to see you. He depends on you, John."

"We work well together. But his own boys are getting bigger now, and he'll have them to help more with the work. Robbie and Charley are good strong workers. I've just about had all the farm work I can stand." They rode along in silence for a bit before he mused aloud, "I'll see if I can get another school. I enjoyed teaching."

Indeed, the following October, John sat in another schoolroom not too many miles north – in a Hutterite Community. The last student had left for the day. What had just happened reminded him of his own childhood when he felt alone surrounded by strangers. He thought of the time early in his stay on the farm when Mrs. Coyne broke forth in a tirade of anger and abuse using every curse word she knew in her guttural German tongue. He didn't know what the words meant, but eventually he learned the language, including the swear words. He never spoke much German, but he understood it. In fact, that was how he got this position so easily in a German settlement – because of his knowledge of the language. Most of the students were bilingual, but the parents knew how important it was for the teacher to understand what the children said in either language.

Mrs. Coyne had picked up his muddy boots, grabbed his arm in a viselike grip, and marched him to the door where with her other hand she had flung his boots into the yard. Tears had sprung to his eyes both from the pain and from confusion. He mumbled, "Sorry," but she didn't stop scolding him, nor let go of her death grip. The word "*Dummkopf*" was the one word he knew.

Later, Mr. Coyne explained that she had washed the floor and was frustrated to find it muddy. He also told him that because the baby, Anna, coughed all night, she'd had little sleep. "You'll learn some colorful language if you keep leaving your boots in the middle of the kitchen floor," he chuckled. "My advice is to take them off and leave them near the door before you go into the house."

"Yes, Mr. Coyne." John caressed his arm, still feeling the sting of her grasp.

"Good boy!" the farmer smiled. "You'll find she's fine when you go into supper. She'll be over it."

Earlier that afternoon John had sat looking over student papers. The children had left, but his helper Friedrich stayed to help clean the classroom. Suddenly the door burst open, and in strode Frau Reinartz shouting German obscenities. John stood and greeted her, "*Guten Tag.*" He asked her gently, "*Was ist los?*"

She was about to continue her tirade when he pulled up the teacher chair for her and said, "*Welkommen, Frau Reinartz. Setchen sie auch, bitte.*"

She was disarmed. The man with the name of Herr Donahue could speak her language. She told him in German that she came to defend her son, Hermann, who came home, crying everyday from school. In fact, today he was so distraught he couldn't tell her what had happened.

John listened intently, and then called Friedrich over. "Friedrich, tell Frau Reinartz what her son does. Tell her he fights with the other boys, that he refuses to speak English and that today, he ran out of school." The woman watched John's face while Friedrich translated. "Tell her it is important for all the children to speak English when they're in school. It's all right to speak German at home, but now that you've come to America, it is important to speak the language of your new home. Once Hermann learns English, he'll teach you and Herr Reinartz."

When Friedrich finished, John asked, "*Verstehen sie?*" She nodded. He went on, "Your son will be fine when he gets to know the other boys. They are all German, but they've learned to speak both languages. Hermann will learn if he just gives himself time. He's frightened. He misses his home in Heilbronn. Tell him to learn a few words every day." He smiled at the mother kindly, adding, "He's a good boy."

When Friedrich translated, she tried to smile. "*Danke. Ja. Hermann ist eine gute Sohn.*" Frau Reinartz looked at Hermann's teacher with his striking blue eyes, knowing he was not the monster that her son was making him out to be. He looked hardly more than a boy himself. So young. Her new friend, Frau Schmitt, told her that this teacher was a good one – not like the one they had last year, who she said beat the children everyday. Her face softened, knowing that her son was in good hands. He would come, she told Friedrich to tell the teacher. She stood, shook John's hand briskly, and left.

Proud of his diplomatic ability, John smiled. He turned to his young helper and said, "Thank you for your help, Friedrich. You may go now. I'll see you tomorrow."

"Mr. Donahue," Friedrich said. "Hermann has sisters at home but his mother won't let them come to school."

"We'll teach Hermann first, and then get the girls to come later. Thanks for telling me." *One battle at a time.*

That night he wrote in his journal. *Am I teaching school because I can? Because I want to get off the farm? Because I like children? Maybe for all those reasons. But I can't continue. How can I save money to establish a home and family on a teacher's salary?*

John returned to the farm at the end of the term, but he had made a decision. He'd move off the farm and into town. Finally, in this year of 1900, he'd be on his own. Mr. Coyne met him at the depot with the wagon. "You look good, John." He stepped back to get a good look at him, "Teaching seems to agree with you." They walked together to the wagon. "You plan on going back in the fall?"

"I think my teaching days might be over. Not enough money in it. I want to try something else." When he saw the older man flinch, he reassured him, "It won't happen right away. You can count on me this spring for the planting."

As they rode along, Mr. Coyne said, "The boys will be glad to see you. And Ma and Anna too. We miss you when you're away."

"I miss you all, too, but it's time I was on my own. After all, I'm almost twenty-three. Time to move on."

"What kind of work are you hoping for?"

"You remember, I talked to Jim Tobin before Christmas. He may be prepared to offer me a position in the land office. Told me to think about it. If the offer's still good, I may take it."

"So you'll go from working the land to selling it, is that it?" Mr. Coyne slapped him on the knee. They laughed.

Robbie, age sixteen, and Charley, fifteen, greeted him with warm familiarity; thirteen-year-old Anna said her hello with a shy smile; the baby cooed from his chair; Mrs. Coyne greeted him with her ordinary aloofness in her mixture of German and English, "*Welkommen, Johan. Ve glad to haf you here. Ve haf stew.*" She pointed to the pot bubbling on the stove. "*You like?*" She turned back to her work, adding under her breath. "*Ya, I know.*"

He said, "Thank you. I'll enjoy it." He looked around and, when he didn't see Willie, asked, "Where's the little one?"

Robbie said, "Off exploring somewhere. He'll be back."

"His stomach tells him when it's time to eat," Charley added.

At that moment, seven-year-old Willie came banging into the kitchen. John didn't know him very well since he'd been away so much the last several years. But, he was good with children, and they responded quickly to him. Willie stopped at the door to greet him shyly. John sat on the nearest chair. "Willie, come and see if you can find the candy." He extended both hands, palms down, closed in a fist. "You have to guess which hand."

Willie stepped forward shyly and poked John's right knuckle with his forefinger. John opened his empty hand.

The child's face darkened in disappointment.

"What do you think?" John asked Will, "Is the other hand empty, too?"

The child lightly touched the outstretched hand. He turned it over and there lay a sweet treat. Willie snatched it up and popped it into his mouth. "You're spoiling his dinner," their father remonstrated with a laugh.

"What about us?" Charley asked, stepping forward. "Do you have anything for us?"

His father teased him, "For you? Why would a great lug like you be wanting candy?"

John leaned down and pulled a sack out of his suitcase and put it on the table. He looked around at the assembly. "For the family," he said, smiling at Robbie and Charley.

"Why don't you take your bag upstairs?" Mr. Coyne asked. "Supper's almost ready. You can unpack later."

"I'll do that." He stood looking around at the family before heading up to his little room. Even though he shared the room with Robbie (the other two boys were across the hall), he thought of it as his room.

Not too many weeks later with much of the planting finished, John donned his new blue serge suit for his interview with Mr. Tobin. The Coyne family waited in the kitchen, mostly silent, Mr. Coyne pacing, Mrs. Coyne fussing at the stove, the children sitting or standing around. "Where are you, John? Are you almost ready?" Robbie called up the stairs. "We're waiting to see the show."

John adjusted his collar and cuffs and tugged on his jacket. He headed down to the kitchen. Mr. Coyne whistled. Even Mrs. Coyne turned and smiled, while the children clapped in approval. "What do you think?" he asked the assembled family members. "Will Mr. Tobin hire me if I look like a business man?"

"He'd be a fool not to. You certainly cut a fine figure," Mr. Coyne said. "Turn around. Let's get a good look at you."

He did as told. Anna stepped forward. "Wait a minute, John. You have a loose thread here." She plucked a thread from the back of his jacket. "Now you're perfect." She stepped back quickly.

"Thanks." He turned and gave her a smile. Then he looked to the others. "Don't stand there gawking."

"Forgive us, John. It's not every day you have a new suit," Mr. Coyne said as he fingered the sleeve. "That's beautiful material."

"I read somewhere that clothes make the man," John said, standing tall, squaring his shoulders. "It can't hurt to look your best."

As he had dressed, he'd remembered the farmer saying to him again several days ago as he had said often lately, "I'm sorry, John, but I still don't understand why you can't just stay here and do farm work. You know you're welcome to work here."

"Thanks, Mr. Coyne." He'd looked at the farmer evenly in the face of this old argument. "I appreciate your offer, but I think I'd like to try some other kind of work. I don't think I'm cut out to be a farmer."

"Nonsense." Mr. Coyne had turned away to stare dejectedly out the window at his fields. "You do a fine job. I couldn't hire a better farm hand." He added quietly, almost to himself, "I really don't know how I can replace you."

"I may be able to do the work, but my heart's not in it," John had said, looking at his back. "I want to see what else I can do."

Mrs. Coyne turned away from her work at the stove and asked, "*Vat time ist meeting?*"

She wants me out of her kitchen, out of her hair, out of her life. He took his watch out of its fob. "I've got plenty of time. Over an hour."

Willie moved closer. "I wanna see."

He showed the boy the new pocket watch and held it to the child's ear. Willie liked this better than the suit. The three teenagers also took a turn to look at the timepiece. After a few minutes, John closed the cover and returned it to its pocket. "Now I've got to be going. I do want to be there in plenty of time. I'll see you when I get back. I'll tell you all about it."

Robbie put out his hand to wish him, "Good luck." The others repeated, "Good luck."

Mr. Coyne and Robbie walked out with John to the yard where the horse waited, saddled and ready. Mr. Coyne shook his hand, saying awkwardly, "I hope it goes well, John." Robbie gave him a hand in mounting his horse. The children stood in the doorway to see him go.

Journal entry – May 15, 1900

A great relief. I start a new life, my own life, away from the daily grind of farm work. No longer am I a slave to the whims of the Coynes and weather. Glad I can make this change. Some may say what happened to Tom and me was charity, that the sisters in the Orphan Home who sent us here and the families who took us in were acting in our best interest. But what they did to us was sinful. That we as children were forced to work as slaves, and that's what indentured servitude is, is shameful.

And how did they keep their slavery a secret? They called us their foster family and they offered to adopt us. Not out of love, nor out of concern for us, but out of greed. Here was an opportunity for free labor. If I had been adopted, I would not have been free. One thing I've always wanted to ask, but can never ask – who gave you the right, Mr. Coyne, to exploit a child? How do you feel at night when you say your prayers, asking God for protection for your children? Do you ever give a thought to the man who fathered me?

The Home should have told us that we would never see our father. We believed that we were only to work for a short time and then return to Boston. I might've known the truth if I'd just paid attention. Playmates used to disappear suddenly from the Home – whole groups of them – never to return. But I was too young to understand.

This family is decent, and even though lately Mr. Coyne has been kinder to me, all the years of growing up, they never gave me any love or attention. Who knows what awaits me! Finally, I will choose my own life.

John stepped out of the farmhouse to face a large crowd of people in the yard. He believed they could help him. Instead they turned from him. When he begged for help, they gave no response. He looked back where Mr. Coyne stood impassive in the doorway. He turned again toward to the crowd, but they'd become a pack of wolves, baring their teeth. They would tear him apart. He turned back to the farmer. He was gone and the door was locked and barred. His heart pounded and his body jumped. He awoke with a start. It was a dream. He lay panting with dread and fear as he faced the unknown. How would he survive on his own?

He rose, dressed, and then stood in the doorway looking at the room he'd slept in for all these years. Suddenly, he realized how lucky he was to have a room all these years. He'd heard of boys in his situation that had slept for years in a barn.

After breakfast, he carried his few belongings down the stairs and out to the waiting wagon. The family sat at the kitchen table, silently waiting to say good-bye. Mr. Coyne stood when he reentered the kitchen. "Are you ready, John?" The two older boys rose also.

"Yes, I have everything." He looked around at them all. He went to Mrs. Coyne first, standing at the end of the table collecting dishes. She put them down and wiped her hands on her apron. He took her hands in his and said, "Thank you for all you've done for me over the years." He looked at her warmly with his penetrating blue eyes. *"Danke und auf wiedersehen."*

Tears sprang into both their eyes. Gently, John pulled free from her and moved along the table where he tousled the hair of Willie and Ed, shook Anna's hand warmly, and embraced Robbie and Charley each in a bear hug.

At dinner the evening before, they'd sat around outside in the yard and quietly talked of the years that he had lived with them. Mr. Coyne had said, "We'll miss you, John. You're part of the family."

He nodded but said nothing. *Yes, you will miss my help with the farm work, and Mrs. Coyne will miss me in the kitchen and helping with the children.*

He stepped to the door, then turned back and said, "Goodbye. I'm sure we'll meet ..." His voice broke, and the tears came again. He was saying goodbye, not just to the family and to this home, but also to his childhood and his innocence. Quickly, he left the house, down the few stairs, and pulled himself up onto the Coyne wagon. The farmer joined him and started the team of horses. John looked back and saw the children in the yard, waving at him. Mrs. Coyne held the baby and stood in the doorway to see him off.

Their drive took them two miles north, then five miles west to the town of Ethan. John pictured it in his mind's eye as they rode along, silently thinking it was like something a meteor shower left with its cluster of buildings plunked down in the middle of the open prairie, all huddled together as if for warmth or protection. He knew of similar towns as if randomly thrown down, but when you looked closely, you saw that a ribbon of railroad tracks connected them, snaking along from Yankton in the south to Mitchell and on to Aberdeen in the north.

As often as he'd been to Ethan, it would be different now. He mused aloud, "You know the town was named for the Ethan Allen of Revolutionary fame. I find that interesting."

Mr. Coyne shifted in his seat and spoke slowly, as if speaking into the distance. "I remember when Si Gillis moved his building with the post office and trading post from Rome up here. Fifteen or twenty years ago. About the time we arrived. The Milwaukee Railroad platted the town with the streets running east and west and north and south. Many changes since then."

They lapsed back into silence. When they arrived at the Tobin house, where he would board, Mrs. Tobin greeted him warmly. Mr. Coyne helped him bring his belongings into the second floor bedroom. After depositing his bags, John walked Mr. Coyne back to the wagon. They embraced awkwardly. "You know, John," the farmer said, "you'll always have a home with us. If things don't work out or ..." He trailed off. They embraced again, both in tears. Embarrassed, they separated. The man who'd been his foster father hopped up onto the wagon and gave a signal to the horses.

John wiped his eyes, watched him go until he disappeared around a corner. He went back into the house. Mrs. Tobin stepped out of the kitchen. "John, Jim said you can go to the office anytime. I think he didn't expect you this early, but he's there."

"Thanks, Mrs. Tobin. I'll go down now, then." He turned to leave.

"John, you're to call me Till. We don't need to be formal in this house."

"Till?" he looked at her quizzically. "An interesting name. And your real name is?"

"My name is Matilda, but when my sister Mattie was small, she couldn't manage that, so I became Till."

"And Mattie's name is ...?" he asked as he leaned easily against the doorjamb.

"Martha." With her arms folded, she stood at the end of the table where her daily baking awaited her. Her two small children played nearby on the hearthrug.

"And Bessie is Elizabeth?" he asked. He was reluctant to leave this pleasant woman.

She laughed lightly, "Yes, but that's her middle name. Her first name is Theresa, but no one has ever called her that."

"How many Craigs are there? I always forget."

"Ten. Two boys and eight girls. Half of them still live on the farm. My brothers look like they'll never marry, and the three youngest, Mattie, Bessie, and Katie, still live at home."

He shook himself, "I better let you get back to work and get myself over to the office." He smiled gratefully at her warm hospitality and headed out. *Yes, I'll feel at home with the Tobins.* He walked along Ash, and at Second turned north. He looked at the houses, brave structures exposed to the harsh Dakota weather. He saw that the gardens, both flower and vegetable, gave color to the otherwise bleak landscape. On Main street he looked to the block of businesses: the Commercial Hotel, the Rosenquist Blacksmith Shop, Snow's General Store, Tobey's Restaurant, Nalt's Lumberyard, the bank run by Bronson, the post office run by Jud Annis, Donk and Stopher's Hardware (with the land office where he would work on the second floor). These familiar places – these familiar folks. A town he knew that always had a population of about

300, a town where he knew everyone.

When he reached the land office, Mr. Tobin rose to greet him with a warm handshake. "Welcome, John. I have everything for you here on your desk. I hope you find everything satisfactory. Look at the papers to get a feel for what you'll be doing."

John said, "Mr. Tobin, I want to look at those parcels of land east of Mitchell you talked about yesterday. I could take the early afternoon train and survey the area." He was anxious to begin.

"Yes, you can do that. But John, you're to call me Jim. We don't have to be that formal in this office." He smiled warmly at him and then pointed to the typewriter on a third desk. "Remember, you can use that anytime you need. You young fellows amaze me. I'm just learning how to use it." He moved to his own desk, found the papers, and handed them to John, who had followed him across the room. "You sure you want to plunge right in?"

"I'm ready." John took the papers and returned to his own place with a smile. "Thank you for giving me this chance." *I can do this. Open a new chapter in my life.*

Chapter Six
Finding a Family

John lived with the Tobins for two years. When the family relocated to Iowa, he moved into the Craig farmhouse until he could find a more permanent boarding place. He had taken over the land office business and began to feel more secure in his future. On a cool Saturday morning he and Bessie Craig stepped out the back door to weed the garden. "These plants should do quite nicely," she said as she attacked the weeds with her trowel. "We've got to clean up this area." She pointed to several nearby flowerbeds.

He stepped back to watch her work. Now he was sure he wanted this woman to be his wife. Every fiber of his being ached for her. He couldn't remember when he'd first met her, but they must have been very young. Over the years, he had seen her often in town, at church, at the festivals, at the dances. But now he felt something new. Feeling his eyes on her, she looked up at his gentle expression with his clear blue eyes fixed on her.

"How long have we known one another?" he asked.

She sat back on her heels and repeated his question. "How long have we known one another? I don't know. Since we were children." He watched the color rise in her cheeks. She turned back to her work, throwing a handful of weeds away from the plot and concentrating on another stubborn patch. "Why?" she asked softly. He did not answer, but stood gazing at her. She spoke again without looking up, "Why don't you see what you can do in that flower bed over there." She gestured with her free hand. "Take care of the weeds and aphids."

He moved to where the early crocus bloomed, with the tulips and hyacinths almost ready. He placed himself so that he faced her. The day before, when she'd come home for the weekend from her teaching position, he had watched her. Elizabeth Craig. Why hadn't he paid attention to her before? For years he'd known her and hadn't really seen her. Now that he lived in her house, he listened to the stories her mother told and watched her interact with her brothers and sisters. He found himself looking forward to Fridays. He'd think, *She'll be here tonight.*

Everything in the house and garden spoke of her and her capable hands. She was beautiful; she had delicate features, dark brown luxuriant hair, snapping dark eyes, fair skin, and a dainty girlish figure. She always spoke softly and calmly, but with conviction because she knew her own mind. She was clever and kind and good. And the wonder was that he thought she liked him, too. *Yes, we might make a life together, have a family and share a home. Dare I hope? Can I believe in such good fortune for me?*

Just then Bessie's father, Will with his pipe clamped in his mouth, stepped out of the back door, banging the screen door behind him. "John," he said. "I'm going over to the south forty. Want to come along?" He glanced at his daughter. "That is, if Bessie can spare you."

Deferring to her, John asked, "Is that all right?"

"Yes," she said, without looking up. "You two go along."

That evening John found his chance to talk to her. After supper, they walked out to the apple orchard beyond the barn.

"Bessie," he spoke haltingly, "I think you know I love you and that I want to marry you."

"John, I ..." she began.

He held up his hand to stop her from speaking. "No, don't say anything yet. Let me finish." He took a breath. He looked at her, and seeing her rising color and the look in her eyes, found courage to go on. "I have nothing to offer you but what you see before you. No family." He added quickly, "I will not shame you, I promise. I'm determined to establish a home and have as fine a family as you deserve."

Again she started to speak, and again he stopped her. He took her hands in his and looked into her warm dark eyes. "I don't know by experience what a real family is, but I want to work at making a family with *you*. I lived with a family, but it wasn't my family, and they never made me feel a part of their family. I hope you can love and trust me." He paused to take another breath. "I think I can support us. I'm doing all right in the land office. And I have the grain elevator work seasonally. Since the age of seventeen, I've been saving what I can of my earnings. Mr. Coyne paid me for my work the last several years I was on the farm, and I taught school for several years. He reached up and plucked an apple blossom. He placed it gently in her hand. "I love you. Will you marry me?"

She cupped it in her hand lightly. "Oh John," she whispered. Now she was speechless.

"I want to give you a room full of blossoms, not just this one." He looked at her steadily, trying to read her thoughts.

"John, I'll be happy to marry you." They gazed at one another, facing the setting sun, their faces suffused with a warm glow. His red hair and her dark locks so close together sparkled in the light.

"You make me so happy ..." His voice faltered, and tears came to his eyes. "I come to you with empty hands. I have only a sad history."

"John, money is not the important thing. You're a good man. You have talents and abilities. You're intelligent and ambitious." She spoke warmly. "Look at all you've accomplished since you left the farm. People admire and respect you."

They stood quietly content to be together. John's mind raced. He hadn't thought everything through. "Do you mind terribly waiting until next year? I have a plot of land where I want to put up a house in town."

"Yes, if you think that's best. I can wait. But, John, the house is not as important as the people who will live in it." She touched his arm gently. "And you're going to let *me* contribute to this marriage. I've been teaching for several years, and I've set aside some savings too. If I can get a position next year, I'll have even more."

As they walked back to the house, he stopped her and asked, "Did your Mother tell you I'm moving out to the Davis place tomorrow?" He took her by the arm. "Old Bill needs someone to look after him."

"Yes. Wouldn't the tongues wag if we were living in the same house before we marry!"

"Seriously, it has nothing to do with that. It just happens that his son asked me to help out. With free lodging, I'll save on living expenses." They took several steps forward. "I can still come and see you on weekends."

A month later John presented Bessie with an engagement ring – a pledge of his love, he told her. They walked out in the yard, and when they returned to the house, they spoke to her parents, Sarah and Will, who welcomed the proposal gladly. They told him he would make a good addition to their family. They had always admired how he overcame his difficult childhood with ambition and hard work. They knew he respected their daughter and treated others with dignity.

The four sat in the parlor; the Craigs in their matching easy chairs faced Bessie and John sitting side by side on the davenport. "I've got to be honest with you," John said, looking first at Will, then at Sarah. "When Tom and I were sent here as children, we knew our father was ill. Several years ago I wrote to Massachusetts to see if I could find him. I got word he's in a mental institution. You should know that."

Will said, "That has nothing to do with you, John. You're a fine gentleman who has proved yourself. You have nothing to be ashamed of.

Sarah added, "What you are is what you've made of yourself, John. Don't think your father's illness has anything to do with who you are or our acceptance of you as a husband for our Bessie."

"I will always respect her. I'll be good to her," he promised.

"We expect you mean it," William said warmly and rose to shake John's hand.

One evening John visited the Craigs. When he saw that their grass needed cutting, he took out the mower and got to work. Sarah insisted he stay for supper with the family, Will, her two sons, Katie and herself. Afterwards, he and Sarah sat on the porch chatting in the fading summer light. John reported on the progress of his house and about the folks in town. She talked about her married daughters and the latest letters she'd received from them.

The following day around noon, thinking about lunch, he put his hand into his jacket pocket. No billfold. "Dadgum," he said under his breath. His heart sank. He broke out in a cold sweat. "*Where's my money? Where did I leave it?*" He checked his pockets. He looked through his desk drawers and around the office. No luck. There was nothing to do but retrace his steps. He had to find that money. He was in a panic because all the money he had saved was gone – all $130. He had bills for the house he was building.

Josiah looked up from his desk on the other side of the room. "What was that, John? I didn't hear you. Did you want something?"

"No, nothing," John said, irritated with himself. He couldn't tell Josiah just now. If and when he found it, he would. "I have to go out on an errand. Be back shortly." He grabbed his fedora from the rack.

"What about lunch?" Josiah called after him.

"I'll eat later," John shot back as he hurried out the door and down the stairs. "I've got to take care of some personal business."

He would look first in his room, and then retrace his steps over the past twenty-four hours. He did that – walked everywhere he'd been, along the road, at the blacksmith's, in the lunchroom. He racked his brain trying to remember if he had taken it out and put it somewhere. He stopped at several businesses and inquired, but no one had seen it. His feeling of panic increased. He went to the Craig farm and told Sarah.

"I didn't find it," she said sympathetically, wiping her hands on her apron. "But you're welcome to look around. I'll look, too." She headed toward the kitchen. "Let's see. You were in the kitchen and we sat on the porch. Anywhere else?"

"It's not here. I'll go look in the shed and in the yard. Maybe I dropped it when I took out the mower, or maybe somewhere on the lawn."

"All right, I'll keep looking. Maybe Dad picked it up and put it somewhere. He could do that, you know, and not tell me." She headed toward the dining room.

More agitated by the minute, John walked out to the back and into the shed. When his eyes adjusted to the semi-darkness, he looked around. He moved the mower, and lo and behold, there was his wallet in the corner! He opened it and saw that all the money was there. All $130. He heaved a sigh of relief, and put the wallet into his inside breast pocket.

"I found it," he shouted to Sarah, who had stepped out onto the porch.

"Thank God," she said. "What a relief! Come in and have a cool glass of lemonade. Or can I get you some lunch?" she asked hopefully.

"No," John said. "Thank you anyway, but I've got to get back to the office. I left in the middle of things. I'll see you again soon." He saluted her.

He hurried back to the office with a lighter heart. He wished Bessie were here so he could tell her, but he'd write her a letter. He missed her so much. Iowa might as well be on the other side of the world. However, in less than a year's time, once they were wed, they'd be together.

Office of The J. L. Donahue Real Estate and Loan Co.
Lands Bought and Sold, Loans Negotiated
Room 9, Stopher Building
July 21, 1903

Dear Bess,

You asked me if I wanted you to come home. Nothing you could do now would please me more. But you must not come. I don't want to be so selfish as to have you come home now. It would be mean of me. I hope you like down there quite well. You must go and see everything you can and enjoy yourself all you can. I always miss you most on Sundays. I have been so used to seeing you then.

Do you know dear that I sometimes think I am the most miserable being in the world when I ought to be happy as I have every reason I could possibly have, except perhaps if I would some morning wake up and find myself a rich man. I am not sure that would make me happy. I hardly think it would, yet

I cannot overcome that desire to get rich. I was out at your place Sunday evening and got the mower and mowed down some of the weeds in the yard, and lost my pocketbook and $130 in it but was fortunate enough to find it. I did not miss it for nearly a half day afterward. I tell you I bounced around like a rubber ball for awhile, as it was the size of my pile now.

It doesn't seem very long till you will be mine. Won't you, darling? I will not get poetical this time dear but I hope this finds my darling well and happy and I know it will be a welcome missive. I am loath to leave off, will promise to do better next time and say good night.

Your own John

August 16, 1903

My dearest Bess,

In a talk with your folks this morning, your mother told me of the little girl that Ella has taken. Finally we got to speaking of myself at Coynes and the kind of a time I had there. Your mother thought all boys on a farm had quite hard times and said that "Our John" also had had his share. "But these young kids of ours, they've had good times and it spoils them. But never mind they'll come down and then they'll see."

So you see what a bad girl you are. Your mother didn't mean it though. She wouldn't have anything happen to one of you for the world. Sometimes she gets mad because you aren't kids anymore.

I used to think I was the most abused kid that ever lived. Maybe I was mean, but I never got convinced of the fact either from argument or more strenuous evidence forcibly administered. I don't believe that it is necessary to have hard times in order to get the proper conception of what a decent person's life should be. I can't imagine anyone wishing to see sorrow or necessity come to those who are dear to them.

I have an unbounded respect for all mothers; I would give a great deal if I could have my mother. But the love I have for you is a thousand times greater. This may seem absurd but I was young when mother died. During all the lonely years of boyhood I had a longing in my heart. It must have been for the mother's love that I never knew after I was old enough to realize its worth. We never know the value of such things until actually deprived of them. When I have you with me I do not think then that perhaps I might lose you. But when you are away I know how much I love you. And each day I am away from you makes you dearer to me. I think it is well you went to Sheldon this summer. I know I love you more now and I never doubt your love like I used to.

I must close now. Let me know how everyone is. Is your certificate all right for this fall term? Write soon and tell me when you will come home.

Your own John

Several months later John stood across the street and admired the house he had lovingly labored on for the past year. He surveyed his neighbors' houses to the east and to the west. When he saw a train sitting on the tracks, he felt a sharp pang of anxiety. As a child, he often wondered where the home was for him. He wondered if he could crawl back into the black beast and be carried back to where he belonged. Could he go home to Boston? Or could home be transplanted to the wilderness? But the doubts nagged at him still. What was home to him? It wasn't Boston, with its long-lost image of family. It wasn't the orphan home that he hated. It wasn't the Coyne farmhouse. No, he never knew a real home. Soon he and Bessie would marry and live in this fine structure. *That's what makes a home – two people who love each other. No longer a dream, but soon a reality.*

Suddenly he heard the wail of the train, startling him. Often when he heard it, he became the terrified child thrown into the belly of the monster where he lay for days and was carried away into this wilderness – away from the familiar and toward strangers and unrelenting work. Often in his nightmares as a child, he relived the train journey across the country and, when waking, he felt like Jonah in the belly of the whale spat out onto alien soil. *God, why? Who decided?* He smelled the acrid black smoke that the beast belched and heard the wailing, an echo of his wailing child's soul.

He shook himself. The terrors of childhood were over. He owned his own home. He would share it with Bessie Craig, soon to be his wife, and they would make a family. Smiling, he entered the house. He watched the play of light on the floor from the large front window. *Our family home. No longer alone or haunted by fear.*

A few days later John shelved his books in the parlor and put his clothes into the wardrobe and chest of drawers in the bedroom. He stepped back to see how much space was left. *Yes, plenty of room for Bessie's things.* He looked out the window to see the Craigs' wagon pulling up in front. He hurried out and down the few stairs to greet them. Her brother Joe hopped down first and reached out to shake John's hand. John helped Bess down, holding her hand and smiling whispered, "Soon." The color rose in her cheeks, giving her a glow of health and beauty.

Her father Will got down more slowly and approached John with his hand extended. "Wait'll you see all the things this girl has." He gestured where John could see several trunks and bags. "I'm afraid to go back home. I'll probably find *our* house empty." The three men laughed.

All business, Bessie ignored them and moved to the rear of the wagon. She pointed to the smaller of the chests. "That one goes in the dining room. It has my linen."

Joe pulled it forward and said, "I can carry that. John and Father, you two bring in the other one together." He hefted the trunk to his shoulder and headed into the house.

She pointed to the other trunk. "This holds my clothes and goes in the bedroom." She stopped John as he jumped up on the back of the wagon. "John, hand me the satchels first. I can carry those in."

He handed the bags down, then John and Mr. Craig lifted the trunk and carried it between them to the house, up the four stairs, across the porch, and into the house. Bessie followed them.

When everything was in, the three men stood in the doorway chatting. Bessie said, "Go about your business." She pushed them out. "It won't take me long to put these things away."

John paused and asked solicitously, "Bess … Can I … help you with anything?"

"No, you go, too. Leave me alone. I have to do this organizing by myself."

Will turned and called to him, "Come on, John. We're going to the blacksmith." He linked his arm in John's. "You'll learn when to leave womenfolk to themselves."

When they returned a half-hour later, Bessie was standing at the front door. She called to John and asked him to come in for a minute. Her father and brother waited by the wagon. She showed him the Bible her parents were giving them, and the statue of the Sacred Heart from her sister Ella. "We'll keep the Bible in the parlor and the statue in the bedroom. Is that all right?"

He ran his hand over the cover of the Bible, his eyes misting, so touched was he by their generosity. *This for us, for our new home.* After a few minutes, he said, "We are truly blessed." They exchanged glances, the looks of expectant, even nervous anticipation.

John sat on his bed at the Davis place, his gaze fixed on his new suit. Beside him on the bed, he'd laid out his linen. He still had to press his collar and cuffs. He put his hand to his brow. His mind raced, his heart pounded. *What am I doing? Do I really love Bessie Craig? Does she love me? What does that mean? Love.*

He went over in his mind the married couples he knew. The Coynes never showed outward affection. Suddenly he remembered a day when he was about thirteen and he came upon them in the kitchen, giggling like teenagers. Mr. Coyne was tickling Mrs. Coyne while she was half-heartedly pushing him away. Embarrassed, he'd left the house and returned to the barn.

This past year as he realized his love, proposed, and prepared for married life, he had watched how the Craigs treated one another. This couple was full of banter and teasing with easy familiarity. But he had not seen them physically demonstrative.

Since he had decided to wed, he wanted to talk to someone. But who? Could he talk to Tom? His poor brother, he sighed. He couldn't talk to him. He wouldn't even be here from Alexandria to the wedding as he and his wife Belle awaited the birth of their second child. Maybe already born. They were still grieving the loss of their first born, whom they had named John. His doubts paled in comparison.

Who else? Mr. Craig would probably be embarrassed. Nor could he talk to Mr. Coyne. If his father were here, *he'd* help him. No, he was truly on his own as he had been for everything since childhood. He realized, as he fingered the wool jacket sleeve, that if he survived childhood, he could survive anything. Now he had Bessie's love and their life together to help him do more than survive.

In the morning John rose early. He was glad to be alone – alone since last week when old Bill with whom he was staying had gone to the hospital. This was the day. He dressed and stepped out onto the porch to breathe in the fresh spring morning. Everything was ready. He listened to the birds as he watched the sun make its slow progression in the east. The morning dew sparkled on the grass like diamonds. His heart sang.

He shook himself and went back inside to adjust his collar and cuffs. The sound of the carriage wheels in the yard startled him, even though he was listening for them. *That would be Robbie to fetch me.*

"Good morning. You're right on time," he called as he stepped out to greet his friend.

Robbie jumped down, took his hand and said, "Good morning, John. I must say you certainly look handsome." The friends looked at one another with affection. Even though John had moved out of the Coyne farm four years before, he saw Robbie often enough to maintain his love for the young man who had become even closer to him than his brother. *A worthy substitute as witness.* Robbie said, "Let's go. You don't want to be late for your own wedding." He clapped him on the shoulder affectionately.

As they rode along, John went over in his mind the events of the day. They would have the wedding during Mass, friends and his new family would be there, and he would come away with his beautiful bride. Then they'd have breakfast at the Craigs' house, and after that go on to the depot to take the train south to Iowa. They'd stay a few days in Sioux City and from there to Minneapolis. *To spend all that time with his bride – in fact a long life with her stretched ahead.* He smiled. His bag was packed; the wedding ring was in his pocket. His thoughts flew back to Tom who couldn't come. *I stood for him last year when he married Belle. Today, he can't even be here.*

Robbie pulled the wagon in front of the white frame church with its steeple pointing high into the sky. His brother Charley had saved a place for the wagon outside the front door. Robbie jumped down to secure the horse. The Craig family had arrived and sat in the front pews. The Coynes assembled on the groom's side. Some friends and town folks took places behind them. The groom, waiting in the sanctuary, looked toward Sarah, who smiled at him from her place. Finally, John saw his bride, and his heart leapt at the sight of her. Dressed all in white, Bessie carried a simple rose bouquet. Her hat with its flowers and feathers added a few inches to her five-foot frame. The organ trumpeted a triumphal refrain, and Katie, the maid of honor, in a lovely ash-rose dress, led the party down the aisle. Bessie walked with her father. When they reached the altar, the strains of the organ tapered off. Will put his daughter's hand into John's. He bowed his head as if to give a silent blessing, and turned to join Sarah.

During Mass, John was aware of Bessie close to him. He could smell the faint fragrance of her flowers. The flickering candlelight sent a ripple of doubt through him. *Was this right?* He barely paid attention to the familiar ritual, nor did he listen to the Latin prayers. He stood, knelt, and sat automatically when the others did. He prayed silently, *God, help us to make this marriage work. May I learn to trust you and may I make Bessie happy.* As they exchanged vows, his voice trembled. *A wife, a family. Finally.* He looked into Bessie's face. In her warm eyes, he saw acceptance and love. She spoke her vows with confidence. When John placed the small gold ring on her finger, he felt a joyful surge of determination. *We will make this work.* He smiled nervously at her.

Later, as they walked down the aisle to the front door, John knew the eyes of well-wishers were on them. He felt the warmth of Bessie's hand securely holding onto him as she confidently smiled up at him. *She's the strong one.* Outside the church, they greeted their family and friends, who, after congratulating them, moved into small groups, the women talking of the wedding or of the dresses, the men of the crops and the hopes for the season. Each of the Craig men and all the brothers-in-law clapped John on the shoulder. Bessie's sisters embraced them. Michael and Rosa Coyne, with their children, Charley and Anna, stepped forward in their turn. Gradually, they all moved to their wagons. Only the wedding party and the bride's parents would take the two-mile trip for breakfast at the Craig homestead. Most of the men had to return to the fields, the women to their household chores.

𝕿𝖍𝖊 𝕰𝖓𝖙𝖊𝖗𝖕𝖗𝖎𝖘𝖊
April 14, 1904

Donahue-Craig Wedding at
St. Peter's and Paul's Church, Starr

On Thursday morning at eight o'clock the marriage of Mr. John L. Donahue and Miss Elizabeth Craig was solemnized at St. Peter's and Paul's Church in the presence of numerous friends and relatives. After the impressive marriage ceremony the bridal party returned to the home of the bride's parents, where an elegant breakfast had been prepared and later, coming to Ethan, took the 11:30 train for the south.

After a short bridal tour to points in Iowa and Minnesota, they will take up their residence in this place. Both Miss Craig and Mr. Donahue are too well known to the majority of our readers to require an introduction, having lived in this vicinity since childhood, late-Miss

Craig becoming a very successful teacher and Mr. Donahue being well known as a popular grain buyer and real estate agent. Their many friends with one voice wish them success and happiness, and *The Enterprise* adds its hearty congratulations and throws its handful of rice with the rest.

John and Bessie sat side by side on the bench in the Minneapolis Art Museum. They gazed at the paintings, he dressed in his navy blue suit with white shirt and starched collar and cuffs, she in a light tan spring coat with the hint of her pink frock underneath. His fine head of red hair contrasted with her dark, almost black tresses, which she had pinned up under her brown hat trimmed with bright pheasant feathers. However, one saw an even more striking contrast in their eyes, his a liquid blue, made more brilliant by his clothing, and hers, dark and snapping. They had set aside a day on their trip to visit the newly opened museum.

Comfortable with one another, they sat holding hands in silence. He turned slightly to her, "What do you think? Could I have been that lad?"

"What did you say?" She moved her eyes away from the portrait of a lady she had been studying.

He squeezed her hand and drew her even closer to him. "This picture of the newsboy." He pointed slightly to the right. "If I had stayed in Boston I might perhaps have sold papers to help the family. What do you think?" He stood, pulling her with him to get a closer look at the painting.

As they neared it, Bessie smiled. "I like this lad. His rosy cheeks and bright eyes make him look healthy and well cared-for. And his beautiful suit, hat, and boots! I'd say he's having an easier life than you did."

"It's hard to tell. I read an article in the paper that talked of the hard life of poor children in New York and Boston and how they make a living any way they can. The honest ones sell newspapers. I shudder to think what some others are driven to." As she waited for him to go on, he thought for some minutes. "It pains me that children are in such a state. At least I wasn't abandoned like some are. My father put us in a home. Imagine if that home hadn't sent me to Dakota to do farm work; I wouldn't be sitting here in Minneapolis with you." He fell silent, staring at the painting. "In any event, our children will have a better childhood than I did."

"I agree. But children must also learn to work. We need to fit them for success in life and teach them the value of labor."

"We'll teach them the important values, don't worry." They sat quietly for several minutes, lost in their own thoughts. "Bessie, it's good to be here. I'm surrounded by beauty, and the most wonderful beauty is sitting right beside me."

Finally, in their new home, John and Bessie sat in their matching dark red velvet overstuffed chairs. The table between them held the kerosene lamp, giving them both light for their reading. Opposite them stood their settee and beyond that the double door, open to the dining room with its new oak table, chairs, and china closet. He read a book with stories of the Greek heroes, and she had the newspaper she had picked up in Minneapolis. They sat in companionable silence.

She put the paper down and watched him for a few minutes, then she said gently, "Excuse me, John."

He put his bookmark in the page and closed the book. He looked at her and smiled.

"I don't know about you, but I want an early night."

"All right, you go ahead and I'll come along in a few minutes. Take the candle with you." He gestured across the room. "I'll stoke the fire."

She didn't move, but sat on. Together they watched the hearth fire. "When is our wedding portrait coming?" she asked, suppressing a yawn.

"The photographer said to give him a couple of weeks."

"I'm thinking," she said gesturing, "that the wedding portrait should look nice on the wall behind the settee. Don't you agree?" When he nodded, she went on, "and the art prints from the museum on the opposite wall."

He looked to where she pointed. "Yes, that sounds good."

"That Curtis Hotel was certainly fine, wasn't it? Robbie gave you good advice when he suggested we stay there."

"It certainly was." They smiled at one another. Finally, after sitting silently for some minutes, she rose and kissed him.

Earlier that day when they had alighted from the train in Ethan, John handled the luggage. When he'd seen the two lads playing by the side of the Commercial Hotel, he called them over. "Joseph, Francis. How would you like to earn some money?"

Their eyes lit up. "Yes, Mr. Donahue," they said.

"Take these grips to our house. You know our new white house?" He reached into his pocket for some coins.

Joseph said, "We know your house, Mr. Donahue."

"Leave them on the front porch. We're coming right along behind you." He handed them each a nickel.

"Thank you, Mr. Donahue." They grinned, pocketed their coins, then hoisted the luggage and headed down the street in front of the newlyweds.

The couple walked arm in arm to their new home. The two boys dashed by to take up their post again near the hotel. When John and Bess approached the yard, they stopped in front of the house.

"We need to get started on the garden," Bessie said. "What do you think? A vegetable garden over there to the east, and along here in the front, the flowers, marigolds, zinnias, and sweet William. And maybe hollyhocks in the back?" She inspected the area and added, "And cosmos. I want cosmos."

"Good. How about a lilac bush at the corner of the house?" When she nodded, he said, "I'll get the soil ready tomorrow." The spring air caressed their faces.

After they unpacked, they went into the kitchen to prepare their meal. Bessie asked, "What do you suppose we can have for supper?"

"Robbie promised to leave something. Let's see what he left us in the larder. Ah, pork chops, potatoes, and green beans. As good as his word. We'll have a good meal, don't you think? I'll get the fire going and start the meat. Why don't you start the vegetables?" Once the meat had started cooking, he said, "I'll set the table."

"I can do that in a minute," she said, looking up from the beans. "You must be tired after the long ride. Why don't you go in and rest a bit?" The potatoes had started to boil on the stove.

He looked at her for a moment, went over to her, took the knife from her hand, put it down on the table, clasped her hands in his, and said, "Listen to me, Bessie. This marriage is a partnership, and you and I are going to share the work. You took the same trip. You're just as tired as I am. After supper, I'll wash the dishes. You can dry them, and then we can rest together."

"All right, John. Whatever you say."

"That's the way it will be." He turned to the larder. "I just had a great idea. Do you suppose we could have some muffins with our meal?"

"Good idea."

"I'll get the corn meal and flour. And how about some peaches? We can open one of the jars you put up last season. That would sure finish up things in style." When she nodded, he asked, "Do I get to lick the bowl?"

She laughed, "What?"

"I never got to lick the bowl as a child. First, it was Robbie's turn, then Charley's, then each of the others. Whoever was youngest. Simple as that. I never had a turn."

"Don't tell me you never ..." She laughed again.

"Sometimes Robbie or Charley would share some when it was their turn. Remember, I was a deprived child."

"John, you can do whatever you want. This is your home. If you want to lick the bowl, go right ahead." She returned to her work.

"I'll even let you have some if you want," he said with a twinkle in his eye, as he disappeared into the larder.

Several months later John left church, still seething as he had from the sermon to the end of Mass. Folks lingered as always on this Sunday, the men in one group, the women in another. John told his group, "I'm so tired of it. That priest just hammers away for money. I don't want to hear anymore from him."

"He thinks it's important," Anthony shrugged.

"I don't care what he thinks," John fumed. "We don't need a new church. Where does he think we're supposed to get the money to build a church? And he wants a rectory."

Alf teased, "Come on, John. You must have a fine stash hidden away. You're working all the time – in the office and at the grain elevator."

"Well, if I do," John said heatedly. "I have no extra money for a church. Living in a home with wife and family seven days a week is more important than going to church one day a week for an hour."

Anthony looked at John, suppressing a smile, "What would Father Brones say to that?" They all looked to John. "Shouldn't God be first in all we do?"

"I don't like the man. He's so pompous and pious." He felt frustrated at these demands on his pocketbook.

"You worry too much." Peter reached over and patted him on the arm. "If you don't want to give money for the church, you don't have to. Everyone knows you're starting out and need every penny you have."

John ignored him, "I ask you. Why do we need a new church? With a spire that reaches 112 feet." He mimicked the priest, "'so it can be a visible landmark for many miles.' Tell me why we need that. Most folks are struggling. No one has money."

"Have you told the priest how you feel?" Alf asked gently.

"I'm not talking to him. He wouldn't listen to me."

They stood in an uncomfortable silence. After a few minutes, Anthony shifted the conversation to tell a joke that had them laughing, and they all relaxed.

Before they went their separate ways, Anthony said, "Relax, John. Don't worry about the church or the priest's house."

John apologized. "I'm sorry for my tirade. I just had to vent my frustration. Thanks for listening. I apologize to you all. You shouldn't have to listen to my ranting. At least you saved Bess from hearing these complaints."

Anthony said, "We understand, John. None of us in this group has money. We're going to give what we can afford and not worry about it. Money is tight when you're starting out with a wife and young family. Besides, we don't have to match the richest man in town with a donation. We'll give what we can and forget it. You do the same." The other two nodded in agreement. They shook hands all around.

When John walked into the kitchen, Bess looked up from her work. "Did you get that off your chest?"

"Yes, those three were sympathetic and said they don't have much to give either. I think I don't have to be embarrassed with a small donation. And there's an end to it."

Boston Beginnings

John Donahue was born in a
house on Silver Street,
South Boston.

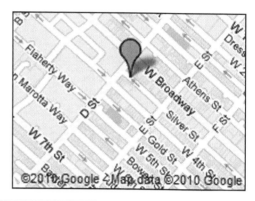

Above: Home for Catholic Children,
Harrison Avenue, Boston.
Courtesy of Daughters of Charity
Archives Northeast Province.

Ethan Beginnings

Above: John Donahue standing on the porch of the bungalow he built before he married. Below left: Bessie Craig and John Donahue wedding portrait. Below right: portraits of John and Bessie before they married.

Business and Family
Right: John Donahue
stands outside The
Enterprise office about
1910. Below left: from
left, Craig, Bess, John,
and Kathleen, 1908.
Below right: Craig and
Kathleen about 1912.

Adult Children
Above left: Fred and Kathleen
Kappenman on their wedding day
in 1930. Above right: Kathleen
pictured in 1945. Right: the
newlyweds, Irene and Terry
Donahue. Below: Terry Donahue
poses in 1942 as a naval officer.

The Ten Grandchildren
Right: photo of the seven cousins taken about 1939: Back row: Sheila and Joyce Donahue; middle row: Lois and Tom Kappenman; front row: Sharon, Judy and Jim Kappenman.
Below: photo taken about 1943: back row: John and Bess Donahue, Kathleen and Fred Kappenman; front row: two cousins, Dennis Donahue and Terry Kappenman. Lower right: Pat Kappenman, 1950

Partners through the Years
Right: taken in 1950. Below:
celebrating 50 years in 1954.
Below: right celebrating 55
years in 1959.

The Coyne Family
Left: Michael, Rosa, Anna, Robbie and Charley. Right, front row: Michael, Rosa, Robbie; middle row: Leo, Edmund; back row: Charley, Anna, William.
Below: Coyne farm.

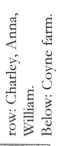

Chapter Seven
Husband and Father

About a year after their marriage, John and Bess rose early to finish their packing. Some of their belongings were already in the wagon outside the door. They were abandoning their home – the home he'd built – to move to Tyndall thirty-five miles south. They stood side by side at the stove. He started the coffee while she made the oats.

"Did you remember the books in the dining room?" she asked.

"Yes, they're tied together. All ready. What about your sewing things? Are they ready?"

"It'll just take me a minute to pack those, Everything's in one place."

While the coffee brewed, he set the table. He watched Bess stirring the cereal. She turned around and with furrowed brow asked, "What will happen to this house?"

"I don't know. At least we have a tenant for right now."

"Are we sure we want to do this?"

He shook himself, forcing a smile. "Yes, it's all settled. We'll try this liquor business in Tyndall. Your brother-in-law Phil offered a deal too good to pass by. The land office isn't paying right now. We've got to give it a chance. It's not the end of the world. If it works, fine. If not, we can move back here." He moved across the floor to take her hands in his. "It doesn't matter where we are as long as we're together."

After they embraced for a long moment, she spooned the cereal into the two bowls. "Let's eat." The room looked stripped and lonely without the familiar decorations. They sat. After a few minutes they both spoke at once.

"I wonder if ..."

"We can always ..."

They burst out laughing.

"Go ahead," he said.

"No, you." She laughed again. "I forgot what I was going to say."

"If we do decide to come back and this place isn't available, and there's not an empty house in town, we can always live with your folks."

"They would love that. I'm not worried about being without a home. You'll do fine whatever you do, wherever we go." They sipped their coffee. They didn't know that this breakfast was the last they would have in this house.

And sure enough, in less than a year, they had moved back to Ethan with John again at the land office, as well as at the grain elevator. He had decided the liquor business was not for him. Besides, Ethan called them back. However, they did not take up residence in the bungalow he had built, but moved into a larger house on Main street. With a baby coming, they knew they needed more than the four rooms of the house he had built.

They weren't back in town long when John received a letter from Charley Coyne telling him he was buying the *Beadle County Herald*, inviting him to become editor. He read the letter to Bessie. "What do you think? I might get into a whole new line of work." He looked at her hopefully. "I'd love to try."

"Beadle County?" she asked. "Not another move? Where's the office?"

"In Wolsey. A little train ride, but directly north. Just seventy miles. I can go straight from the depot here to Wolsey depot. The print shop is right up the street, he says. Since the job just takes two or three days a week, I'd like to try it and see what it's like. I'd be home the rest of the week. I'm not asking you to pack up and move north like we did when I took the job in Tyndall. This is different. We can stay right here in Ethan."

"And the office can spare you?" She looked up in alarm. "You'll keep the land office job? We do need the money."

"Yes, I'll continue the work here when I'm not working on the paper. Neither one pays much, but who knows what the future holds?" He saw her wince. "Are you all right?"

"Just tired. And my back hurts, but it won't be long now." She arched herself and rubbed her back. "What does an editor do at a newspaper?"

"Nothing glamorous – more like journeyman work – setting type, running the press, distributing the paper. I think that's basically it. It's something Charley says I can learn. Also, he writes that Mr. Johns, the present editor, will stay on for a few weeks to teach me. You know if I like this work, and if *The Enterprise* is ever in need, I might like to work right here in town on the paper."

"It sounds good, John. You're more suited to that kind of work." She picked up her sewing. "Can Charley wait a few weeks until after the baby comes? I want you here when I deliver."

"I'll write him a letter tonight and see what he says. If he can wait a few weeks, I'll have the position. If he can't and wants to get someone else, I'll know it's not to be for me." He stood and stretched. "Right now, I'm going to the workshop and see if I can get started on my next project. Now that the cradle is finished, I can start the little side table for the baby's room."

A week later, after a long and difficult labor, Bessie gave birth to their first child – a son. Her sister Fanny and mother Sarah acted as midwives. For the most part, John stayed out of the way. When he saw his son for the first time, he gazed in awe at the infant lying beside his wife. The new mother looked up and smiled, pleased with herself. "How are you, Mother?" he asked as he took her hand gently in his.

"I'm all right," she said weakly. "Just tired and sore."

"He's a beautiful baby. Such dark hair. I guess he'll look like his mother."

Bess smiled, but said nothing.

"What's his name?" He cradled the baby gently, looking lovingly at the tiny features and fingers. The baby whimpered.

"Careful," she cautioned. "Hold his head. Do you mind terribly if we don't name him John? You're John and I have a brother John. There'd be too much confusion with another John in the family." She lay quietly smiling at her husband and the baby. "We've gone over so many names in the last several months, but I keep coming back to the same one."

"What's that? What have you decided?"

"Terence." She spoke the name softly, reverently.

"A fine Irish name! He certainly looks like a Terence. You know I like the name."

She hesitated.

"And for a middle name as we said, why don't we use my family name?"

"Terence Craig Donahue, he is then." He smiled at her, and then turned to his son. "Does the name suit you, young man? Sure, and he's happy with his name. Aren't you?" They gazed at the child. "Why don't you rest a bit? I'll get you a cup of tea and a bite to eat."

"Thanks. Leave the baby here with me." She reached out her arms, but he didn't want to give him up yet. She lay back again.

Finally he handed the infant to her and, humming, danced into the kitchen. Suddenly he thought of his father. *He knew this joy. Three times. Two boys and a girl.* He prayed, *God, keep your hand over him wherever he is.*

Several weeks later he boarded the train in Wolsey to head home. As the journey took him south, he looked out the window at the flat land, the landscape with its wide range of possibilities, greening on this June evening. Tired, he was tired. It was a long trip from Ethan for the job on the newspaper. But at the same time, he was learning so much, and he felt pride as he saw so many people around him reading or carrying the *Beadle County Herald*. Almost two months ago he didn't know the paper existed, and now he was the editor.

Since his son's birth nothing bothered him. He was proud of his tan suit and his brown fedora. He moved his eyes to look at his hands with the fingers and fingernails stained with printers' ink. *It isn't the dirt of some farm.* He wished that he could have some mark on him that said that he was a father. That's what made him proudest. After thirty years as an orphan, feeling alone in the world, now he had his own family, a wife and child. He removed his eyeglasses and rubbed his eyes. *Yes, a good choice to have agreed to work for Charley on the paper.*

As he walked down the street in Ethan, he smiled in anticipation of holding his son. *I'll be a real father. I'll not let anything harm him.*

Little did he know that in six months, Charley would sell the paper, and John would lose his job. But rather than being sad, he was relieved not to have the separation during the week from Bessie and the baby. Again he worked at the grain elevator, and selling real estate. However, with his experience in printing, he eventually convinced Mr. Blackman to hire him occasionally at *The Enterprise*.

On Christmas night, John sat admiring the small tree with its tiny Christmas decorations. They had lit the small candles for a short time earlier, but now the tree just reflected the light of the lamp at his elbow. The table was spread with the gifts they'd exchanged. He could hear Bess as she sang the baby to sleep. The house spoke to him of content and peacefulness. Just a few years earlier he'd been on his own, boarding at someone else's house. Now he had a wife and son, and they awaited the birth of their second child. They had their health. He counted his neighbors as friends. When one pursuit didn't work, he always found something else to support his family. These facts were his gifts. He didn't look for anything else.

He remembered a Christmas when he lived on the farm. He had gone with Mr. Coyne and the two older boys to the bank of the James river where they'd found a tree, the first time they'd had one. Not many trees in the area, so they usually used a branch as decoration. Following a German tradition, on the feast of Saint Nicholas, Mrs. Coyne filled her children's shoes with nuts and fruit. But not his; he wasn't her child. On Christmas morning each of her children found a small toy, perhaps a wooden figure that their father had carved or a new shirt, hat, or mittens their mother had made. In other years, perhaps a store-bought toy, a yo-yo or top or blocks. He never expected a gift. He never found a gift.

Growing up, he'd watched the Coyne family and wondered why he couldn't live with his own family. He used to think that having time occasionally to read was his gift. In the winter, he did have a little more time to himself – to read and study. He lost himself with the lives of the characters; he traveled to faraway places and lands of enchantment. Now in adulthood, he had all this abundance. He had looked for someone, and Bessie answered his desire. Here was a woman who gave him her love. That morning, they'd gone to Christmas Mass proudly carrying their son. Later they'd shared dinner with the Craig family.

When Bessie came into the sitting room, John showed her the little wooden carved figure he held in his hand.

"Where did you get it?" she asked, taking and examining it. "Did you carve it?"

"No, I stole it when I was a child. It belonged to one of the boys."

"John, I'm ashamed of you," she clucked and handed it back to him.

He held it almost reverently. "When I took it, I thought Mr. Coyne carved it. I found out later that a logger gave him several when he was living as a boy in Yankton."

"Are you going to return it?"

He ignored her question. "Let me tell you a story about an orphan boy, living with a family. Every Christmas their children played with their new toys. He had nothing. Their old toys sat in the box. He thought to himself, 'Why can't I have one toy? They'll never miss it.' He slipped it into his pocket. At night he put it under his pillow, and during the day he hid it with his clothes. Remember. He had nothing."

"Oh, John," she said, her face softening. After a few moments of silence, she asked, "Will you give it to Craig?"

"Maybe when he's older. He'd just chew on it now. You know I'd give him the world if I could." They sat admiring the tree. This time he was the one to break the silence, "You know this is the best Christmas I've ever had. Thanks for coming into my life and giving me a son. These are the only gifts I need."

The following April on a bright and pleasant day, John walked down Main street with a spring in his step. Bursting with excitement, he bounded into the house where he found Bess in the kitchen shelling peas. Craig sat on the floor nearby, playing with his blocks. The child toddled over to his father with his arms raised. John reached down and swung him in the air, then sat, dandling him on his knee. He announced, "It looks like Steve Oathout is definitely interested in giving up the paper, and I'll take it. I talked to him again today."

"Good! You enjoyed the work at the Herald. This'll be good for you." She watched him as he played with Craig, squealing with delight. "You'll be glad to be out of the land office."

"I will. I'll have to borrow some money from our savings to buy it and to pay fees to the news agencies." He furrowed his brow, calculating. "But I figure we have enough. I think it'll be a good investment."

She stopped her work, wiping her hands on her apron. "We'll be able to build it up again. Don't you fuss about money."

"I wonder if my brother Tom can help in the shop. You know with him back in town, he might be glad of a little extra work. He has time in between his well-digging jobs, and the money – little as it'll be – will help. I might have to ask for your help. Steve says help is hard to come by."

"I think I'd like that," she nodded as she moved to check on the several pots bubbling on the range. "We can take Craig along; he's no trouble. And when this baby comes," she patted herself, "I'll work something out, too."

"The best thing about this is I'll be able to spend more time with you and the children." Carrying Craig, he walked over to her and put his hand gently on her arm, "I hope it's a girl."

"A boy or girl. It doesn't make any difference. As long as the baby is healthy." She stirred the gravy. "Change is good. You'll do a fine job with the paper."

He went back to the rocker, picked up a children's book, sat, and began to read to Craig, who snuggled into him.

On a hot August day, John lifted the newborn into his arms. "Oh, Bess, she's so tiny. She looks fragile. What do you think? About five pounds?"

"Tiny and fragile, maybe, but she's perfect," Bessie said. "The right number of fingers and toes. She's smaller than Craig, but she is a girl. Maybe to be expected." Bessie looked hot in the bed. She wiped her brow.

He sat gingerly on the edge of the bed, cradling the infant. "How are you feeling?" he asked, looking at her carefully. "Fanny said you had a hard time of it again."

"Fine. Just tired now." She paused and lay quiet. "She was a long time coming. Yes, I'm glad to have Fanny's help. Mother was here most of the day, too. She's in the kitchen getting supper ready. I decided, since I chose the name for our son, perhaps you want to name our daughter."

"How does Kathleen suit you?" he asked. During the months of waiting, they had run down the list of boys' and girls' names they liked. Suddenly he knew by looking at her that this child was Kathleen. "Another fine Irish name."

"Kathleen Donahue. Sounds good. And for a second name?"

"Why don't we give her your name like we said?" he asked. "Elizabeth. Kathleen Elizabeth Donahue."

"A lot of name for such a little baby.

"She'll grow into it."

Both watched the sleeping infant for a few minutes. Then she asked, "Did you finish this week's edition?" When he nodded, she asked, "What about the other print job?"

"Both done. The newspaper is ready to go out tomorrow. And the print job is ready to be picked up."

After resting a few minutes she said, "Why don't you introduce Kathleen to her brother. He hasn't met her yet."

"Good idea. Then, shall I get you a cup of tea?"

"Yes, thank you." She lay back, closing her eyes.

When he entered the kitchen, Craig toddled over to him, saying, "Dada."

John found his mother-in-law Sarah checking on the roast. She smiled at him and exclaimed, pointing at Craig, "Land's sake! That child is active. How does Bessie keep up with him?"

He laughed as he sat in the rocker, "He's a challenge."

The two-year-old stopped when he saw the bundle in his father's arms and asked in a small voice, "What is it?"

"It's your sister. Say hello to Kathleen." He took Craig's hand and guided it to Kathleen's. "See how soft she is."

"Oh." He saw the awe in his son's face.

"You have to be very gentle with her." The baby gave a little cry, and Craig stepped back in surprise.

"Will she break?"

John chuckled. "Yes, she might break if we drop her. So we'll be very careful. You won't let anything bad happen to her, will you?" He reached over, guided Craig's hand again to stroke the baby. "See, she likes it.

She's smiling." After a few minutes, he asked Sarah, "Is the water ready? Bessie could use a cup of tea."

"Already steeping in the pot. I'll bring it in to her and then be on my way."

"We're grateful. Bessie was glad to have you here." He stood and said to his son, "Come with me, Craig, and you can say hello to your Mother."

They entered the bedroom together. Craig saw his mother lying in bed with her eyes closed and asked his father in a small voice, "Is she sick?"

"No, Mama is not sick. She's just resting."

Bess opened her eyes and pushed herself into a sitting position, pulling the sheet over her. "Come here, my little man. Give your Mama a hug."

Craig climbed up and hugged his mother. Then he snuggled in beside her. John put the baby in her cradle. "Your mother has a cup of tea for you." He cleared a space on the bedside table for the tray.

"Here you are, Bessie." Sarah came in, poured a cup of tea, and handed it to her. She turned to John. "Everything's ready for dinner on the stove. You can take care of that?"

"He certainly can," Bessie spoke up. "John is very much at ease in the kitchen."

Sarah left the room, returning in a few minutes, folding her apron. "You let John wait on you for a few days, Bessie." She bent down and hugged her. "Give your Grandma a kiss, Craig." He reached up his face. "Goodbye, John," she said giving him an affectionate hug.

He walked her to the door, "Thanks again for everything. I don't know what we'd do without you."

When he returned to the bedroom, he heard Bess telling Craig that the fairies brought the baby because they decided that he needed a sister. "Not right now," she said conspiratorially, "but later when she gets bigger and can talk and walk, you can play with her. Won't that be grand?"

On a cold December day Bessie put the apple pie in the oven. When she heard the knock on the door, she hurried to open it. She found Tom Donahue, stomping his feet and chafing his gloved hands. "Mercy, Tom. Come in out of the cold. This is certainly a pleasant surprise. What brings you to these parts?" Tom removed his coat and hat, which she took and hung on the coat tree while he removed his boots. "I'm afraid John isn't home. He went to Mitchell on business and won't be back till late. You're welcome to stay for dinner. Or can I get you something now to eat or drink? A cup of coffee?" She led him into the sitting room near the fire.

"No, really it's all right," he said. "I came to town to settle some business and thought I'd just stop by. I just need to talk. I miss you folks in Ethan."

"But Alexandria is home for you now," she assured him. "That's where Belle is happiest. Sit down. What can I do for you?" When he didn't answer but sat gazing into the fire, she asked, "How are Belle and the children?" As an afterthought, she asked about his wife's twin, "And Dora?"

He shook himself. "They're fine."

She ventured, "Belle and Dora have a unique relationship?"

"Indeed they do. First because they're twins and then because they both have hearing problems. They don't talk to many people, but they understand each other."

"Do they have some hearing?"

"A little. But for them to understand, the speaker has to face them and speak very clearly."

He looked into the fire and mused, "I can't imagine what life would be without them."

"You've had more sorrow than anyone can imagine, losing two babies as you did." She reached out a comforting hand to him. "I don't know how Belle can go on. Your little ones must give you joy."

"It's hard on Belle even with two healthy children," he agreed. "We're always afraid something may happen to them." He paused before going on. "You know when I was a child, I thought nothing could touch me after losing my parents and sister and being separated from my brother. But losing those babies has been horrible. Now with both Grandpa and Grandma Coyne gone, I feel like I've been orphaned again. Like my own parents, they were – good to me – treated me like one of their own. Sure they made me work, but all farm children work. John doesn't feel the same way toward Mike and Rosa." He took out his pipe, filled it, and lit it, puffing thoughtfully. "Shoot, he still calls them Mr. and Mrs. Coyne. Maybe they treated him different because they had their own children." He paused to draw on his pipe. "Good people. Grandpa Coyne grew up an orphan himself."

"Really?" Bess settled back in her chair. Tom needed to talk. She would listen.

"His parents were killed in a freak storm in Ireland when he was three years old. He called it the 'Big Blow.' A lot of people in his village died, including his folks. He said he was too ornery to die. After that some relatives brought him up. Maybe that was why he was so good to me. He knew what it was to be an orphan." He puffed slowly, watching the smoke rise. "Then, when he was a teen, he left Ireland, moved to England for a time before he came to this country. Both Coynes told stories of how horrible life was because of the potato famine in Ireland. Grandma used to tell how when she was a child, after the English superintendent spread turnips out in the sheep-lot for his livestock, she would sneak through the hedge and gather up enough turnips to feed the family for the day." He shook his head. "They hated the English. Because of English laws, Grandpa never learned to read and write. Many Irish immigrants can tell the same story. Not John and me though. Our story is lost."

Bess sat forward and asked, "Do you remember much of your childhood home?"

"No, not much. I wasn't even six when my mother died. I don't even remember what my parents looked like." They sat quietly listening to the clock ticking. He slowly roused himself. "I remember more of the Orphan Home than John does, but not much. No child should have to go through what we did. Living in the Home was bad enough, but being shipped across the country, forced to do farm work all those years, and then losing your only sister and being separated from your brother was horrible." They sat in silence.

Suddenly a small figure stood in the doorway. "Mama."

Bess said, "Oh, Craig. Is it time for you to be up from your nap?"

Tom put his pipe down and put out his arms, "Come see your Uncle Tom."

Craig walked over slowly, "Dada."

"No," Tom laughed. "I'm not your Daddy. I'm your Daddy's big brother. But you can still give me a big hug." The child toddled over and Tom lifted and swung him around. Craig squealed in delight. When Tom put him down, he climbed up beside his mother, and then looked at Tom with wide eyes. Just then they heard a soft cry from the baby in the next room. "That's Kathleen. You'll get to see her." She returned shortly, cradling the infant. The baby cooed and smiled when Tom spoke to her.

"Your children think I'm their father."

"You certainly look alike. Anyone would know you were brothers."

He shook himself. "I have to go." She walked to the front door with the children and watched as he donned his boots, coat and hat. He gave

Kathleen a kiss and embraced Craig and finally Bessie. "Thank you for listening, Bess. It helps when I can share the story."

"Say hello to Belle and Dora for me," she said. "John will be sorry he missed you. And next time you come, plan on staying for a meal."

"Thanks. I'll do that," he said as he opened the door, stepping into the biting winter wind.

One afternoon, John burst into the kitchen, waved a large envelope, and said excitedly, "Look what came in the mail today." He put it on the table and quickly walked over to where the children were playing, stooped down, and picked up Kathleen. He sat down and, when Craig toddled over, picked him up also and put him on his other knee.

Bessie moved away from her work to look at the return address. She exclaimed, "The portraits. How did they come out?"

"I haven't opened them yet. I want you to see them first." He bounced the children up and down, one on each knee.

Bess dried her hands on her apron, opened the package, and spread out the pictures. "Oh, dear!" She exclaimed in dismay, "These are horrid."

"All of them?" He leaned forward to get a closer look. "Don't touch." He held Craig's hand. "What about the one on the left?"

"Well, I guess that's all right," she conceded. "But look at Kathleen. Her eyes are closed." She put it down and picked up another one. "This one is all right, too," she became more positive, "but look at Craig's mouth hanging open. Mercy!" She put the two photos side by side. "Maybe, on second thought, this one is better, don't you think? Look at Kathleen. What a beauty!"

"She surely is. And we're not even prejudiced in her favor." The baby, knowing they were talking about her, laughed with delight. "This one, though, doesn't do her justice."

"Maybe if we'd removed her hat," she suggested.

"But we're all wearing hats," John protested mildly.

"You're not," she contradicted him. "You have yours in your hand."

"Well ..."

She interrupted him, "Maybe if we go again in six months, we could do the indoor portrait without the coats and hats?" She picked up the pictures and put them back into their envelope. "How many will we order?" She carried it to the next room and put it on the desk.

He counted on his fingers. When she returned he said, "We decided on one each for your folks, brother and sisters, my brother and the

Coynes, and Robert. With a couple for us. That's fourteen." She went back to her work at the stove. He picked up a book and settled into the rocker to read a story to the children before supper. One child on each knee.

Later that evening, after the children were put to bed, John and Bessie sat in their regular places in the sitting room. He turned to her suddenly with a sense of urgency. "Are we ready to have another child?"

She took several more stitches in her handwork before looking up. "No, John. I think two is just fine. We have a son and daughter. We want to give them all our love and attention." She took several more stitches. She paused for a minute and shook her head slightly. She spoke with conviction, "I won't go through that birth pain again. Twice is quite enough."

He had stopped his work of sketching a plan for a chair, and he looked at her bent head. "I know you had pain, but I thought it was worth it for the children."

"It is for these two. But I won't endure such agony again. It was horrid. I don't even like to be reminded."

He put his paper and pencil down, got up from his chair, and knelt in front of her, taking the sewing from her hands. "Thank you, Bessie, for giving me our two children." He kissed her hands one after the other.

"Just think of how much attention we can give these two," she said, softening.

"Bessie, I won't make you suffer again if that's what you want." He rose and walked over to the family portrait and looked at his family of four for a long time in silence.

Elizabeth Donahue
Ethan, South Dakota
April 30, 1909

Dear Till and Jim,

I'm sending you the latest family portraits. We're quite pleased with how well they came out, especially the one of just the two children. Don't they look grand? We think they're better than the ones we sent you last fall. They've a bit of both their mother and father in them, don't you agree? John and I celebrated our fifth wedding anniversary two weeks ago with a quiet dinner at home. Or, as quiet as things can be with two active children. Thank you for the card. John enjoys the work on the newspaper, especially because he works in town and can come home for lunch. Occasionally I've been called on to help at the print shop. I enjoy it. It's interesting work.

We're well. We see Mother and Father every day when they come over to see their grandchildren. They're fine, enjoying town life. Mother especially is glad to be away from the daily grind of farm work, although they're up early in the mornings still. They can't seem to break the habit of a lifetime.

Write with the news. How are you, Jim and the children? Remember the summer when I stayed with you in Iowa to help with the children? In spite of the fact that you were ill at that time, we had a wonderful summer, didn't we?

Your sister, Bessie

Elizabeth Donahue
Ethan, South Dakota
July 30, 1909

Dear Till,

I write this letter with a heavy heart. The two children of Tom and Belle Donahue died within a month of one another. Their five-year-old, Dora, died at the end of June, and Louis, barely a year old, died last week — both of childhood cholera. Sick for only a few days, they died all too soon and too young. The funerals and burials were here in town at Trinity. As you can imagine, the parents are distraught. To lose one child is a horror, but to lose four is beyond comprehension. They're childless again. I can't even imagine their grief.

Belle's twin, Dora, lives with them to offer her sister what consolation she can and help her to cope with her loss. Tom tries to keep himself busy with work, but their hearts are bereft. Last winter, after the death of the elder Mr. Coyne, Tom came to talk about the loss of his foster parents. He said he felt lost without the only parents he ever really knew. But at this blow, how can anyone ease their burden?

I look at the latest family portrait — a copy of which I sent to you in April. I look at our children, Craig and Kathleen, and just can't imagine losing one of my babies, never mind both. We do worry about Kathleen, who is a fragile child. I have no other news. My heart is too heavy.

Your sister, Bessie

Chapter Eight
A Man of Influence

One Sunday afternoon Bess and John read while Kathleen took her nap and Craig played on the rug with his toy soldiers. The knock on the door startled them. "Are we expecting someone, Mother?" he asked as he rose and headed to the front door. Mr. and Mrs. Coyne were standing on the porch. As he ushered them into the parlor, he called, "Bessie, come see who's here. We have company."

She joined them, greeting them warmly, "Can I get you something? A cup of tea or coffee? A cold drink?"

"No, no, we're not staying," Mr. Coyne shook his head. "We came to bring you a gift." He held a flat package under his arm. The visitors exchanged a conspiratorial smile. They sat together on the davenport opposite John and Bess, who took their seats on the overstuffed chairs.

Mr. Coyne untied the cord and took the brown wrapping off the package. He moved almost reverently. "We've brought you a copy of the family portrait," he announced as he handed the framed photo to John.

"The whole family." John took the frame to examine each face. "Lovely."

"We had two sittings," Mr. Coyne said, beaming as he handed John a second framed portrait. John passed the first one to Bessie.

John said, "I think I like this one better. Look how good Robbie looks here."

"I knew you'd say that." Mr. Coyne turned to his wife. "Didn't I say he'd like that one better, Ma?"

"Ya," Mrs. Coyne nodded.

"I'm glad you like them," Mr. Coyne said. "We want you to have one of each."

"Thank you so much. They're … lovely." John placed them on the table. The Coynes stayed to talk of their children, of the farm and their neighbors. Mr. Coyne did much of the talking. Suddenly, he pointed to the bookcase on the south wall. "You finished another piece of furniture, John."

"I did," John said proudly. "Last month."

Mr. Coyne rose to examine it more closely. "Beautiful!" he exclaimed. "You've come a long way from the first little stool you made. Remember?" John nodded. "Look at this, Ma." Mr. Coyne said to his wife. "He's put glass doors on his book case. The books will be protected from dust." He ran his hand appreciatively along the top and edges. "Fine work."

He resumed his place, but John, instead of listening, remembered the first time he helped with a project. The farmer was building a hog pen and told him, "Hold that board steady, Boy." John strained, "I can't. It's too heavy." But he did hold it while the farmer hammered in the nails. "There," he said. "Good and stout." He remembered how, when he could, he let his arms drop in relief. He came out of his reverie when the visitors stood to leave. He and Bess walked them to the front door.

When they moved back into their sitting room, John brought the photos with him and looked at them for a long time. Bessie, standing next to him with her hands on her hips, asked, "What do we want with pictures of the Coyne family?"

"I'm glad to have them," John said defensively. "After all, I lived with them for fifteen years. Before I had a family of my own, these folks were all I had."

"But they were so horrid to you. Why are you always so nice to them?"

"I'm nice to them because, as I said, they're the only family I knew growing up. And they're my friends."

"Friends? The way they treated you? You owe them nothing, John."

"No, but it doesn't hurt to be nice to folks. I've learned it's no good holding on to anger or vindictiveness. The only one that hurts is yourself."

"Even if they abused you."

"They were no worse to me than many parents who strongly discipline their children. Especially farm families where there's so much work."

"Oh, John. You've told me stories of life in that home. They did not treat you as one of their own. They mistreated you."

"Perhaps you're right. But it's not in my nature to hate them for it. In the game of life it seemed I was dealt a bad hand. But I can't be angry at the dealer of the cards nor at those who took advantage of my ill fortune. I'll just play out what I have."

"You make me angry." She gestured to Craig, who seemed oblivious to the disagreement. "What about us?"

At this, Craig looked up at his parents with a quizzical look.

After a thoughtful moment John said, "When I met you I had a complete change of luck and all the cards have come up aces since. Or should I say I found the Queen of Hearts?" He smiled warmly at Bess.

"Oh, you," Bess laughed in spite of herself. "You are good. Just too good." She pointed to the two portraits, "But their pictures won't be placed with our family portraits."

"I wouldn't do that, Bess. I'll put them away." *I may have painful memories, but they're all I have.*

John opened the kitchen door quietly and stepped in, shaking the snow off before removing his boots and hanging up his coat and hat. He chaffed his hands and smiled at Bessie, standing at the stove. "Where are the children?"

"Craig is at Mother's." She turned slightly to him. "She said she'd bring him home before supper. Soon I hope."

"Kathleen?" he asked hopefully.

"She's better," she said with a tired sigh. "I'm just fixing her some gruel. You can take it up to her. Sit down a minute and tell me what happened at your meeting."

"Good. Everything's fine." he sat at the kitchen table. "All we need to do now is sign the papers tomorrow, and the house is sold."

"Did you give Stephen a tour?" She stirred the gruel.

"Yes, he was quite pleased. He praised the good workmanship."

"Of course he would," Bess said simply. "It's a beautiful house." She looked up from her work and asked solicitously, "This week's edition is ready?"

"Yes, we put the paper to bed today." John shivered even though the kitchen felt warm. "Brr, it's nasty out there. In some ways, I wish we could have lived in that house longer. Just didn't happen." He paused; when he spoke again he was more positive. "Even though I worked hard on building that bungalow, I'm not heart-broken that we only lived there for a year. A house is not a home. It's the people who live in the house that count." John stood and walked over to Bessie, embracing his wife in a bear hug.

"Get away," she laughed. "You'll make me spill the cereal." She poured it into a bowl, and he took it from her, heading to the next room. As he left the kitchen, she admonished, "Don't wake her if she's sleeping. We can feed her later."

John fed and changed Kathleen, then dressed her and carried her to the kitchen where he found Bessie's mother, Sarah and Craig. "Here she is. All better thanks to Nurse Bessie here. If I ever get sick I want her to nurse me." John handed the baby to Sarah. "Then I know I'd be fully cured." He leaned down and tousled his son's hair.

John Donahue
Ethan, South Dakota
January 15, 1910

Dear Jim,

I'm writing to thank you again for the advice you gave me years ago concerning the purchase of the lots in the Drake addition. Recently, I sold most of them to Shaw and netted myself a tidy profit in just over six years. Of course, if I developed them by building houses as we talked about at the time, I might have made even more. But I found myself too busy, and now it is impossible with running a newspaper and print shop. With this sale of properties, I'm almost out of the land office work. Not bad for an orphan farm boy. Thanks again for giving me a chance.

Steve Oathout is buying out the last lots — among them the one where Bessie and I built our first home. We've been holding onto that one for sentimental reasons, but it's time to let it go. We'll miss the rental income, but since Steve is interested, Bessie and I agree that it's time.

Your brother-in-law,
John

John sat in the parlor reading, and when Bessie returned from putting the children to sleep, she picked up her sewing, took several stitches, and said, "Excuse me, John. What about us getting a piano? Winifred could give lessons to Craig."

"Amazing!" He lifted his head in surprise.

"What's that?" she asked without missing a stitch.

"I was thinking the same thing."

"Winifred said even children as young as five or six can learn."

"We all heard how he learned that little melody last week on our visit to your sister."

"They have a sale of pianos at Brady's."

"I saw that. I'll check into it when I go to town on Monday. Yes, a piano is a good idea."

They went back to their work. The house settled down in quiet. The children slept upstairs. John had opened his book but did not read. He moved his eyes off the page, looking into the fire where he read some pages in his memory book. The first time John had visited the Craig family home was the Sunday he went with Jim and Till Tobin and their children soon after he'd moved into Ethan. The youngest Craig children, Ella, Bessie, and Katie, had taken turns sitting at the piano, each playing her favorite piece.

Another memory came to him from the farm when he was about twelve. On a warm summer night they'd all sat outside, watching darkness come on. Mr. Coyne had produced a tin whistle from his pocket and gently coaxed a lilting Irish tune. They all listened. John remembered thinking that even the animals delighted in the sweet melody. The dog lifted his head and perked up his ears. When he finished the first tune, a horse in the barn snorted his approval.

Wrapped in the warmth of a long day of work with a rare "job well done" compliment, John had sat contentedly, delighting in the music and looking up at the stars. Mr. Coyne announced the name of the first piece and went on to the next. Even in the dim light the windows looked unblinking at the orphan with wide eyes, as if uncomprehending. The stars stood afar off and faint, offering no warmth or brightness. He felt lost in the sad melodies, always an outsider.

In too short a time Mrs. Coyne had said, *"Kinder.* Robbie. *Schlafenzeit."*

"Ah, Ma," Robbie and Charley groaned. "We don't want to go to bed."

The older brother added, "We want to stay and listen to the music."

Their father wiped the instrument on his shirttail and said, "That's it. Concert's over. We're all going to bed."

But no one moved or spoke. The strains of the music hung in the air. After a few minutes Mrs. Coyne rose slowly and went into the house with Anna close behind her. John got up, picked up her chair and carried it into the kitchen. He heard Mr. Coyne say, "Go on, you two. I'm coming right behind you."

Only rarely when they sat out on warm nights did they have music. Sometimes they listened to the sounds of the night, sometimes they talked of the work, or sometimes Mr. Coyne told stories – mostly of his childhood.

"A penny for your thoughts," Bessie broke into his reveries.

John turned to her with a grin, "I was remembering the first time I visited the Craig farm and you girls took turns playing the piano."

"I don't remember that," she frowned.

"I came with Till and Jim. It was your mother's birthday. I had just moved into town and was living with them. Just started working in the business. I don't know why they invited me. Maybe they felt sorry for me and thought I needed some social life. Anyway, after I met the two eligible Craig girls, I knew it was only a matter of time till I decided which one I'd marry."

"How long ago was that?" she asked absently.

"About the turn of the century. Eleven years ago."

She put the sewing down. "Ah, yes." After a pause she said, "No, I mean when you decided I was the one." When he ignored her and didn't answer, she went on, "I remember how the Tobins and Navins always teased you." With furrowed brow she asked, "That first time you came, I thought the men spent most of the time out on the porch and we girls stayed in the parlor."

"We did. But when the piano playing started, Little Jim and I came in to listen. Big Jim and Phil stayed outside with the children."

She asked insistently again, "So when did you decide you wanted to marry me?"

"The day in the garden a couple of years later. I guess you started to grow on me." When she winced, he said, "Pardon the pun."

"You mean the day you proposed?"

"That's right."

"That's when you decided?" she asked incredulously.

"Yes. I was rather slow."

"You decided? Then proposed?"

"Right. Overnight, I decided." They sat in silence for a moment. "And when did you decide *I* was the one?" he asked her.

"Very soon after you started coming regularly to the house." She laughed, picking up her sewing again. "It sure took you long enough."

"I was looking for family so long I didn't know it when it stared me in the face."

"But, John, you lived all those years with a family. It isn't like you grew up in an orphan home."

"That doesn't mean anything. I've told you. They never treated me like family. I was always an outsider. When I saw how your family treated one another and all your visitors, I saw a difference. Your family would never treat an orphan the way the Coynes treated me."

"Yes, we did have a happy home." She folded up her sewing and stretched. "I'm going up to bed. Will you come?"

He shook his head and opened up the book, "In a bit. I want to finish this chapter."

"Don't forget to bank the fire," she reminded him.

"Take the brick up with you, so the bed will be warm and toasty by the time I get there." He reached up his face, and she leaned down to kiss him. He sat on, thinking of his blessings – family, home, wife, and children. He had the best of everything. He had work that challenged him, and the best part was that it wasn't farm work. He wondered if things would've been different if he'd agreed to be adopted. No, he would've been even more under their thumb and probably stuck permanently on the farm. He opened his book to read. His family was safe upstairs, and all was at peace. Once they bought a piano the house would fill with the sound of music.

One hot July day, mid-afternoon, Fanny's husband Herman and his brother Conrad stopped in to see John at the print shop. They stood awkwardly in the middle of the shop. When they finished their small talk about the farm work and families, Conrad asked, "So, John, when's the Harvest Festival?"

"You tell me. When will most farmers be finished bringing in the crops? Mid August?"

Herman pulled on a straw and thought on it. "Give us another couple of weeks and all of Dakota's crops'll be harvested. Some fellows have already started, but we've got a couple days before ours are ready." He looked to Conrad for affirmation.

His brother leaned against the desk and added, "Looks like a good year. Folks'll be ready to celebrate."

John pointed to the calendar hanging on the wall behind his desk. "Today is July 25. How about August 15?"

"Sounds about right," Conrad said. "What do you think we should have for activities?"

"Something for the children," John said.

Herman added, "Something for adults."

"How about a baseball game?" John asked. "Remember the year we had the fats against the leans?"

"I remember that," Conrad said. "You were the best of the leans." He turned to his brother. "Wasn't he, Herman?" They both chuckled.

"Don't remind me." John picked up his pencil, took up a pad, and started jotting down ideas as the three of them talked over different activities: contest, games, races, and the people they could ask to lead the events. When they finished, John said, "Thanks, fellows, for stopping by and getting my work done for me. I'll get this ready for the paper and have it in this week's edition. If it's in several times, we'll get a good crowd."

"And you'll talk to the other fellows?" Conrad asked.

"You bet." John shook their hands. "Thanks, Herman, for agreeing to oversee the tug of war."

The day of the Fair dawned to bright clear sunshine, the streets clogged with folks from early in the day till late. John walked around, checking on activities, making sure they were running smoothly. Early in the day he looked over the display of pies and breads, knit goods and quilts and made sure the judges were lined up to decide the prize winners. He stopped by where the tug of war contests were underway and saw the other contestants of different ages lined up to try their strength. He walked to the east end of town where the baseball games played continually. He stayed a long time where the children's races were going on. He stopped into the hall where Mr. Weepie had opened it for dancing. He talked to so many folks who were visiting their neighbors, marveling at how the children had grown. *Everything is under control. I have hardly anything to do.*

At the end of the day, John and Bess sat on the porch relaxing in the cool, evening breeze. The children slept after the day of excitement, even though Kathleen had spent part of the day sick in bed. He said to her, "Sorry you had to miss some of the activities."

"It couldn't be helped" She smiled and patted his hand. "Thank God, she's better."

John said, "Well, finally a successful Harvest Festival in town. Don't you agree?"

"Yes, folks enjoyed themselves," she agreed, "and we certainly had a crowd."

"I must tell you, after last year's disaster," he confessed, "I was rather nervous."

"This was a better year for farmers. And we had better weather," she said thoughtfully. "Of course, your article in the paper made it sound so inviting – people came from all the surrounding towns, Worthen, Tobin, Starr, Mitchell."

"I don't think it was anything I did," he replied. "It was because folks had good crops, and then everyone – so many people – helped. I couldn't believe the enthusiasm."

"Oh John," she said, exasperated. "Take some credit for yourself once in awhile. It's the best festival around because you organize it and publicize it so well. People know it's a good one."

"No," he said. "I can't take any credit. Herman and Conrad did it all. They're the ones who deserve the credit."

"They didn't write the article, and they didn't scare up the volunteers. Land's sake! You've lived in town a dozen years and have run the paper for four. People admire and respect you. You wield more influence than you think."

"Of course, the Craig connection is helpful," he offered.

"John, you have to let it go." She touched him gently on the arm. "Forget the fact that you're a farm boy. Forget you're an orphan. Everyone else has. And even if they remember, they know you as a man of influence. You're a family man and a good businessman. Trust yourself more and what you can do."

He looked chagrined and, taking her hand, said, "Yes, Mother. Whatever you say."

A year later, and just before another successful Harvest Festival, John kept an eye on the machine as it printed the newspaper. He looked up to see Bess exultantly waving an envelope. "John, you have mail from the Post Office Department in Washington."

Nodding to his assistant Elmer, he walked over to where she stood in the front of the shop. "What's that? I can't hear you over the racket."

She handed him the letter, "You want to open this." She could barely contain her excitement.

He stared at the return address. He sat at his desk to open the envelope. Before he took out the letter, he looked up at Bess. "What do you think? Is it an appointment? Or a rejection?"

"I'm sure it's an appointment. You saw the scores on the Civil Service examination. They have to give it to you. Just open it," she said, irritated at his delay.

He opened the envelope and read the letter:

July 30, 1913

Dear John L. Donahue,

This is to notify you that you are appointed Postmaster for Rome effective as of August 29, 1913.

He beamed, both relieved and pleased.

Bess took the letter from him and read the rest of the details in the letter. "Wonderful!" she exulted. "This extra income will really help."

"Oh, let me see that." He looked over her shoulder at the rest of the official letter. Mentally, he started his plans. "I'll talk to Andy tomorrow and arrange to move the equipment in here. I'm glad he encouraged me to take the test." He looked around. "We've got this wonderful space right up front where we can set up, and I can keep an eye on both operations. Just have to move a few things around."

Bess offered, "And I can help with either job."

"Yes, good." He folded the letter, returned it to its envelope, and handed it to her. "Take this home and put it on the desk."

"Right! I'm going to check on the children and start supper."

"We won't be much longer. We're almost finished for today." The noisy press stopped its clangor, and after she left, he moved to the rear of the shop to help sort and fold the paper. "It looks good, Elmer," he said, giving an approving nod.

Six months earlier, when he had gone into the post office to collect the mail, he'd seen the notice for the Civil Service exam. When he'd taken an application, Andy had said, "Good for you, John. Take the test. This is a job you'd be good at. I think I'll be finishing up here next summer. Me and the Missus plan to move on."

"Thanks for the tip." With this encouragement and after talking to Bess, John had filled out the application and mailed it in. On the test day he took the train to Sioux Falls and reported to the test center. When he got home late that afternoon, he told Bess, "I think I did all right."

"Of course you did all right. You probably did very well. When do you get the results?"

"Not for months. Andy said when dealing with the government you've got to expect to wait for everything."

Now, as he stood in the print shop, he envisioned how he would balance the two jobs – the space and his time. A happy challenge.

When they'd heard the news of Ella's death, John and Bess dropped everything and rushed to the Schurz farm. Bessie was devastated at the news of the accident and death of her sister Fanny's youngest child. They found the family in the parlor. Bess embraced her sister, brother-in-law, and the three children, and then stepped over to view the body.

John followed her. After some minutes of prayer, and when they'd all resumed their places, he asked his brother-in-law, "Tell us what happened."

Herman told the story almost in a daze. "I took the two older girls to Mitchell. Fanny was in the house sewing, and Oswald and Ella were playing in the yard. Fanny saw them there about five o'clock. Then Oswald must've gone to the barn to do his chores – he's very responsible for a thirteen-year-older." He paused to take a breath and wipe his eyes.

Fanny leaned forward and picked up the story. "I didn't think anything about not seeing her because she usually followed her brother in his work. I went about six to gather the eggs and met Oswald coming out of the barn. When I asked him where his sister was, he said he left her playing in the yard." She started to shake again with weeping.

Herman soothed her, holding her close. After a few minutes, he picked up the story. "They called her, and when she didn't answer, they looked in the machine shed. Fanny found her beneath the grindstone, which evidently toppled over and crushed her. She doesn't know how she did it but she managed to lift the stone and carried her to the house. She thought she could revive her. She thought maybe she was only stunned. She tried to reach me in Mitchell but I'd already started for home. When I got here, I called the doctor. He came right away. He said she must have died instantly."

John said, "Not yet four years old. Too horrible to die so young!"

"Where are Craig and Kathleen?" Fanny asked suddenly.

"They're with the folks," she said.

"And the funeral …?" John asked.

"Sunday. Father Burkel was here earlier, praying with us." She broke down again in sobs.

John found Bess sewing in the sitting room on a cool, crisp mid-October day of 1916. He told her, "I'm going out to Rob's farm to get information on the accident at the Nelson farm and see how he's doing. I heard he has some bad burns."

"Tell him we're praying for him." Bess looked up from her work at her Singer sewing machine.

When John rode onto the Coyne farm, he tethered his horse outside the house. Robbie and his wife Martha sat in the kitchen. George lay in a crib nearby where his mother could watch him while their two other children, Emmet, aged eight, and Celestine, two, played in the yard. Martha poured John a cup of coffee.

Rob said, "I don't know what I'd do if something like this happened to one of mine." He looked out the open door at his children. "Celestine is about the same age as the Nelson girl."

"How bad are your burns?" John asked.

"Not too bad. This will heal," he said as he held up his bandaged hands.

"What about your farm work?" John asked solicitously. "How will you manage?"

Rob said with a grin, "I thought I'd hire you." When he saw John's surprised look, he laughed. "My brothers will help me for a few days."

Martha firmly corrected him, "More like a few weeks." She appealed to John. "I keep telling him he's got to let his hands heal."

"Can you tell me what happened?" Suddenly full of business, he took out a pad and pencil. When Rob shook his head, he added, "I have to put something in the newspaper."

"You don't want to write about me," he protested.

"Well, it'll be hard to leave you out," John explained, "because I do have to write about the fire and the death of the child."

"It was horrible." Rob put his hands to his eyes as if blocking out the memory. "I had finished my evening chores. When I came out of the barn," he gestured across the yard, "I heard the alarm. I saw smoke in the east in the direction of the Nelson place. So I rode over there as quick as I could. A couple of fellows – the workers helping in the field and the neighbors to the east – had already formed a bucket brigade trying to douse the flames shooting out of the barn. They had started beating the flames with brooms. It was pretty hopeless. Mrs. Nelson, clinging to her four-year-old George, was screaming that her baby was still in the barn. So I told the fellows to wrap me in a blanket. They soaked me good with water, and I ran in. I was lucky to find her right away, but it was already too late for her. I grabbed her and ran out. The flames were fierce all around me. She was cooked like a roast. Poor little pet. I see her every time I close my eyes." He shuddered.

"Don't say any more," Martha said.

"It's all right. I feel better when I can talk about it." He looked at her gratefully.

"Do they know what started the blaze?" John asked.

"Evidently the children were playing with matches, and when George saw the fire he panicked and ran out, but little Sarah must have frozen and the flames just engulfed her. I hate to think what she must have suffered."

John offered, "Perhaps she was overcome by smoke and didn't feel the flames."

"I hope so. Poor George. He doesn't quite grasp what happened.

And the parents are distraught. But they don't blame him. They know it was an accident."

John changed his questioning, "Did they lose any stock?"

"They lost a horse." Rob said. "They had the others in the field. Just coming in. One of the hands was first on the scene, heard the horse screaming, and saw the flames. They sat in silence for a few minutes. John looked at his notes. *Sufficient.*

Rob shook himself. "Do you remember the fire we had in the barn at home?"

"You mean when the lamp fell over and the things near the door caught fire? I was about sixteen," he said as he pocketed his pad and pencil. "That was nothing."

Rob nodded. "To a ten-year-old it was big. I watched you and Dad put out that fire. I thought you were the bravest men in the world. I wanted to grow up to be just like you."

John protested, "I don't know if I'd have the courage to do what you did, Rob."

"If I know John Donahue, I know you'd do what had to be done," Rob asserted.

"The accident I remember on the farm is the time I gashed your leg with the pitchfork."

Rob, laughing, looked down at his left leg. "Is that where I got that scar? I don't even remember what happened." Martha stood and began to gather lunch things. "You two with your memories. You'll stay for lunch, John." She stated it as a fact.

"No, I'm sorry I can't." He knew he had work to do, but he didn't move. "But thanks for the invitation. Rob and I don't see each other often enough."

"You're busy in town with the paper and the post office, and I'm busy on the farm. Tell me what happened with the pitchfork? I've forgotten."

"You ran right into me. You were about six." He smiled, remembering. "I was so afraid I killed you. There was a lot of blood. You were crying. Your mother was screaming." He laughed lightly, "Then for weeks, you limped around, so proud of your hurt leg."

Martha put a plate and flatware in front of John.

"No, really, I can't stay," John protested to her. "I've got to get back to work."

Rob said, "Nonsense, you've got to eat somewhere. It might as well be here."

Martha added, "It's simple fare, and you're welcome to it." She put bread, cheese and salads on the table. Then she went to the door and called in the children.

"I don't want to impose on your hospitality," John said, giving in.

"You're not imposing. Just take what you want and eat. We have plenty." Martha poured milk for the children. She took her place and asked, "John, you were like a big brother to Rob and Charley?"

"Yes. They followed me around everywhere."

"No, you were incredibly brave," Rob said. "Remember the time you faced the angry bull?"

"That was nothing. I was close enough to the fence so I could just hop over." While they ate, they shared stories of other mishaps and accidents on the farm.

In another half hour John said, "Thanks for the lunch. I must really be off." He rose and patted Robbie lightly on the shoulder. "I'm proud of what you did, and this story will be printed in *The Enterprise*." He thanked Martha for the lunch and left.

A few months later, Bess and the children were in the print shop when John became aware of the darkening sky, heavy with the threat of a storm. He walked to the back of the print shop where Bess was setting type. He said, "I'm afraid we're in for a downpour. The clouds look like they're building up for a humdinger of a storm."

She glanced up at him and said, "Oh, I just have a few more lines to do on this story. Can we leave the other jobs for tomorrow?" As she spoke, she looked toward the front of the shop and saw through the window the black sky. "My goodness! It does look bad. Maybe I should get the children home before they get wet. They can't afford to get colds. Especially Kathleen. Can you finish this?"

"Yes," he said, urging her along. "You go ahead. How far are you?"

She pointed to the typewritten copy. "I just finished this sentence."

"Fine. Go along. I'll finish up here."

She called to the children, sitting on the couch, fully engrossed in their books. "Craig, Kathleen, get your jackets. We're going home." When they didn't move immediately, she urged them on as she handed them their jackets, "Come along. You can read when you get home. There's a storm coming and we don't want to get wet."

They had taken only a few steps when the drops of heavy rain fell on their faces, and they smelled the acrid rain as it hit the dry earth. She hurried the children along, but when they arrived home, they were already wet. She sent them to their rooms to change into dry clothes. She set about building up the fire in the stove so she could make them a hot drink.

Kathleen came back into the kitchen and asked, "Can I have a cookie, Mother?"

"Say 'May I have a cookie?'" her mother said. "Let me look at you, Kathleen. Did you change your shoes and stockings?" She looked down at her daughter's wet shoes. "No, you didn't. Off you go again and put dry things on your feet."

Craig poked his sister on her way out and said pointedly to his mother, "May I have a cookie with the chocolate, Mother?"

Kathleen stood in the doorway to see if her brother got a cookie, but her mother waved her along, "Off with you. Now!"

Back at the shop John finished the layout of the story Bess had started. Then he walked to the window and watched the storm flood the street, his heart heavy with the thought of the ugly war in Europe. And with Americans having lost their lives in the sinking of the *Lusitania*, it looked like the United States would have to be involved. He returned to his desk to write an editorial on the war in Europe. The rain pounded on the roof. He wrote, "The storm clouds have been hovering over Europe for some time, and when the rains came, they brought destruction to all the land." He knew all too well the destruction that rain could wreak on the land.

He stopped and considered what he had written, then continued typing, "What was our first concern when we saw the clouds today? We wanted to protect the children. Have the Huns shown a belief in protecting children? Or the innocent? I think rather that they have displayed a blatant disregard for the rights of the most vulnerable in our world. I have seen often enough how rain and hail destroy crops and endanger lives. The Huns have acted as the destructive force in Europe, blazing a path of death and woe."

He continued, "How do we respond? We do all in our power to protect the innocent. Cruelty and oppression must be stopped. Enlist today to join the fight against oppression and murder. Our country depends on us to support the cause of democracy and freedom for all."

He reread this section. *Yes, this is what I want to say.*

At Sunday dinner, Craig with his brow furrowed in concentration said to his mother, "I see Grandma and Granddad going to church every Sunday and they never walk on the same side of the street. He always crosses over as soon as he leaves their house. She comes out with him but walks on the other side until she gets across from the church. Then she crosses the street. Why do they do that?"

Bess said, "I don't rightly know. I never noticed."

Craig appealed to his father. "They leave the house at the same time. They sit together in church. Why don't they walk down the street together?"

"That's just what they do." John thought for a minute. He looked at Bess, but addressed Craig, "Maybe because they're together so much of the time he needs to get away from her for a few minutes."

Bess protested, "Dad. Don't give the child the wrong idea."

"I'm telling Craig that sometimes in life when you live with a person a long time you need to get away from her, even if it's a few minutes walking to church on opposite sides of the street." He winked at Craig.

Craig looked carefully at his father. "You and mother never do that. You're always together. You work together in the print shop and the post office, and you work here in the house and in the garden." He pushed the carrots around on his plate.

"We have our moments," John said, repressing a grin. "Your mother visits your aunts sometimes without me." He gestured to his son's plate. "Don't play with your food."

"And your father goes to meetings in Mitchell and Sioux Falls without me," Bess added.

John said, "And we both go to the dentist or shopping without the other one. So you see. We're not together as much as you think."

Craig frowned, and then persisted in getting an answer to his original question, "But what about Grandma and Granddad?"

Bess explained, "Maybe that's just what they do. He likes the north side of the street, and she likes the south side." She pointed to his plate, "Eat your carrots, Craig."

John watched him take a bite of the ham and watched him chew for a few minutes.

Craig had another question. "I saw Granddad yesterday at his house, and he had his head over a bowl, and his head was covered with a towel. Grandma said it was a Turkish bath he had to have on account of his asthma. What's asthma?"

"It's a disease of the lungs," Bessie explained. "It means he has trouble breathing. The steam helps to clear the passageways. It's because he worked as a farmer all those years and now he's allergic to dirt and pollen."

Kathleen had been eating and following their conversation quietly, but in a lull in the conversation she spoke up, "They've got wrinkles."

John explained, "That's because they're old. All old people have wrinkles."

"I don't want wrinkles," Kathleen said. "I'm not going to get old."

Craig said triumphantly, "Yes, you are. Everybody gets old." He took his last bite of ham.

"Not me. Am I, Dad?" she asked her father.

"Afraid so," he said with a smile. "Everybody gets old."

"Maybe I'll get old," she persisted. "But I'm not getting wrinkles."

Her mother said, "I'm afraid you won't have much to say about it."

"You're old," Kathleen said, "and you don't have wrinkles."

John and Bess exchanged a glance. John said, "You're right, so perhaps you'll escape like we did."

Kathleen turned to Craig. "See, I told you I'm not getting wrinkles."

"Such a lovely service." John and Bess sat on the porch with her parents after the children had gone to bed. "I liked the way Bishop O'Gorman used the comparison of the draft law of the United States to confirmation making the children soldiers of Christ. I'll be sure to include that in the paper."

Sarah said, "Didn't the children look wonderful? The boys, so handsome in their suits and the girls, so lovely in their dresses and veils. It's too bad they had to go to Mass twice."

Bess sighed, "Such a long day for them. Craig takes such things in stride, but it's hard on Kathleen with her delicate constitution. I hope she doesn't get sick."

John patted her hand. "She'll be all right. Imagine how long it would've been if the 114 children all received two sacraments in the same Mass – Eucharist and Confirmation." He paused. Then he added, "I was twenty years old when I made Confirmation, and I remember it was a large group. Did you make it the same day?"

"I must have. The bishop doesn't come often." She looked at him. "I was confirmed in 1897 in Saints Peter and Paul Church."

Sarah said, "Yes, Katie and Mattie were confirmed that day, too." Will nodded in agreement.

John added, "My brother Tom was twenty-two, and Robbie was thirteen." They sat in silence for a few minutes. He went on, "Father Goggin asked me to thank folks in the paper for the help he got. No easy task to accommodate all those people from so many areas, the bishop and all those priests. He said he told the bishop that the church was certainly going to be adding many more soldiers in the future, attested to by the chorus of babies who sang all through the service."

"You like this priest, don't you?" Will asked.

"I do. We've worked together on so many projects. I hope he stays awhile. We don't seem to keep a priest here long." He paused. "I've liked most of the priests we've had."

"Except Father Brones," Will said, giving him a sideways glance.

"Don't remind me of that man. Money, money, money all the time." He made a face. "He stayed too long. You can't make me believe we needed a new church. He was always harping on building a grand, big church."

"You have to admit Holy Trinity is a lovely church." Sarah didn't wait for an answer, but rose. "Come along, Dad. Time we went to bed." He joined her, and they walked across the street to their home.

One March evening in 1918 Father Goggin and John met in the print shop to settle some of the future talks by the newly formed group called the Four-Minute Men – the propaganda effort of the Great War. The war had dragged on in Europe while President Wilson struggled in getting support for the cause. The opposition came mainly from immigrants – the German Americans who didn't want to take up arms against their own people and the Irish Americans who wouldn't fight on the same side as the English.

As they finished their meeting, John assured the priest, "I will be careful not to foster prejudice against Germans."

Father Goggin stood to leave and, putting his hand on John's arm, said, "Good. We must not give in to the climate of war and hatred in our world."

"I'm fighting a war of words for this country," John said. "I'm supporting those bearing arms for us. That's why I agreed to be the chair of the local Red Cross and have led it for over a year and why I'm agreeing to be a Four-Minute Man." He reached for his hat. They left the office and walked together down the street. "Let me tell you what I believe," John continued. "I'd stake my life on Al Freidel and Conrad Schurz. They're German Americans, have lived in this country most of their lives, and are as loyal to America as you and I. The ones I'm angry at are the Germans who have committed such terrible atrocities we've been reading about in the newspapers."

"You wrote words to that effect in *The Enterprise* last year," Father said.

"I did. We don't hate the German people. We hate the barbarism their leaders are pursuing."

The week before this conversation, a group of businessmen, on John's invitation, had met at the priest's house to organize those who would speak on behalf of the war effort. Father Goggin had nominated John to head the group. "He's already done so much for the war effort as chair of the Red Cross," he had explained, "and with him at the newspaper, choosing anyone else would be a mockery."

"No one will do a better job," they all agreed. "He's the obvious choice."

John had received the information in the post office and called the meeting. "Speakers are asked to address topics as outlined in these papers from George Creel in Washington. You only have to talk four minutes, and that's during the reel changes of films. We'll be designated as 'spokesmen of the National Cause,' to lift local morale and morals. They'll send the information weekly from Washington. I'll put most of the information they send in the paper so people can read it, but they need to hear it as well." He paused and looked around. "So, who's willing to join us as speakers? As I see it, we need four or five." He added quickly, "Let me be the first to volunteer."

Father Goggin, Doctor Stockdale, and Charles Boresson took John's cue and expressed their willingness, and the team was formed. Father Goggin said he would begin on Saturday at the movies by outlining the "Four-Minute Man" idea. Doctor Stockdale could end the first evening session, he said, by taking up the matter of organizing a home guard.

"John, as one who keeps a wonderful garden," Father Goggin said, "you're the best one to talk about the importance of food conservation."

"I'll speak on Sunday evening," John said as he picked up one of the papers and read, "'Advocate avoiding waste and planting victory gardens.' It explains too that a serious wheat shortage is threatened because last year's crop was so poor. What about next Wednesday? Father, can you urge Red Cross support?" He looked up to see the priest nod. "And Charles, can you explain the income tax law?" He was putting initials next to each item on the list.

"Will do," Charles said.

"Let's meet once a week for the duration of this effort," John said. "Another thing: there'll be training sessions in Sioux Falls to learn effective speaking strategies. I'll let you know when that is, and if at least some of us go, we can bring back the information for the others."

"I think folks will be receptive," Doctor Stockdale said. "They all want to know what they can do to help. And let me say for everyone in town, John, we owe you a big debt of gratitude for all you do."

Even though John raised his hand in dismissal, he was pleased with the affirmation. "I couldn't do it alone." He looked around at the small group. Everyone here is important." As they left, they shook hands all around.

Chapter Nine
Raising Children

On a hot, dry August day, Bess prepared the party for Kathleen's tenth birthday with her five friends. She would serve sandwiches, pickles, fruit treats, and of course the birthday cake with homemade ice cream. Late in the morning Craig found his mother on the back stoop working the crank for the ice cream. "Just in time," she said, "to finish the last turns. My arm is breaking." He laughed easily. She massaged her upper arm as she watched him take over. "Is your father almost finished?"

"Well, we finished the Johnson job, but he wants me to go back this afternoon to help with another project. And tomorrow we'll have the work on the newspaper." He grinned up at her. "He told me to take a break because, he said, 'All work and no play make Jack a dull boy.' I told him he was Jack, not me, and he isn't dull at all."

She laughed lightly, shook herself, and said, "Well, I better see to the rest of lunch. Kathleen's friends will be here shortly." She touched him lightly on the shoulder. "Thanks, Craig. This will be a nice treat for them. Your lunch is ready in the kitchen. Get yourself a glass of milk."

On August 9, the actual anniversary of Kathleen's birth, the family shared a special dinner – the birthday girl's choice – shepherd's pie. Before they cut the cake, John handed her a small gift-wrapped box. "Happy birthday!" he said.

Kathleen untied the ribbon, pulled off the paper, and, when she opened the box, she gasped, "It's beautiful!" She took the small gold locket on a chain out of the red velvet-lined box and examined it. The heart-shaped piece had leaves and three round blossoms etched on the front.

"Now, Kathleen," her mother admonished, "You want to take good care of it. You'll wear it only on special occasions. We thought because you're ten we should give you something really special."

Kathleen showed it to her brother, who was straining to see over her shoulder. "See, it's got a flower and leaves on it." He glanced at it and went back to his place across from her. He had a gift to give her too; but he would wait until their parents gave their gifts.

Her mother repeated, "Whatever you do, don't lose it."

John picked up another box from the side cabinet and said, "Look, your mother has a matching one. See how they open up so you can put something inside as a keepsake." He opened Bessie's and showed it to her.

Bess said, "I'll put a lock of hair from my two children in mine, one on either side."

"Yours is different." Kathleen looked back and forth from hers to her mother's. "You have a heart and I have a flower."

"That's all right. That way you won't get them mixed up," John said laughing.

"Dad," she protested. "Mine is smaller."

Craig asked, "What'll you put in yours?"

"I can't open it," she said, struggling with the clasp.

Her mother reached over. "Let me help you." She opened it and handed it back to her.

"There you are."

Kathleen said, "I don't know what to put in it. I can put a picture or something."

"You don't have to decide right now," John said as he handed her a much larger box. "Besides, we have another gift." Kathleen put down the locket and undid the wrappings to find a doll. "Oh, Mother, Dad, she's beautiful." She stroked the doll's hair.

Craig said, "I have something for you, too," and he handed her a small package, which he had wrapped himself. She opened to find one of the books by Beatrix Potter. "Oh, thank you, Craig." She smiled at him. "I can't wait to read it."

They set the gifts aside, and Bessie served the cake. When they finished, Bessie said, "Now you two go into the parlor while your father and I do the dishes. Craig, you want to play something in honor of your sister's birthday. Kathleen, tell your brother what you want to hear."

The children went to look through the piano pieces. "Do you want to hear the Bach piece I've been practicing?" he asked her. "Or something popular?"

"Why don't you start with the Bach and then when they come in, some songs we can sing?" Kathleen suggested.

Their father poked his head in and said, "Good suggestion. Go ahead. Start. We can hear you in the kitchen."

A month before, John and Bess had gone into Mitchell to buy Kathleen's gifts. They had bought her the doll first, knowing how much she wanted it. Then they had stepped into the jewelers to see about a ring, but when they saw the lockets, they knew they'd found the perfect gift.

John saw them in the case. "Look at these, Bessie. We can buy one for you and one for her. A mother/daughter pair. She won't lose this on a chain. She might lose a ring."

"A locket's a good idea, but mother/daughter," Bess protested. "It's not my birthday."

"You gave birth to her and we should honor the mother on the child's birthday, I think." He smiled at her. When they chose two they agreed on, the salesman boxed them and they left happy with their purchases. "Did Craig get her gift?" John asked as they walked toward the depot.

Bess said, "No, he hasn't. I think he decided on a book, but he'll probably get it at the last minute. You know him."

"Ah, yes, though he may be last minute, he always comes through."

On the ride home in the train they talked about their children. "Such beautiful babies," John mused. "No others as beautiful. Craig looked strong and healthy from the beginning, and Kathleen so tiny and delicate. To think …" He ended lamely. "Certainly she's given us a few worries over the years." They rode in silence for a few minutes. "When I think of how Tom and Belle lost four of their children, I wonder how we've been so fortunate."

"I know. God, keep his hand over us."

"I'm so happy that they have three healthy children now." They sat in silence as they thought of his brother's losses. "We haven't seen them lately. Why don't we invite them to dinner some Sunday?"

"Wonderful idea. What about the Sunday after the birthday?"

"Good idea. I'll write to them and tell them to bring the children and Dora."

Every town has its local characters, and in Ethan four of these local farmers – Don, Pete, Gus and Oscar – sat down in the local diner for lunch after doing their business at the grain elevator. Don carried *The Enterprise* to read the latest news.

Pete asked Don, "What're the headlines?"

"Looks like our boys are finally coming home," Don offered without looking up.

When the waiter came, they ordered the daily special: pork chops, potatoes, and green beans.

"I don't know why we had to get mixed up in that European war," Gus said.

"Well, old timer," Don said, "according to all I've read in the paper and heard from the Four-Minute Men, we just had to stop the piracy of the Germans. And then there was that secret agreement between Germany and Mexico. Too close to our own border."

Gus sipped his coffee. "How many of you fellows been to war? If you haven't been in battle, you've no idea what war is all about."

Oscar buttered his bread and without lifting his head said, "The closest I got to the military was signing up in that Spanish-American War back in '98. We only got as far as Minnesota to the training camp, and then it was already over. John Donahue was with me." He pointed toward the paper with his knife. "It was a terrible experience."

"I find it difficult to believe John signed up to go to war," Pete said. "We couldn't find anyone milder and more peace-loving."

"He did. Caught some kind of a fever. Spent a lot of time in sick bay while the rest of us drilled and marched and did target shooting." Oscar turned to Gus, "How about you, Gus? You ever been in a war?"

"You bet, he said proudly. "My family was living in Pennsylvania when the Civil War broke. I joined the Confederates the last few months. It was a pretty ghastly affair."

While they ate, Don steered the conversation back to the latest news, "About this war now. No one did more for the war effort around here than the Red Cross and the Four-Minute Men. And you know John headed both of those groups. We've got to be proud of him and the others." He shook his head. "Especially Father Goggin. Too bad he has to leave Ethan. It seems we just get a good priest here, and he's gone in a few years."

"There's a farewell dinner for him next week." Don asked, "You all going?"

"We'll be there," Pete said. "We're going to miss him. I hope the new priest is half as good. Did you hear? John is master of ceremonies at the dinner. He'll do a great job." They all nodded in agreement.

A few days after the priest's dinner, Bess brought chicken broth to the bedroom where John lay ill with influenza. It was 1918, the year of the epidemic that killed so many. When she said his name softly, he rolled over slowly. She put the tray down on the table and said, "I've brought you some hot broth."

"I don't want anything," he moaned.

"You have to take some nourishment. You'll never get well without something in your stomach." She took the extra pillows and put them behind his head. "Let me help you to sit up a little. I'll feed you." She took him by the arm and between her pulling and him pushing, he half sat up against the pillows. "Mercy! We have to break this fever. But first some chicken broth." She picked up the bowl and spoon, sat on the edge of the bed and managed to get him to swallow most of it. This time, he kept it down.

"Thank you," John said weakly. "That did feel good."

"I'll take these to the kitchen, then I'll be back to give you an alcohol rub to see if we can get your temperature down."

A week later, John finally came downstairs. He had slowly regained his strength. He found Bessie with her sisters, Mattie and Ella, drinking tea. Their children played outside with Craig and Kathleen. Mattie said, "Goodness, John. You've lost weight. Look how your clothes hang on you."

He sat down to join them. "I think I've never been that sick," he smiled ruefully. "I've decided that all those articles in the newspaper about influenza were right on the money."

Ella said, "Some of my neighbors said the same thing. You're lucky to be alive."

"He got sick because he's been working too hard," Bess complained. "Out every night to some meeting, the Red Cross or the Four-Minute Man or some other group." She turned to her sisters. "And that's after working all day in the print shop and the post office." She turned to scold him, "You've got to slow down."

"I imagine now that the Armistice has been signed there won't be any need for all the meetings." He smiled conspiratorially at his sisters-in-law. "I'll come home and be a good boy."

"Life went on while you were sick," Bess sniffed.

John appealed to Ella and Mattie. "See how expendable I am. Bessie just takes over. You know who ran the paper and the post office while I lolled in bed."

Mattie interrupted them. "Bessie, I want to show you the new dress pattern I have. Where did I leave my bag?" She rose to retrieve her satchel from the parlor.

John got up slowly. "I'll go get the children. It's time they came in from the cold."

"Good," Bess said. "After they have their hot drinks, they can take turns playing a piece on the piano. Put on your heavy coat. And your hat. We don't want you to have a relapse."

"Yes, Mother." He turned to Ella and Mattie once again, this time winking. "See what good care Nurse Donahue takes of me."

For years John and Bess had talked about plans for their son, and now that he was twelve, it was time to make a change. Early in May John once again went over the plan. "We've agreed we want Craig to attend a first-rate college, and we know he'll have little chance of acceptance with the town school not being accredited. So, is now the time to send him to Mitchell to school? He could live with your sister Ella during the week. We know she'll take good care of him. He can go to school with his cousins, Virgil and Ken, and they could study together. I talked to the principal this week, and he said the school would welcome him. And we agreed that paying the tuition would be well worth it, a good investment, in fact. Can we make the final arrangements with your sister on Sunday?"

Bess had dreaded this day. "I guess you're right. Just wondering why we can't wait a couple of years? He's so young."

"He'll be fine," he assured her. "He adapts easily. He's just dog paddling here. He's capable of striking out to the deep water, and I don't want to hold him back. He needs a challenge with more students and better teachers. The world is changing, and young men need a college degree to get ahead in the world. I want him to have better advantages than I did."

"You're right, of course. It's just we'll miss him so much."

"I know. But he can come home every weekend, and during school breaks. Besides, he'll be here all summer."

"It is best for him. What about Kathleen? We won't be sending her off to Mitchell, will we?"

"No, I'll get on the Ethan school board this fall and work to get the school accredited by the time she enters high school. We've got a few years."

In August when Craig moved to Mitchell, Bess decided to take in a boarder. She told John, "We have the empty bedroom and we can use the extra money." She continued to do that for many years, usually one of the teachers in the school.

"Sure, and your mother was a grand lady." Everyone in the kitchen turned to look at Will Craig, who stood in the doorway. When no one spoke, he said with a twinkle in his eye, "She married me, didn't she?"

Relieved, Bess and her sisters laughed lightly. They were putting the final touches on the lunch for the gathering after their mother's funeral. Bess took her Dad's arm. "Come along and sit here." She led him into the parlor to a large easy chair. "Tell the children about living in a sod house." The grandchildren gathered around. Some sat huddled together on the davenport while others took places in a semicircle on the floor. He needed no further invitation.

"I like to think of those days when we first came to Dakota, your grandmother and me." He added as an afterthought, "And all our kids. You never saw a more desolate spot – no trees anywhere around. So I built my family a fine sod house. Kept us warm in winter and cool in summer. Nothing like it."

Kathleen interrupted him. "What's a sod house?"

He laughed lightly, "Why sod is nothing but dirt." He watched their amazed faces.

"You lived in a house of dirt?' queried little Ella Navin.

"But how did you do it?" asked his grandson John.

"Well, you see, when we first arrived … let's see, 1882. A long time ago. This whole area was simply covered with prairie grass. And the prairie grass has deep roots. So when we used our plows to dig up blocks of sod – almost like bricks, we had the building blocks for our house. I had some good help in your uncle John." He looked at their young faces and explained, "You don't remember him. He died in 1908."

"That was the year I was born," Kathleen said in awe.

He went on, "And your aunt Anna was married, so your uncle Phil Tobin helped too."

Craig said, "I don't know them."

"No, none of you would. They moved to Canada years ago. Let me get on with my story. Your grandmother. Wasn't she after me to build a proper house? I told her this sod house is fine. No, she kept insisting. So, I said, 'I have to build the barn first.' She kept after me, and then I said, 'Let me put the seeds in the ground.' She asked again, but now it was harvest time. No time at all to be building a house. Finally I had to get the lumber and give her a house to keep the peace."

A little voice piped up imperiously, "Where did you get the wood if there were no trees?"

Everyone laughed, but Will waved his hand and went on, "That's a good question. We had to go all the way to Yankton to the lumber mill. Took several days down and several days to get back home." He smiled, "Your Uncle John and I had quite the trip." He looked toward the door where Bess stood ready to announce that lunch was ready. He said to her, "Do you remember the house made of earth?"

She nodded. "Yes, I lived in it till I was about eleven."

"You young ones were such a help to your mother. And what would we have done during the past year if you weren't here to help me take care of her." Suddenly his face crumpled and he began sobbing.

John stepped over to put his arm around him. "You stay here, Dad, and Craig'll fix you a plate. You need to eat something." Joe had pulled over a chair to sit beside his father. The children, ushered by their mothers, went into the kitchen for their meal. Craig brought him a plate, and surprisingly, he did eat a little.

The Enterprise
December 8, 1919

Mrs. William Craig Loses Long Fight
Succumbs to Grim Reaper after Heroic Struggle
Lasting Many Weary Months

Mrs. William Craig died at her home on East Main street at six o'clock Monday morning. Mrs. Craig had been in failing health for more than a year. Last July her condition became so serious that she was confined to her home entirely. At times there seemed some improvement. Later a dropsical condition developed, but disappeared entirely before her death. Owing to heart lesions, she was unable to lie down and had sat in a chair during her entire illness.

Sarah Alice Doyle was born in the county of Dublin Ireland on June 1, 1841, and came to America in 1849 with her parents and settled at Portage, Wisconsin. She was married at that place to William Craig on November 1, 1862. They lived at Eau Claire, Wisconsin a short time, moved to Missouri in 1866 and settled near Cameron. In 1882 they came to Dakota and settled on a farm southeast of Ethan where they lived until 1905 when they moved to Ethan where they have lived since then. She was the mother of ten children.

"Now Kathleen," Bess said one cool fall afternoon to her daughter who had just finished practicing her piano pieces, "I bought you nice kitchen towels and good thread. I'm going to teach you how to do cross-stitch. Once you learn to sew on towels, I'll buy good linen and you can start getting your things ready for your trunk."

"Do I have to?" Kathleen folded her arms and pouted as her mother patted the place beside her on the couch. When she reluctantly sat, Bess showed her the towels, the threads, and the different designs.

Just then her father came in the room to get his glasses, and Kathleen whined, "Dad, Mother says I have to learn needlework and get ready for when I get married. I'm only twelve. I'm too young to get married."

John warned her. "Just wait and see all that you have to do. It'll take you years. Why, you'll be forty before you marry." He grinned at the two of them, sitting side by side.

"Dad," Kathleen whined again.

He ignored her and listed on his fingers, "Dining room: table cloth and napkins, runner for the china closet; bedroom: sheets and pillow covers, dresser scarves; and for the parlor: …"

Bess interrupted him, "Dad, leave us be." She turned to her daughter, "Kathleen, don't fuss. You've already done tatting on fine linen. This is just the next step. Let me see your hands. Are they clean?" She took her daughter's hands and inspected them. "No, just as I thought. Go wash your hands. You know that's always the first step in doing any needlework. If you don't, the work will be horribly soiled."

"But you have to wash it anyway," she pointed out.

"Go," Bess said imperiously, waving toward the kitchen and continuing to grumble, "And you should have clean hands when you play the piano. I suppose the keys are all dirty again." Bess turned to John who had sat at his desk to watch the scene. "She finds more excuses. I despair of that child."

"Do you think she'll work with you this time? You sent her to Mrs. Conway to learn how to tat."

"I'd like to try. I'll see how it goes. But as you say, she always argues with me." She tapped her thimble idly on the arm of the couch.

"Heaven knows she always sees her mother with busy hands."

Bess ignored his comment. "You'd think she'd take inspiration from her father doing two jobs." She'd picked up her sewing and took several stitches before looking up him. "How much longer are you going to continue with this schedule?"

"Maybe it's almost time to give up the newspaper," John admitted.

She gave him a sharp look. "Is it? And you'll keep the post office?"

"I think so. I don't like the job every week of soliciting advertisements. And I don't appreciate all the Republican drivel I have to print. It's getting to me. After all, I've been at it a long time. I bought the newspaper just before Kathleen was born."

"What about Kathleen?" their daughter asked, hearing her name as she reentered the room.

He teased, "Just that you're the most beautiful young woman in town and I have to fight off all the young men who want to marry my daughter."

"Oh, Dad," she laughed in spite of herself.

"Leave us women alone so we can get to our work," Bess said with a dismissive wave of her hand.

A week later, after several sessions marked by frustration and tears, Bess asked Mrs. Conway if she would teach Kathleen how to work cross-stitch. "She just won't work for me. She listened to you in the tatting and does fine work. Can you help her?"

"I'd be happy to," her friend said. "Your daughter is a lovely child! We get along fine. You know, Bessie, they say some mothers and daughters just don't get along. Like oil and water, they don't mix."

After supper Bess reminded Kathleen, "Time to practice. You haven't played today." When her daughter didn't move, she said again, "Go on. Play some of your scales."

Kathleen slowly went to the bench and sat. She started playing and almost immediately hit several wrong notes. John and Bess winced but said nothing. She stopped and put her head down. Her father urged her to play a Bach piece.

She stared at the keyboard, not moving. "Play that piece 'Narcissus.'" Bess said without stopping her work. "That's a lovely piece."

She rifled through her music sheets and in a few minutes began the Bach. After a few bars, she again hit wrong notes. She tried again from the beginning and hit even more wrong notes. Suddenly she banged the cover down over the keys and cried, "I don't want to play this piece. I don't want to play piano anymore. I quit." She put her head down on the piano and sobbed.

John went over to sit beside her on the bench. He put his arm around her shoulders and hugged her. "That's enough for today. You can try again tomorrow."

"I don't want to play anymore," she said in a muffled voice, her head in her arms. "I'm no good."

"You're very good," Bess said quietly from her place on the other side of the room. "Don't worry about a few wrong notes when you're practicing."

"But Craig plays so good, and no matter how hard I try," Kathleen complained, "I can never be as good as he is. He plays Mozart and all I can play are the Bach exercises. And I'm not even good at that."

Her parents knew that their daughter was jealous of her brother, who could play by ear as well as read music. John said, "Don't worry, Kathleen. You and Craig have different talents. That's all." He took out a clean handkerchief from his breast pocket and handed it to her. "Wipe your eyes. That's enough practice for today. Go upstairs and read. We'll talk tomorrow." He hugged her.

"Thanks, Dad," she said, sniffling. She added defiantly, "But I won't play the piano ever again."

Two days later he took Kathleen into Mitchell. On the train he said, "We'll find something special for you that Craig doesn't have."

Kathleen repeated what she'd said for the past several days, "I'm not playing the piano ever again."

And John repeated as he'd said each time, "We'll see."

They went into the music store on Main street, but instead of looking at the sheet music or books of piano pieces, he led her to the back of the store where they saw new and used instruments for sale. When the proprietor, Mr. Zweigler, came over to them, John told him they were looking for something special for his daughter. The owner said, "The little lady wants perhaps to buy a trumpet?" He turned to Kathleen and asked, "Are you wanting to blow your own horn?" He pointed to the brass instruments on the wall. She giggled.

John said, "We might be interested in a violin." He pointed to one sitting in an open case. "What about that one? Can we look at it?"

"Look at it you can, but for this little lady," he said with a twinkle in his eye, "I have something very special. Wait here." He ducked through a heavy dark curtain hung in the doorway. In a few minutes he returned carrying a small case. "For such a small lady we have a special violin," he said opening the case, and tucking it under his chin, made a few adjustments with the frets and lightly played "Twinkle, Twinkle, Little Star." During the short performance John watched his daughter, pleased to see that she was fascinated. "I've just restrung this, and it's ready for a new owner. You don't mind having something used?" he asked, bending down and handing her the delicate instrument.

"What do you think?" John asked. "Do you want to try it?"

She looked at him hopefully. "You mean if I learn to play this I won't have to play the piano?"

"Try it and we'll see what happens. Maybe you'll want to go back to the piano." He teased her, "Who knows? You may hate the violin and be glad to return to the keyboard."

She shuddered. "I don't think so."

"Winifred will be sad to lose one of her star pupils," he said with twinkle in his eye.

"I don't care," Kathleen said obstinately.

John turned to Mr. Zweigler. "I didn't know that they came in different sizes. Are they just as good as a regular one?" He pointed to the full-sized violin displayed on the shelf.

"They make some half-size violins for children. It sounds the same – maybe not as loud. It would be difficult for a little lady like this to play a full size violin. And I can give you a good price on this. If it doesn't work for her, I'll buy it back from you."

"What else do we need?" John asked. "Music, supplies?"

Mr. Zweigler gathered what they needed and put everything in the case. "Do you have a teacher? The violin is a difficult instrument to learn without a teacher."

"We have a teacher," John assured him.

Kathleen looked up at her father, "Who?"

"Mrs. Oathout. Do you think you can work with her?"

"It looks hard," she said, hesitating.

The salesman patted her hand, "It's hard for the one who doesn't try, but you will try very hard. And practice, practice, practice."

"I'll practice if I don't have to play the piano," Kathleen asserted.

After John paid for everything, Mr. Zweigler handed him the case and said, "You need anything – replacement parts, repairs – you come back and see me. I'll take good care of you."

"Thank you," John said as he shook his hand.

"Good luck, little lady," he said taking Kathleen's hand, giving her a warm handclasp. "Such tiny hands. Hard to reach on the piano. Hard to reach an octave. Fine with the violin."

When they stepped out onto the street, her father handed the case to Kathleen. "This belongs to you. Take good care of it," he said gently.

"I will," she beamed up at him. "Thanks, Dad."

Several months later, John came home unexpectedly in the middle of the afternoon and found Kathleen playing the piano. He stood in the doorway, listening. When she stopped, he applauded. "Sounds wonderful. Have you been sneaking behind our backs practicing the piano?"

Chagrined, she turned to her father. "No, I thought I'd try again and see if I remembered. It's like I've been playing all along."

"You're not giving up the violin?" he asked.

"No. I like the violin. But I just wondered if …" She trailed off.

"Your mother and I'll be glad to hear you play either one. Go ahead, continue what you're doing." He went to his desk to find some papers. She started again, and then stopped. He looked over at her. "Too bad you can't play both at the same time." They laughed together.

"Mrs. Oathout gave me some pieces where the piano accompanies the violin. Maybe Craig and I can try it when he comes home."

"Wonderful! But you'll have to play the violin part." He had hoped for such a proposal, but knew it must come from her. She seemed ready. He smiled fondly. "Play some more."

Later when they were alone, Bess told John, "You said all we needed was to give her something that was her own. Look at her. Fairly good on violin and even better on piano. Those months of not playing don't seem to have hurt her."

The two Ethan old-timers, Gus and Oscar, ate breakfast at the diner every Friday regular as clockwork, and every week Gus found something to complain about in *The Enterprise*, which he carried in with him and read to his companion. Oscar believed this time that maybe Gus had a legitimate gripe.

"Don't that beat all! Did you see this letter in the paper?" he asked.

"What's that?" They had finished eating and were drinking their coffee. As usual Oscar was mentally planning his day while his companion read, but he was ready to listen to this week's complaint.

Gus shook the paper in his friend's face, "This here letter says we shouldn't have a column of Worthen news. Shoot! Of course we should. Don't most of those folks come and do business in town? Aren't they our neighbors and friends?"

Oscar reached a hand across the table. "Let me see that. Who wrote it?"

Gus held onto the paper. "Danged if I know. It's not signed. Says if you want to know you can get the name at *The Enterprise* office. If a fellow's gonna criticize, he oughtta put his name down, don't you think? Wait'll I see John Donahue. I'm gonna give him a piece of my mind." He shook the paper again. "Listen to this. He talks about the double-headed baseball game on Sunday afternoon 'In the Shade of the Old Mennonite Village.' What's that supposed to mean? We're not supposed to have fun on Sunday?" Oscar again reached across for the paper. This time Gus handed it over. "See in the second column. Read it for yourself."

He read silently while his friend fumed opposite him, "I don't know about you, but I like to know what's up with those folks." This is what he read.

The Enterprise
June 16, 1921

An Appeal

Mr. Editor:

We trust that you will read these few lines in the same spirit in which they are written, the spirit of justice rather than criticism. But we feel that it is time that someone register an emphatic protest, concerning a certain department of the dear Enterprise. Now we refer to those articles under the heading, "Worthen News."

Oh! Mr. Editor, where is Worthen? What is Worthen, and why is Worthen? Is it a place, or just a condition? Is it a new fad in ladies' hats, or is it a disease? Mr. Editor, please have a heart and lift the clouds of bewilderment from our troubled minds. Think of it, Mr. Editor – nearly a whole column in our dear paper devoted to a proposition of which few know, and no one cares! In the name of common sense, Mr. Editor, is this fair? Why not devote a part of this space to some topic of common interest such as baseball, prohibition or "Bringing Up Father?" We feel that if you did, you would be making an affirmative response to a long felt want!

As we think of it, we recollect that a recent outburst of the "Worthen News" gives the impression that everyone from Granddad down are baseball artists, including the gentle sex. Think of it, a double headed baseball game on Sunday afternoon, "In the Shade of the Old Mennonite Village." Yea, verily, a piece no artist dare attempt.

Now does that sort of so-called news concern you? Does it concern any of your readers? Does it concern anyone else? We say NO, and we say it with a vengeance!

We humbly suggest that you instruct the editorial staff to cast about a little, and see if it is at all possible to do something to relieve the situation. We know you will agree that an emergency exists. The cause of the common people is pitted against the interests of the few. "Few" means Worthen.

We trust that you will think wisely and act quickly on a matter so close to everyone's heart.

Again we ask, who, what, and why is Worthen? I thank you.

– Contributed

Name furnished on request.

(Editor's note – The above article was printed merely to allow our capable Worthen correspondent to inform this "fresh party" about Worthen and what it will not stand for. We are from Worthen ourself and no one can kick her shins and get away with it.)

Oscar scratched his head. "I don't get it. Is it bosh? Or sour grapes?" He shifted in his chair. "I'll ask John when I get my mail why Worthen news shouldn't be printed. Hell, he prints news of all the towns around here, Starr, Tobin, even Mitchell."

"Makes no sense to me," his friend agreed. "You tell him to keep Worthen news in the paper. Tell whoever wrote that letter he better get used to it."

"This is the funny thing. I think John grew up on the Coyne farm out there in Worthen. Isn't that the damnedest thing you ever heard?" He shook his head perplexed. "And then he lets this letter get in the paper. He's not mad at Mike for some reason, is he?"

"John don't get mad. He's too mild mannered for that. I just don't get it."

A week later, they met again. As they waited for their meal, Gus asked his friend, "Did you hear anything about that Worthen flap in the last week's paper? I don't see anything on the first page." He folded the paper back and skimmed the second page.

"When I talked to John last week, he said I'd have to wait until today to find out. Isn't that the darndest!" Oscar watched him look for the article. "I guess there's gonna be a response."

When their breakfast of eggs, sausage, potatoes, and toast came, Gus put the paper down on the chair next to him. They went right to eating with little conversation. When they finished, he picked up the paper and looked through the next page. "Ah," he said. "Here it is. An apology." He looked up. "Did you hear that?" he asked. "An Apology." He read aloud.

𝕿𝖍𝖊 𝕰𝖓𝖙𝖊𝖗𝖕𝖗𝖎𝖘𝖊
June 23, 1921

An Apology

The editor of *The Enterprise*, in connection with the article which appeared in these columns last week, labeled, "An Appeal," desires to explain that the whole thing was merely a joke. The article was written by a Worthenite in the spirit of fun, with the knowledge and sanction of the editor. No harm was intended to anyone and no offense should be taken. The idea which prompted the article was merely to create a little interest, and it did! In fact, it created a sensation! But when the whole thing was explained, it is easy to see that only a spirit of fun prompted the article.

This writer offers his apologies to any who have been offended and assures them that both the editor and the writer of the "Appeal" have none but the kindliest feelings for the Worthen Correspondent and the good people of Worthen township. The picnic and the ball game at Rockport was one of the finest kind of things for the people. A chance for relaxation and clean, wholesome amusements do not desecrate the Sabbath and the writer had no such idea in mind. We sincerely hope that this explanation will remove any ill feeling that may have been caused by the article.

"Well, I'll be hornswoggled," said Oscar laughing. "John was just having fun with us. He's something else. Just a joke."

"Don't that beat all!" Gus scratched his head. "So this explains the part about the ball game being a chance for 'relaxation and clean wholesome, amusement.' That John Donahue does enjoy a good time."

"You know what I think? I think he wrote both the letter and the apology. I think he is the Worthen correspondent. When I see him I'm gonna tell him, 'You got us good.'" He paused and shook his head. "Why didn't we catch this as a joke? We're losing it, pal."

John and his worker, Lester Williams, reviewed the articles for the next week's edition. Suddenly, he put the papers down. "I can't do it anymore, Lester."

Lester looked at him. "What's the matter?"

"I can't print all this drivel about Republicans. I'm going to have to give up the paper." He looked at his young assistant. "Do you want to be the editor?"

John saw the astonished look on Lester's face. "But, Mr. Donahue, you are *The Enterprise*."

"Please Lester, answer my question before I change my mind," John said.

"Are you selling the paper?" Lester looked into John's face, incredulous.

"No, just handing over the daily job of operating it. You know my political views are so opposite to most folks around here. I find it hard to maintain the integrity of my beliefs. Besides, some businessmen are refusing to advertise because they say they don't like the Democratic slant of the paper." John looked beyond Lester out the large front window into the afternoon sun where he could see the sign for the newspaper hanging from its brackets. "This paper is too old and has too good a reputation for me to allow it to die. Ethan needs *The Enterprise*, so if I must give it up, I will. You've been working here now for a while, so you know the routine. You're a capable writer." He touched Lester's arm gently, "I ask you again. Are you willing to take the job of editor?"

"Well, if you put it that way ... well ... I guess, yes," the young man smiled gratefully. "Yes, I am."

"I'll be here in the post office. I'll even work in the print shop some. And, maybe, when it's not a question of politics, I'll even write some pieces. Keep my hand in it. This is how I started newspaper work, as editor. I worked for Charley Coyne up in Wolsey on the *Herald*. He was the owner and did nothing in the day-to-day operations of the paper. In fact most papers are run that way. You're young. You'll learn all there is to know about the job."

"I think I'd like to try," Lester said with more confidence. "When do you want me to start? I know I'm learning from a good teacher."

John smiled. "How about immediately? I'll write a valedictory for this edition. Why don't you get started on setting up these pieces?" He handed Lester the articles they had agreed on. "Just save me half a column on page three." He put a fresh piece of paper in the typewriter and began his last official editorial.

Later, when John told Bess what he had done, she said with relief, "I'm glad you've finally done that. You've been working too hard. And you don't need all that worry about printing political views you don't agree with."

The Enterprise
July 7, 1921

Valedictory

After thirteen years and one month, the undersigned releases control of *The Enterprise*. Two thirds of the twenty years the paper has been in existence, it has been conducted by us. During the past thirteen years we have tried to give the people of this town and community the best newspaper possible under the circumstances. How well we succeeded is hard to say. Certainly, we would be ungrateful if we failed to thank the hundreds of friends, and loyal businessmen of Ethan for their unwavering support, without which no newspaper can live, much less thrive and

---

become an influence for the good of the community. It is only on account of being unable to continue the mechanical work of getting out the paper regularly week after week that influences us to lay down the work at this time.

Our earnest hope is that you will continue to support your home paper in the future as you have in the past and that the new editor will deserve your support, which we believe he will.

John L. Donahue

On a crisp, cool March evening in 1922 a smiling John walked down Main street on his way home. He looked up at the stars. As one of the organizers of the evening for businessmen, he was among the last to leave Green's. Everything had gone well; people seemed pleased and now the town had its first business group – something he had tried to organize for years. He found Bess working on a rag rug. He stood in the doorway. "You're still up?" The electric overhead light blazed.

"I want to hear all about it," she exclaimed. "How did everything go? Sit down and tell me." She pushed a stray lock of her dark hair back into its place behind her ear.

John pulled a chair over and sat opposite her next to the rug frame. "This looks good. You've done so much." He picked up some threads and began to weave.

"Never mind the rug," she said impatiently. "Tell me about the meeting."

"The good news is that the Commercial Club is up and running."

"A success then?"

"I'd say so. Jim counted fifty people who signed on. He's the treasurer and will collect dues; Bob's the chairman; George took notes as secretary. Yes, it was a good meeting." He stopped working and stared at the design. "They talked about plans and motives for the group. Finally we have some organization for the businesses in town, and things may work more smoothly."

"Not that you haven't tried to get something going for years. Who's on the board?"

"Rob Coyne, of course. Herb, Henry, Harry, Will," he listed the prominent townsmen. "Looks like a good group of workers."

"But not you," she said with relief as she looked across at him.

"No. I've had enough activities for a lifetime. Time to hand it over to the young people."

"Good. How about the dinner? How did that go?"

"Fine. Green cooked up a fine pot roast with potatoes and gravy, carrots, and green beans, and his special cherry cobbler for dessert. A good meal." He looked at her across the rug and said, "A good meal, but not as good as a meal in this house."

"What did folks think of the cards you had printed?" she asked as she picked up the threads again.

"They were a great hit. And just like you said, half of them ignored the side that said, 'Do not turn over.' Joe said after he read the opposite side, 'As if any of us would be here except to cooperate.' The speeches were good. Not too long. 'Course folks were glad to see Father Goggin again. Nice that he came."

"You must be pleased."

"The planning committee did a fine job. The best part of it was to see everybody come together for the interests of the town. Too bad Lester couldn't be here."

"Well, I'm sure he'll join the group once he heals," Bess assured him. "You took notes?"

"Yes, after thirteen years of newspaper business, I took notes." John reached toward his breast pocket, patting the small notebook. "And if I missed anything, I can check with George." He stood up to tie the end of a row. We'll be able to finish this in a few days. It's coming together beautifully. Let's go to bed," he said stretching. "We're both tired."

"You don't want a cup of tea before you go up?"

"No, I just want to go to bed. Come along." They climbed the stairs together.

The Enterprise
April 20, 1922

Editorial

After an absence of nearly three weeks from home the writer returned a week ago yesterday from the M. E. hospital at Mitchell, where he had undergone several operations, making recovery slow. The care received was the best that could have been given anywhere, and the writer hopes within a few days to again take up the work and management of *The Enterprise*, which the former editor J. L. Donahue and wife have so kindly attended to during his absence. The writer wishes at this time to thank the members of the Woodman lodge of Ethan and Mitchell, fellow editors, and many other friends for their kind

acts and words while he was in the hospital and since his return, which have gone a long way in cheering him and hastening his recovery.
Lester H. Williams, Editor

John sat in the post office, frustrated and worried. What to do? His helper, Edward had returned to the post office empty-handed from the depot where he'd gone to pick up the mail. "I don't understand it, Mr. Donahue. No mail today."

John looked at him in astonishment. "That's impossible. Of course there's mail. We have mail every day." Not only did the mail contain the week's edition of the ongoing story for *The Enterprise*, but also all the area mail. What do you say to the carriers and customers? "It just wouldn't happen that *no one* in town would receive mail," John said in disbelief. He took his jacket from its hook, put on his hat, and headed to the depot. He asked everyone he saw about the mail sacks, but no one had seen them. He used the telephone in the restaurant to call the railroad to verify that the mailbags had in fact been delivered to the Ethan Depot. Yes, the agent said, the four bags had been deposited at the regular time this morning at 7 a. m. on the dot. But Edward had left the post office as the train was pulling out, and when he arrived there were no bags to be found. Whoever took the bags must've done so immediately, and disappeared fast.

For several weeks John had continued to fuss over the loss of the mail, and Bess tried to soothe him, "Worrying about the lost mail will not bring it back."

"I know," he'd said. "It's like the robbers stole something from me personally. So many folks are complaining. Some were expecting important mail that never arrived." One day when he was working at home, he heard a knock on the kitchen door. Irritated at the interruption, he opened the door where he found a young couple from town, Marie and Dominique, standing in the doorway, each holding two mailbags. "Where did you find them?" he asked astounded.

"Down near the railroad track," Dominique said.

"We went out this morning looking for flowers to decorate the hall for the party tonight," Marie said. "We wouldn't have found them except that we crossed over to the other side, and when we got to the culvert, there they were. Stacked in a neat pile with a rock holding them down." She turned to Dominique, "Would you say about a mile north of town?"

"No, it was closer – about a half mile – not far at all," he said. "Sorry we couldn't get them to you earlier, but we had to get the flowers in water. We came as quick as we could. We brought them to the post office, but when we saw you weren't there, we thought we'd bring them here."

"Anything in them?" Bess, who had joined him, peeked over John's shoulder. "Those look like they have something, Dominique, but the ones you have, Marie, look empty."

"You're right." She showed the tops of the bags. "See how the straps are cut here and here."

"These have to be the missing bags," John said as he reached to take the bags from the couple. "I'll report this. You may have to come in to sign a statement. I'll let you know." As they turned to leave he added, "Thank you for bringing them."

After the couple left, he put on his jacket and hat, picked up the four bags, and headed to the post office to contact the authorities. He knew without opening them that they contained only the newspaper inserts, that there was no mail. After he talked to officials, he had to wait for one of the two postal agents, Helvik or Green to come to secure the bags and authorize the ordering of replacement bags.

Two days later, another neighbor, Martin Aasleth, brought to the Post Office a small stack of envelopes, very much the worse for being outdoors. "John, look at what I found. Must be some of the mail you lost."

John took it and asked, "Where did you find this?"

"About a mile north of town. You know where we're working on the tracks? We left a stack of railroad ties there a few weeks ago, and when we went back today we found these tucked in between two ties."

John fanned through the pile. "Looks like they've all been opened. So whoever took the bags carried these farther up the tracks to examine them more closely."

"My guess is they were looking for money. They were kind of neat though. Seems like they put the letters back in the envelopes. They didn't just scatter the mail to the four winds."

After Martin left, John examined them more closely. Because of the recent rain a few were almost illegible, but he sorted them. He would deliver the pieces that belonged to folks in town; the ones for the outlying section would have to wait until tomorrow and the rural carrier. John arrived home late that afternoon and told Bess the latest in the story of the stolen mail. "This sorry business is almost at an end. What a nightmare!"

"It's not your fault," Bess said without taking her eyes from her work. "Everyone knows you've done all you could."

"And we'll probably never catch the thieves who did this."

She glanced over at him, "We do have to be grateful to Marie and Dominique and to Martin for turning in what they found."

"Yes, you're right. I'll ask Lester to write an article so folks will know what happened. "

Chapter Ten
Facing Challenges

William Craig died just two and a half years after his wife's death. A few days after his funeral Bess sat by the window trying to catch a little breeze on a hot summer day. She held her sewing but hadn't taken a stitch. Across the room at his desk, John picked up his writing. "Excuse me, Bess." He turned to face her and spoke gently. "Would you listen to this?" She looked over at him. "'He feared his God and loved his fellow man.' Is that what Father Goggin said in his sermon about your Dad?"

"Yes," Bess sighed and kept her eyes fixed on the garden outside the window. The dress and the needle rested lightly on her lap. Earlier she'd begun puckering the fabric of the smocking for the bodice piece of a dress for Kathleen. "I've been fortunate in living close to my parents and being able to care for them in their last illnesses. Poor Dad. He suffered so much the last several years. That accident to his foot really started his decline. Was that two years ago?" She didn't wait for an answer, but continued, "Then all the time he spent in the hospital. That was hard for him. What a blessing he could stay with us for the last several months! Thank you, John, for all you did for him."

She continued to look out the window, seeing nothing but the past. "Poor Mother, what a long, hard illness! Dad was so good in caring for her all those months. I remember standing in the cemetery when we buried her that cold December day, wondering how he would survive without her. But somehow he did. Married nearly sixty years. So devoted to each other." She picked up her sewing. "But I'm not telling you anything you don't already know. You've watched them for the past twenty years."

"Your father did all right for himself."

"Yes, he did, but after Mother's death, he was just lonesome and sad."

He picked up the sheets of paper. "Will you look over the death notice? I want to make sure I've got all the facts right for *The Enterprise*."

Bess set aside her sewing and started to get up.

"No, you sit there. I'll bring it to you. I've tried to write a real tribute. He was one of the pioneers of Dakota, and made a real success for himself and his family." He walked over and handed her the typewritten sheets. "Tell me if this is all right." He sat beside her and watched her as she read.

The Enterprise
August 3, 1922

Respected Pioneer is Called up Higher

William Craig, honored pioneer of this vicinity, passed away July 27 after a month's illness. William Craig was born in County Antrim, Province of Ulster, Ireland October 24, 1837, and at the time of his death was 84 years, 9 months and 3 days of age. He was the son of Francis Craig and Ann McQuillen. His father died while he was still very young. In 1849 his mother brought her family to America. They settled in the then wild state of Wisconsin, near the town of Portage, which was the site of Fort Winnebago. Here he experienced all of the discomforts and hardships of pioneer life and grew to vigorous manhood, schooled in the ways of the hardy settlers who were carving an empire from the vast domain, which was destined to become the veritable garden spot of the earth. Clearing forests, building canals, freighting, lumbering and fighting the elements were the outstanding features of the life of a boy who took up the serious business of life at the age of twelve years.

He was married to Sarah Doyle, November 1, 1862. With his bride he moved to the northern part of Wisconsin, settling at the town of Eau Claire where they lived until 1866. Again answering the call to the West, they moved to the state of Missouri, settling near Cameron where they lived until 1882. Dakota Territory, virgin, fertile and offering a free home for the asking, was beckoning the land-hungry and homeless of the older states and William Craig, ever thoughtful of the welfare of his family, joined the throng which was flocking to its great rolling prairies in the early eighties. Taking up their home near Ethan, enduring genuine pioneer hardships such as drought in summer and blizzard-swept winters of intense cold, he steadfastly sang the praises of the Dakotas when thousands became discouraged and left. In 1905, having wrested a competence from the soil and having reared a family of ten children to honored manhood and womanhood, he and his good wife, who had shared prosperity and adversity for nearly a half century, retired from the farm and moved to Ethan where they lived peacefully until her death December 8, 1918.

The funeral took place Monday, July 31, from the Holy Trinity Catholic church and interment was made in the Catholic cemetery. A magnificent sermon was preached by Rev. James Goggin of Dimock. To extol the virtues of William Craig would be merely to repeat the obvious. No finer tribute can be paid to his memory than to say: he feared his God and loved his fellow man.

When Bess finished reading the pages, she sat unmoving. John rose to kneel beside her. She shook herself. "Thank you, John. It reads well. And you have the facts right."

"You see, I *have* been paying attention to your stories over the years," he smiled sympathetically. He put his arms around her while she cried softly.

While Mother and daughter finished their supper and sat in a strained silence, Kathleen pouted. There were just the two of them; John hadn't returned from his business trip in Sioux Falls. Finally, Bess broke the silence. "You want to wear your navy blue poplin dress tomorrow."

Kathleen folded her arms and said obstinately, "I don't know why I have to go."

Bess ignored her defiance. "And your new shoes." Kathleen glared at the table. Her mother went on, "We're just going to look at the school. After that we'll decide if you should attend Notre Dame Academy next year. You might like what you see. Boarding with other girls should be a good experience for you. Winifred loved it."

"You're trying to get rid of me," Kathleen said. "You're always trying to get rid of me."

Bess looked aggrieved. "You know that's not true."

"Then why over the years have you sent me to stay with the Navins? And the Tobins? For years you've been doing that. Getting rid of me." They sat in stony silence. She challenged her mother, "Why would I want to go to an all-girls school?"

"For one thing, your father and I think you can concentrate on your studies more." She spoke calmly and reasonably. She gave her daughter time to respond. Kathleen remained silent, staring at her plate. "We always thought you enjoyed your visits with your cousin Winifred. You never complained."

"You never listened." She grudgingly added, "Well, when I was little, we had fun, but when we got older, she didn't have time for me any more. After all, she's five years older." She slid down farther in her seat. "I don't have a cousin my age. They're all either older or younger than me."

As Bess started to clear the table, she spoke firmly but kindly to her daughter. "Your father and I are taking you to Notre Dame in Mitchell tomorrow. We have an appointment at ten o'clock, and we expect you to be on your best behavior. All we ask is that you keep an open mind. Other girls are visiting. You might meet someone you like." She looked at her daughter, still pulling a face. "Give me a hand here. You wash and I'll dry."

Kathleen rose slowly and went to fill the dishpan from the kettle of hot water on the stove. "I'll go, but I'm not going to like it."

They worked side by side. "The most important advantage of the place is that the school is accredited, and we think that'll help you when you go to college. We hope you'll continue your studies because you've always had good grades and done well in school. We want you to have all the advantages available."

John came home after Kathleen was asleep, and he and Bess talked about the upcoming trip to Mitchell. He stood by the kitchen table while she poured the boiling water into the teapot. She asked, "What have we done wrong? She bucks me on every side and is never happy no matter what I do. You'd think she'd be glad to try something new. For the last several years, she's been complaining about the town school and has been jealous of Craig because we sent him to school in Mitchell."

"We haven't done anything wrong;" John said, putting a hand on his wife's arm. "She's going through a phase, and we have to be patient with her. Don't you remember being her age? With all the changes she's going through, she doesn't know how to react. Moodiness is a part of growing up."

"I've lost all patience with her. No matter what I do she's unhappy. But at least she washed the dishes tonight without arguing and complaining."

"So there's that," he grinned.

"We didn't have this kind of trouble with Craig."

"Boys and girls are different. Don't forget that she's had a lot of illnesses all her life. That's bound to make her feel different, and then because of it she's more introspective. Amazing that she does as well as she does in her school work with all the days she's missed. She catches up quickly and doesn't seem to suffer in her studies. Craig has always been more outgoing, but he's healthy."

"Remember her first year in school when Craig said she couldn't go because she didn't know how to read?" She poured out the tea and sat opposite him. "Remember the early days at the print shop when you carried her over and she lay on the couch when we both worked on the busy days? Some days we wondered if she'd survive this long." She placed her hands under her chin, her elbows propped on the table, as she watched him sipping his tea.

"Yes, and when she was in sixth grade and missed the last month of school? Spent most of the time in bed. You were run ragged caring for her. And here she is reminding us that she is very much alive. Alive and kicking. I'll talk to her before we leave tomorrow," he reassured her. "I'm sure she'll be willing to visit the campus with an open mind. I'll convince her to try it for at least a year."

"I'm sure she'll listen to you. She always pays more attention to you."

A wonderful, balmy September Sunday afternoon, John stopped his son, whose hand lay on the door handle. "Where do you think you're going, young man?" School had been in session for over a month, but Craig and Kathleen came home from Mitchell most Friday afternoons and returned on Sunday evenings.

Craig turned around to face his father. "I'm going to meet some fellows to play ball." He raised his left hand showing his mitt.

"Don't you have studies?" John spoke sternly.

"I did them. Except the history, and that won't take long. I'll have more than enough time when I get back."

"You may have time. Will you have the energy? And how are you getting back to school?"

"I'm taking the late train."

"Do you think that wise? Your sister has to go with you. You can't think of just yourself anymore."

"Let him go, Dad." Bessie interrupted the father-son debate as she stepped from the kitchen. "He studied yesterday and much of today. He *needs* to get out and clear his head."

Craig smiled at her in relief. "Thanks, Mother."

Bess told John, "Kathleen can take the late train as long as she's with Craig." She turned to Craig. "You'll see her to the school?"

"Yes," Craig looked from one to the other.

"And Rosemary?" John asked. "Does she know about this late arrangement? Or is she going on her own?"

Kathleen, carrying a book, came down the stairs and said, "She's going with us. She's coming into town later today."

"All right," John replied grudgingly. He thought of his own childhood with no time for games, working from dawn to dusk. He patted his son on the shoulder, "It's just that you know you've got to do well in your studies. You go to Notre Dame university next year."

"Don't worry, Dad," Craig said, punching his right hand lightly into his mitt. "I'm doing well in my classes."

Kathleen walked by the three standing in the hall as she headed toward the kitchen.

Craig, with a wink at his father, stepped in front of his sister and said, "Excuse me, Miss. May I have this dance?"

Kathleen looked up startled, laughed and said, "Out of my way, brother."

Craig stood his ground. He told his parents, "You should have seen Kathleen at the dance Friday night. The lads all stepped forward to ask her to dance and she rejected them all."

"I didn't reject anybody," she protested. "I danced."

"Right. You danced with Philip. Watch out. People will think you're a couple."

She ignored this comment. "The only one who asked me to dance was Philip. And," she hesitated, "well, Elmer, too, but I'm not going to dance with him." She turned to her father. "Tell him to leave me alone, Dad."

"I think I don't have to," John chuckled. "By the sounds of things you can take care of yourself. But let's get back to the late train. That's all right with the school?"

"It's fine," she said.

"How will you get to the academy from the station?" he asked.

Craig answered for her, "I'll borrow Ken's auto and drive her over."

Now it was Kathleen's turn to tease her brother. "Maybe you want to see someone at the academy. Maybe her name is Anna." She scooted around her mother into the kitchen to avoid being swatted by him.

Craig headed to the door. "I'll be back soon. We're just going to play a few innings." The screen door banged shut as he disappeared into the sunshine.

Kathleen, biting into an apple, headed back up the stairs. "How about you, Kathleen?" John asked. "Are your studies done?"

"All but a little math. And that won't take long."

"Maybe you should set aside your novel and do your school work first. Then you can read later."

"Now, Dad," Bess began. "Kathleen will get her work done. Stop fussing over your children." She gestured to her daughter, "Go on, dear."

"Thanks, Mother," Kathleen said, skipping up the stairs.

Bess called after her, "And don't leave the apple core on a piece of furniture."

John followed Bess into the kitchen. "You know, Bess we're blessed in our children. We have to be proud."

About a month later Craig, carrying a large box, banged into the print shop announcing buoyantly, "Wait'll you see what I have. A crystal set!"

John cleared off a space on his worktable where Craig deposited the box with a thud. He winced. "What happened to 'Hello, Dad,' and 'How are you?'" He got up and embraced his son. He looked beyond him toward the door. "Where's your sister?"

"She went on home. I wanted to show you this."

"Let's have a look." John peered into the box.

"Dad, you'll be amazed," Craig enthused. "You can listen to broadcasts from all over the country. And Canada. I thought it was about time Ethan was introduced to the modern world." As he talked, he spread the pieces out on the table. "I'll show you how to hook it up, and you can listen." He explained each piece as he worked. "Here you have the tuning coil. Just enamel copper wire wound around the tube. Next to the tuner is a strip of brass that moves along the coil to pick up different stations from their frequency."

"Where does it get its power?"

"From the antenna. See the long wire attached to the other end of the tuner. It's long because it works better if it's strung outside the building. So I'll unroll it and bring it to the window. It's able to pick up more air waves that way."

"What's this gizmo at the other end of the antenna?"

"That's called the crystal diode. It restricts the current flow in one direction. Very important."

"These, of course are the earphones. What's this wire?" John asked, pointing. "You didn't already tell me, did you?"

Craig laughed. "That's the ground wire. The set works best if it's attached to a radiator or pipe." He unrolled the ground wire and wound it around the pipe along the wall.

"Where did you get all this? How much does it cost?"

"I bought it at the Hendrickson shop for practically nothing. He showed us how to put it together and how it works. The Navins have one that Virgil put together. You could buy the parts and sell a set for three or four times the cost." He put the earphones on. "I'll find a station so you can listen." He moved the tuner a little, stopped, moved it back and forth slowly, concentrating with his brow puckered. Suddenly he broke into a smile. "Here, Dad, listen to this." He handed him the earphones.

John listened, suddenly beaming. "Amazing!"

"That's probably coming from Chicago. Incredible, isn't it?"

"Wait'll your mother hears this."

John learned quickly how to put together a set and embarked on this new endeavor. He put an ad in *The Enterprise* and in a few days had several orders. He went to Mitchell and returned, lugging a large box full of radio supplies. Bessie opened the door for him as soon as he stepped up onto the porch. Exclaiming, she stepped back to let him in, "I saw you coming down the street. Mercy! That looks heavy."

"Just awkward." He put the crate down in the workroom. "Glad you were here to open the door."

"I didn't know it would be that big," she said as she followed him.

"I bought enough equipment for more than just the two crystal sets I promised to put together for folks." He knelt, opened the box, and began to separate the pieces. "I'm hoping for more orders. I can have a little side business once word gets out."

"Good. Where will you work? Right here?"

"Oh, no. I'll put the sets together wherever I'm selling them." He took out the pieces he needed for one, placing them carefully into a smaller carton. "I'll go over to Mr. Seitz first. He said he'd be home all day. It shouldn't take long."

When he was ready, Bess opened the door for him again. He walked quickly on the cold November afternoon, his boots making a crunching sound on the icy walkway. He thought of the recent evening when he and Bess sat enjoying one another's company as they often did with reading. He'd worn the earphones to his first crystal set and listened to a Mozart symphony. After a bit he'd taken them off and asked, "Do you want to hear some of the concert? It's lovely."

"No. You enjoy it. I'm fine, sitting in quiet."

He left the phones off and they sat in silence some minutes. He finally said, "I listened to music from Minneapolis the other day, and this concert is coming from Calgary. Amazing! Craig called it the 'wave of the future.'"

"Clever."

He went back to listening, allowing himself to be carried away with the beauty of the music. He reached the Seitz home and knocked. Later he patted his pocket as he walked home. *Great to make some extra money.*

Bessie's nephew, Louis Navin, drove the family Chevrolet to the Donahue house where John, Craig, and their friend and neighbor, Charles Grady, waited with their luggage to travel on this early September morning to South Bend, Indiana. The two cousins, Louis and Craig, would be students at Notre Dame university, Louis in his final year and Craig in his first. Their trip would take them through the states of South Dakota, Iowa, Illinois, and into Indiana. Returning a different way without the two young men, John and Charles would travel through Wisconsin and Minnesota to visit the Grady relatives.

When they arrived on the Notre Dame campus, the four weary travelers stepped out and stretched. Louis, as a seasoned veteran at the university, led them on a tour of the campus. After the boys registered for classes and moved their gear into their rooms, the four shared a supper meal in the dining hall, followed by an evening of orientation and entertainment.

The next morning John and Charles said their goodbyes to the boys after mass and breakfast. John pulled his son aside as he opened his wallet. "Are you sure you have enough money?"

"Thanks, Dad." He pushed his father's hand away, gently but firmly. "Put your money away. I have plenty. Working at the *Tribune* this summer gave me more than enough for the year. I'm grateful to you, because without my years of apprenticeship at *The Enterprise,* I might've been doing farm work."

"Your mother and I will miss you." John put his hand on his son's shoulder.

"It'll be Christmas before you know it, and I'll be home for a month." Craig looked off across the campus.

"You write your mother," John admonished as he embraced his son. "We'll want to hear all about your life here at the university."

"I promise." Craig's voice sounded choked. "Thanks for everything."

At the end of their trip they drove into the Navins' driveway in Mitchell to return the automobile. John checked the mileage and exclaimed, "What do you think of that, Charles? We traveled 1900 miles. Quite a trip!"

"I'm grateful for the chance to see the folks," Charles said. "Thanks."

"I enjoyed having you along." He clapped him on the back. "It would've been a long, lonesome ride without you." They set their luggage on the porch and went inside where Ella had lunch ready for them. Later, they took the late train from Mitchell back to Ethan.

The summer sun shone obliquely into the study where John and Bess sat, he with his book, she with her sewing. They heard Kathleen open the door and drop her bags in the hall. She was returning from a weekend trip with the Camp Fire Girls. She hurried in breathless. "Mom, Dad, I'm home. I had the best time," she said excitedly. "We had so much fun."

John and Bess stood to greet their daughter. John said, "Let us look at you. Looks like you got some sun."

"We took hikes and swam in the lake. We spent almost all our time outdoors," Kathleen enthused. "At night we had dances. I had so much fun." She found it hard to stand still.

John teased her, "Too much fun, I'd say. I thought the Camp Fire Girls were supposed to teach responsibility."

"But we did learn responsibility. We had to take turns preparing the meals and cleaning up." She counted off the chores on her fingers. "We had to keep our cottage clean. We had daily ceremonies. We just had the best time."

Her mother scolded her. "Now, Kathleen, you go and put some cream on that nose. Let me see you." She pushed up her daughter's sleeve to look at her arm. "Maybe your arms too."

"I will, Mother. Before I go to bed." Kathleen pulled away. "But right now I have to unpack and write the notes for the club. We meet again tomorrow, and I have to have them ready." She smiled triumphantly at her father and said, "That's responsibility." She turned to take her things upstairs.

John picked up her larger suitcase and followed her. "Make a copy of your notes for the newspaper."

"I will." She continued chatting about her friends and the fun they had.

Later, as he worked in his shop putting the finishing touches on a chair, he thought of the day about a year ago when Kathleen had come home from school, said a few words to them, then ran angrily up the stairs and slammed her door. John had said to Bess, "I'll go talk to her."

"No, let her be," Bess had said. "She needs time to herself."

"That's the problem. She spends too much time in her room alone."

"What's she doing? Reading. And there's nothing wrong with that."

"But she has few friends. But more importantly, she thinks that we give more attention to her brother. We sent Craig to Mitchell to school all these years. She resents the fact that she's back in the town school. She has to make friends all over again." He ran his hands through his hair. "The irony is that when she was at the academy she was miserable because she missed home so much. Resented us for sending her there." He got up and went to his desk, returning with an envelope that he handed to her. "What do you think about this? I wonder if it might help. It's an organization out of Kansas City, Missouri, called the Camp Fire

Girls."

"It can't be bad if it came out of Missouri." She took the paper. "After all, I was born in Missouri." She skimmed through the pages of information.

John watched her read the highlights and pointed. "See all the activities they have. If we can stir up enough interest to start a club here, she'll be so busy she'll get over her moodiness and maybe even learn a better sense of responsibility. Be easier to live with."

Bess counted on her fingers, "There's Ruby, Florence, and Dorothy. I think there'd be enough for a group. What about an adult? They call her a guardian. Maybe Mrs. Helvik or Gertrude Schurz would be willing to help. They need a younger woman."

"Let's talk to Kathleen tonight and see what she thinks."

That evening their daughter appeared at the supper table in somewhat better spirit. She had finished one book and had started another. When her father told her about the club and some of the activities, she perked up. "I bet Rosemary and Eunice will be interested. Sounds like fun. I'll ask in school on Monday."

"How about advertising around town?" John offered, "I could put up a notice in the post office."

"Great, Dad! Where would we have our meetings?"

Bess said, "You could have the first one here. Next week, after school. Does that give you enough time to spread the word?"

"Yes. This sounds great. I'll write the notice." She had finished her meal. "May I be excused?" She left the kitchen and grabbed a piece of paper from her father's desk to sketch out the announcement.

John and Bess rose from the table, donned their aprons and began the work of clearing the table and doing the dishes. John said, "I'm so glad we found that organization. We have plenty of activities in town for boys, but nothing for girls. This will be good for them all."

"Perfect. Maybe things can be sunnier around here."

At the end of the high school debate the audience of parents, grandparents and children filed out. Bess said to John, "I'm going on home. Tell Kathleen we're proud of her." She gathered her coat, gloves, and purse. "I know you want to see folks."

"All right. I won't be long." He headed to the front of the hall where he saw Kathleen with her friends. Henry Stopfer stopped him by putting his hand on John's forearm. "Delightful evening! Aren't we proud of our children?" He shook his hand. "John, I've said it before, and I want to say again, thanks for all you've done to get our school accredited. That helps all of us in town. And thanks for initiating the Camp Fire Girls. A great organization."

Before John could respond, Ruby and Kathleen joined them. Kathleen put her hands to her face. "I did terrible. I mixed everything up in that fourth paragraph."

Ruby hugged her. "You did great. I was so nervous I forgot a whole section."

The two fathers said, "You did fine. Congratulations."

Rosemary and Bertha interrupted them. After greeting the two men, Bertha said, "Can we have these two for a few minutes?" And the four girls walked off with heads together.

Peter Clark said to John, "Kathleen did a fine job on the debate tonight. Looks like she takes after you. What can't you do, John?"

John, who was secretly pleased, waved his hand in dismissal. "She did that all on her own. She's a good reader. Has a good head on her shoulders."

"You're too modest, John," Pete said. "There isn't a thing that you can't put your hand to. We all owe you so much." They shook hands all around.

John, Bess, and Kathleen finished up their supper. John, who had put on his apron and was scraping the plates, looked up when Bessie asked her daughter, "What about it, Kathleen? Do you want to go along to South Bend to Louis's graduation? Aunt Ella and your father are going." She filled the dishpan with hot water. "Of course, if you're not interested, that's all right because Craig and Louis will return with them, and the car will be crowded enough."

Kathleen's face registered surprise, then delight. "Really? You mean it? I can go?" She clapped her hands. "I'd love to."

"It's too much riding in the car for me," Bess said. "I know I wouldn't enjoy it. Too many hours of just sitting."

"When? What should I wear?" Kathleen shot her questions at her mother. "Where will we stay? How long will we be away?" she turned to her father with the last question.

Bess said, "All in good time. I'll help you pack. You're going the day after tomorrow. You can't take much luggage because there will be five of you on the return trip, and the Navin car is small."

"This'll be fun."

"It'll be a great adventure for you," John said. "Since your mother doesn't want to take the trip, we thought it would be a reward for how well you've done in school this year."

"It was a good year. Especially after we started the Camp Fire Girls."

"Your mother thought that the club would take you away from your studies," he teased Bessie, who was busy putting the leftovers away. She ignored him. He turned to Kathleen. "I knew that it would only help you to do better in school to have those activities."

Kathleen said, "Thanks, Dad, it's been great."

On a lovely May morning two days later, Bess's sister Ella drove the family car from Mitchell to Ethan, where John and his daughter waited with their bags, packed and ready for the trip to Notre Dame. Bessie greeted her sister, and then when the others had climbed in, said goodbye to them all.

They attended the Notre Dame baccalaureate and graduation. They met several professors who spoke to John of Craig's ability and achievements. As they walked around the campus, Kathleen said to Craig, "It's just like a city. Like Mitchell – only bigger." John, a pace behind them, listened. Ella and Louis had gone on ahead.

"What are you studying?"

"All kinds of courses: history, economics, philosophy. They tell us we have to have a wide experience to be a writer. I want to go into newspaper work." He turned to look at his father. "I've had a lot of experience with journalism, thanks to Dad."

"Are you coming back next year?" Kathleen asked.

Craig laughed. "You're full of questions." He turned to his father, "Dad?"

"What can I do for you?"

"Can I come back next year?" he asked.

"If that's what you want," John said with a grin, and he moved up and walked between the two, who each took him by the arm. He had great hopes for his son.

On the return trip, John and Ella sat in the back surrounded by luggage, while the young people sat in the front seat. Kathleen sat between her cousin Louis, who was driving, and her brother. They talked all the way.

Chapter Eleven
More Challenges

Two years later John sat at the kitchen table with the civil service test results in his hand; his jaw was set in a hard line. *So, that's it. After thirteen years I'm pushed out as easy as that. And in spite of the fact that both Bess and I have higher scores than Mrs. Charles Turner. Of all people! Lulu Turner!* When the scores came in the previous Friday, he was pleased to see that he and Bess had done well, their names heading the list. Mrs. Turner scored third. Just then Bess came in from the clothes yard with the laundry. She saw his disgruntled expression and asked, "What is it?"

"I've lost my post office job," he said tonelessly, not raising his head.

She put the laundry basket down and sank into a nearby chair. "What do you mean?"

He answered in the same dull voice, "Mrs. Turner showed me her appointment letter."

"Lulu Turner!" she exploded. "That's ridiculous! Who scored first and second in that test?" She gestured to the paper in his hand; she saw a muscle jump in his neck.

"I know," he said with clenched teeth. "Mrs. Turner takes over on June first. She couldn't wait to show me the official word." His whole body was taut and rigid.

"You've got to protest this decision, John. No one has been more faithful in his duties, more accurate in the work. This is wrong, plain and simple."

"No," he said, somehow finding himself calm and resigned in the face of her anger. "I'll find something else to do. Since it's our building, maybe we can use the space some other way." He sat up and straightened his shoulders, forcing himself to relax. "Maybe it's time to do something different."

"Well, it's just wrong, that's all. You know they don't like us because we're Democrats. They just want a Republican in there. You got pushed out of *The Enterprise* for the same reason. People in this state can't abide a Democrat." They sat quietly for a few minutes. "Being a Democrat in Dakota is like being a mouse in a roomful of cats. No chance at all."

"The wonder is I kept the job as long as I did. Thirteen years is a fairly long time to keep a political appointment, especially when your party is in the minority."

Bess got up, still sputtering. Retrieving her basket of laundry, she went upstairs. John remained sitting. *Maybe I can do something totally different, face a new challenge.* He'd have to think about it. He wondered where Mrs. Turner would set up her post office. Well, it was no concern of his. He had the space. Now what to do with it. He took a deep breath and stretched again. Yes, he had liked the work, but now was the time to move on. God closes a door and opens a window, surely. He folded the paper listing the scores and returned it to its envelope.

Still muttering, Bess came back to finish up the evening meal. John eased out of his chair. He touched her gently on the arm. "It's all right, Bess. Time to move on. Let's see this as an opportunity for a new beginning."

A few days later John stopped at the river on the way home from Mitchell. He'd decided, if he could catch some, fish might be a good meal for supper; it shouldn't take long. He took his pole and bucket out of the trunk of the 1926 Chevrolet and headed to the bank of the river. He sat waiting for a bite with the sky leaden over him, the water barely moving. However, his spirit didn't match the weather or the dull scene before him. His heart was full; he was at peace, even in the face of disappointment and facing, as he was, new challenges. He thought back to the day when as a child he went fishing with Mr. Coyne and the two older boys, when he was about twelve years old, Robbie six, and Charley five. A rare experience because they always had so much work to do on the farm.

He smiled at the memory. In the early days they had made crude poles out of sticks. Rods and reels came later. He didn't fish himself because he was expected to help the boys. For those few hours he had a bit of holiday, a few hours away from drudgery and work. He watched the ripples on the water. He pictured them on the bank of the same river on a day just like this one, dull and very quiet, with no one around. Why did this scene take him back to his own childhood? And not to the times when he brought his own children fishing?

Suddenly the light changed and the sun broke through. A thousand diamonds danced on the water. *What a rich life! With the children doing well in school. Craig on his way to follow in the newspaper business. Kathleen, too, will do well.* He looked into the bucket and saw he had a fine mess of fish. He had grand plans for the grocery business and knew it would succeed.

The one difficulty he and Bess faced was the illness of her sister, who had been placed in the Yankton State Mental Hospital. The news reminded him of the letter he received when he was teaching in Redfield in 1899 saying his father was in an insane hospital in Massachusetts. "All my years growing up on the farm I wanted to find my father," he had told Bess. "I wanted to write to him, but Mr. Coyne always said he was dead. Tom told me, too, we'd never find him, that he'd left us in the Home, and that we should forget him. Then I got the letter proving he was alive. It was too late. There was nothing I could do." Finally, all these years later, he felt some peace with his life; he could let the pain go. He could also understand some of what Bess was going through.

After John helped Lulu Turner and her husband move the post office equipment to its new site, he returned to the bare and empty space of the Craig building and looked around. *Yes, I will make this into a good store. A fine space.* He went home to collect cleaning supplies and tools. Bess was in the kitchen. "Everything's out, and I finally decided," he said as he reached into the bureau for the cleaning cloths, "we'll open a grocer's."

"You're sure?" Bess asked. "There's so much work with running a store. I thought you'd abandoned the idea."

He paused in his task of gathering brushes, soap, mop, broom, and pail to look at her in surprise. "You've never been afraid of work, Bess."

"I'm not afraid of the work. It just seems a big undertaking."

He sat at the table and watched her as she kneaded the dough. "It's something new, something we haven't done before, a challenge maybe, but it should be fun. We have to do something. The newspaper doesn't give us much, and we can't dip into our savings forever. We need more money than we take in with our boarder."

"I don't know. Does Ethan need another store? Can it support another one? You've thought this through?"

"I think Ethan can use another market. I've never seen a business in town that didn't succeed. What do you say? Are you with me? We can make the place different from the others. And from our experience of selling things from Rid-a-worm to radios, we'll do fine."

She grudgingly agreed. "Don't forget I sold Buff rock eggs for setting."

"Right. So, between us we know what to do. I'm going to see how much I get done before lunch."

She raised her hands in resignation. "If that's what you want, John. I'll help, but not today." She went back to her kneading of dough. "I've got my work cut out for me today."

"Fine. There'll be plenty to do later. Today I'll do the cleaning and measure for shelves. I can put those in myself. Tonight we can start looking at the kinds of wares we'll sell. I picked up a list at the supply store in Mitchell."

"All right. You know I'll help with whatever you decide."

Several weeks later, on a fine June day, John and Bess stood in the Donahue Grocers for their final inspection before the grand opening. "Looks mighty fine," he said.

"Indeed it does." Bess gave another swipe with her feather duster on the rows of jars on the shelves.

He nervously edged around the store, straightening shelf items and adjusting the flour and sugar barrels. "What have we forgotten?"

"We haven't forgotten a thing. With the ad in *The Enterprise* today we're sure to have folks stop in tomorrow." She picked up the newspaper and opened to the announcement. "I like the way you put the word service right in the middle of the advertisement. People know and admire you. They'll support you."

"They may well stop in tomorrow, but will they buy?" Now that they were ready to open, he began to have doubts. "After all, the town already has Weepie's Cash Store and Bauer's. Folks have the habit of buying from them."

"We have to wait and see. We've done our part, and we have to trust it'll work for us. Nothing in here except goods that everyone needs and uses."

"I don't know. If we don't sell, then what?"

"Mercy, John! Of course we'll sell these wares. And we'll order more and sell those. Stop worrying. You thought a store was a good idea, and it's going to do well. We'll make it succeed." She stooped to pick up an empty crate. "Come along home. We'll have our supper and an early night, so we're ready for tomorrow."

"Yes, we'll do fine," he said, bolstered by her confidence.

Almost once a week John drove his Chevrolet from Ethan to Mitchell and back. He ordered goods and picked up wares. Business seemed slow, but that was to be expected. He told Bess, "It's still early. Rome wasn't built in a day. It takes time to build up a business, attract customers, and make them want to keep returning." He shaded his eyes in the glare of the hot July sun. As he drove, he reviewed his few hours in Mitchell. He'd even delivered the jams and canning jars to Ella from Bess. *Yes, I did everything I planned.* A sudden dust storm took him off guard. First, he felt the car shake in the wind. He gripped the steering wheel more tightly and slowed almost to a stop. He concentrated on his driving. Suddenly everything disappeared, the road, the fields, the sky. The crash came with a jolt. When he awoke, he couldn't move.

A face peered through the window and asked, "Are you all right?"

John opened his eyes to a stranger. He tried to move, to get up. Pain shot through his back and down his leg. He moaned. The man said, "All right, fellow. Stay where you are. Don't try to move. I'll get you to the hospital."

John wanted to say, *I can't go to the hospital. I've got too much to do. I've got a grocery store to run.* But he couldn't say anything; he could only do what he was told. Several hours later, he lay in a hospital bed in Mitchell. A nurse padded softly around his bed arranging the bedclothes, laying out supplies on the bedside table. Bess arrived with a bunch of wild flowers. She leaned over and said, "John, how are you?"

"I'll be right as rain in a few days. The pain medication will take care of everything." He groaned.

"How did this happen?" she asked. "You're such a careful driver."

"Terrible dust storm. Just blinded. Worst ever. So sudden I couldn't even stop. Nothing I could do."

The nurse interjected, "He stayed on his side of the road. It was the fellow coming from Ethan who crossed over into his lane." She smoothed the sheets.

"How is the other driver?" Bess asked anxiously. "Will he be all right?"

"His knee is shattered," The nurse replied. "Doctor told his wife it's very bad."

"What's his name?" John asked.

"Joseph Shanahan. Salesman," the nurse said.

"How did I get to the hospital?" John asked.

"That's the remarkable thing," the nurse said turning to Bess. "Another salesman – I think his name is Peters – came upon the scene shortly after the accident and put the two of them in his car and brought them here."

"A true Samaritan. I must've blacked out. I remember someone asking if I was all right. Next thing I was in the emergency room. We'll have to send him a thank you," he said to Bess. He closed his eyes, wincing in a spasm of pain. "What about the car? How bad is it?"

"Oh, it's banged up worse than you. Nobody will be driving that auto for awhile."

"What about the goods in the car?"

"Craig got the things to town," Bess assured him. "Don't you fret. I can take care of the grocers for awhile." She patted his hand. "You have one job right now and that's to get better. Now I'm going to sit here quietly. I want you to rest. Let the medicine work."

The nurse nodded at Bess and moved away quietly.

One day in mid-September, John stacked the order of canned goods on the shelf. When he heard the doorbell jangle, he turned to greet his first customers of the day. After Mary and Louise did their business, Mary leaned on the counter. "How are you doing, John? Have you recuperated from your accident? I know you had a hard time there for a bit."

"I'm doing better. Just some back spasms occasionally." He smiled ruefully and stretched.

"Where's that girl of yours?" Louise asked. "I haven't seen Kathleen lately. Such a lovely child."

"I took her to Aberdeen a couple of weeks ago. She's attending Northern State Teachers College. She'll teach school like her mother and father."

"You taught school, John?"

"I did. Three years. And her mother even longer – five years. We both had great experiences in a one-room schoolhouse. Children from age six to sixteen. Some of them just a few years younger than we were."

"Why didn't you stay in teaching, John? I imagine you'd be a good one."

"Because I had an eye on Bessie Craig, and knew I couldn't support a family on a teacher's salary. Also, I needed to save every penny because I knew I'd send my children to college some day."

Louise asked, "But your back, John. Wasn't that hard to drive to Aberdeen with a sore back?"

"I stopped and stretched every few hours. Of course, on the way up, Kathleen kept me distracted. The ride home felt longer."

"And Craig is back at Notre Dame?"

"He is. His last year."

Mary said, "You have to be proud of your children. Both in college. Both doing well."

"Bessie had something to do with that, too."

"Where is Bessie?" the two women asked at the same time.

"Visiting her sister Mattie in Armour. She needed a few days rest."

At the Ethan High School graduation exercises in the previous spring, no father was prouder than he of his daughter. As president of the school board, he had handed the fourteen graduates each a diploma. The others shook his hand, but when Kathleen's turn came she reached up and hugged him. *This is something I never had, a chance to finish high school and go on to college.* He looked at the empty chair on which sat a single rose, set aside for Kathleen's classmate Rosemary, the daughter of Anna Coyne Clark. She'd died in January. He said a silent prayer for her and her family, and added prayers of thanks that Kathleen was spared.

After the ceremony he stood with Ella and watched his son and daughter as they talked with some of the other young people. Bess was talking to a group of mothers of the graduates. "How is it that I have such beautiful children," he asked his sister-in-law, "intelligent, capable and destined for good futures?"

"You do have a beautiful family. How could you miss? You married a Craig." She looked beyond him as if looking into the future. "Theirs is a different world, John. Hopefully, they'll have a better life than we did." They stood in silence. After a pause, she said, "You know, John, many people admire you. You overcame a difficult childhood, and by drive, hard work, and perseverance, achieved a position of a respected businessman in town. And look at what you've done as member of the school board – brought it to accreditation and as good a school as any in Dakota."

John dismissed her praise. "I wish I'd started earlier, then Craig wouldn't have had to live in Mitchell all those years. But then again maybe if he hadn't lived with the Navins, he might not have gone to Notre Dame University like Louis." He gave her a big smile. "Bess and I owe you so much for your care of him all those years. We are grateful."

"And Craig finishes next year?" she asked as she glanced over at him with her sons.

"Yes, and we'll have another newspaperman on our hands. It doesn't seem possible."

After the ceremony the four Donahues enjoyed a delicious dinner. Later the young people took turns at the piano, and Craig accompanied Kathleen as she played her violin. John sat listening. *It will never be the same. Craig is gone most of the year between his studies and summer newspaper work. Kathleen will go to college in the fall. My children will be gone soon.*

On a crisp fall day, Robbie telephoned to tell John that his father had died a few hours earlier. After his friend hung up, John held the receiver to his chest. He sat quietly, his eyes closed. Bess, wiping her hands on her apron, appeared at his side, and putting her hand lightly on his shoulder asked gently, "He's gone? God rest his soul."

For a week they had expected the call. Since his fourth stroke, Mr. Coyne weakened daily. "Yes," he said, putting the earphone back in its cradle. "Robbie said he died quietly in his sleep early this morning. He and Charley were with him. Mrs. Coyne dozed off just before he slipped away."

"I'm sorry."

"Yes. A good man. The funeral is Tuesday. They called Father Eckl, and he said 10 o'clock. Robbie asked if I'd write the piece for *The Enterprise*. I'm sure Lester won't mind."

"He'll be glad."

"I'll go out to the farm later. But first I'll write what I know and have him help me fill in the rest." He wiped his eyes, looking toward the window. "He used to tell us stories about growing up in England and working as a young man when he came to this country."

When he asked Lester if he could write the newspaper article, his friend said, "No one but you, John, should write this tribute."

After he hung up the phone, he sat remembering the years working with Mr. Coyne. Could he say he was a good man? Was there any reason to doubt that? But, how could he reconcile his feelings about his place in that house? He thought of how they made him work all those years. After a few minutes he shook himself. *No need to moan over the past.* He straightened up and went to his desk to set to work.

At lunchtime he joined Bess in the kitchen. He stretched his back and flexed his fingers. Bess said, "I'll call Craig and Kathleen to let them know. Neither of them will be able to come, but they'd want to know. In spite of everything, you liked Mr. Coyne?" She broke the silence after they had eaten in silence for some minutes.

"Yes, in spite of everything, he was good to me. He taught me how to do everything. Of course, when I was a boy I didn't appreciate having so much work. I got frustrated and angry with him often. I thought I was horribly abused. Perhaps I was ... I don't know ... neglected. Left out of things. But after I left the farm, I began to appreciate all he did for me. After all, he was the only father I ever knew." He took several bites before adding, "It was interesting to write down what I remember of his stories."

"Are you finished with the tribute?" When he nodded, she asked, "He's the last of his family?"

"Yes, his brothers and sisters are all gone." When they had finished eating and done the dishes, he said, "I'll have Robbie check what I wrote."

When he arrived at the Coyne farm, he found his friend working in the barn. He expressed his condolences and asked him if he wanted him to leave the paper with him.

"No, I can do this later. I'd like to look it over, and then you can bring it back to the office. It shouldn't take long." They moved into the kitchen and sat on either side of the table. He skimmed through the pages. "It seems rather long."

"It is, but Lester said I could have as much space as I want. These are the stories I remember. And your dad is well known and loved in this area." Robbie took the pages and began to read.

He skimmed the final three paragraphs that listed the survivors, his wife, children, and grandchildren, and then looked up. "Incredible. How did you remember all that?"

After he dropped off the tribute at the newspaper office and returned home, he told Bess he was pleased with how well he had done. "Robbie couldn't find any changes to make." He said wistfully, "I wish I could tell my own family history that way."

"Did you mention yourself?"

"No, I don't really belong. Once I refused adoption I gave up any right to be part of the Coyne story." He gazed out the window beyond her, not seeing anything but the past.

"And you're still not sorry you didn't let them adopt you?"

"No, it was the right decision. Really. And, though I lived with them for so many years, I know I'm not a part of the family. Truth be told, Bess, I was never made to *feel* a part of the family." They sat silently for some minutes, then he mused, "Mrs. Coyne's life will be empty after everything is over and her children go back to their own homes. They were married almost forty-five years."

𝔗𝔥𝔢 𝔈𝔫𝔱𝔢𝔯𝔭𝔯𝔦𝔰𝔢
October 21, 1926

Pioneer of This Community Answers the Final Summons

Michael, Jr., or "Mike" Coyne as he was universally known through-out this section, was born of Irish stock on February 22, 1862 in the coal-mining village of Wolverhampton, Staffordshire, England, where he spent the first six years of his life. His father, a man of no education, in 1867 left his little family to await his quest for fortune, and made his way to this continent alone. After about a year in the iron works at Youngstown, Ohio he accumulated sufficient funds with which to bring his family to America. Michael, Jr., marveled at his first coffee with cream and sugar at Castle Garden, New York, after a stormy and tedious voyage of fourteen days across the Atlantic on the steamship Pennsylvania. Directly after admittance the family made its way to St. Louis, where they were joyfully reunited with the husband and father, and where Michael, Jr., interspersed the acquisition of his three years of schooling with swimming the Missouri river and selling papers on the city's streets.

About 1871 land hunger attracted the family into Iowa in the vicinity of Fort Dodge where both father and boy, Michael, now twelve years old, were employed in the coal mines and jute factories for a year or two. About 1873, not having yet been able to satisfy their craving to own a "bit" of God's green earth, the same urge drew them to Yankton, where the free lands of the Dakotas beckoned with promise of a permanent home at last. On arriving there, Michael, Sr., filed for a homestead seventeen miles north of Yankton, and locating his family thereon, he with Michael, Jr., now fourteen and a man, worked at such employment as they could find around the flourishing young river port of Yankton, earning funds to maintain brothers, sister and mother upon the none too flourishing prairie home.

About 1879, Michael, Jr., then a boy of seventeen, started railroading on various lines of the C. M. and St. P. Railroad, then extending north and west into the new territory and between railroad contracting in the summer and logging operations in the Minnesota woods in winter, he quickly acquired what was at that time considered a nice financial start: this in addition to contributing steadily to the support of his parents and family, until in 1882 at the age of twenty-one he was united in marriage at Tabor, S. D., with Rosa Freidel of local, sturdy pioneer stock, thanks to whose loyal co-operation, high ambition, untiring industry and undying faith in the country and its future, Mr. Coyne rapidly acquired a station of substantial citizenship in the community.

In 1881 he filed on a homestead, preemption and timber claim on Twelve Mile creek in Worthen township, Hanson county, settling there with his bride in the spring of 1883. Here the young couple struggled successfully through years liberally sprinkled with blizzards, floods, drouth, grasshoppers and other vicissitudes. They steadily accumulated more land, and for some time have been regarded as among the largest landowners of the county. Mr. Coyne always kept his lands and never sold any except his original homestead. When crops did not succeed the milk bucket did, with the result that he was accumulating lands while his neighbors were leaving during the hard times. Here the family of five boys and one girl were reared to maturity and by their combined efforts under able leadership prospered until about six years ago, when the time seemed opportune for the parents to begin to enjoy some of the fruits of their labor and hardships, and all of the children but two being settled on farms, or in business for themselves, Mr. and Mrs. Coyne moved to Ethan where declining years for them, and especially for Mr. Coyne, were passed in quiet and peace, at least until his health gave way some two or more years ago, and he suffered his first slight stoke of paralysis in December 1924.

Mike Coyne, typical of the sturdy race from which he sprang, was aggressive and progressive and always in the fore rank of those who labored for the good of their community and their fellowman. No move for the public good was initiated in his county of community but that Mike Coyne was active in supporting it, pushing it with his accustomed zeal and vigor to successful conclusion or honorable defeat. He served several times as one of the commissioners of Hanson county, was for over thirty years school treasurer in his district, brought the first rural mail delivery and first rural telephone service to his community, and during the World war he gave of his time and efforts in the prosecution thereof in a manner reflecting great credit to himself in behalf of his adopted land. He was a man of strong convictions and he expressed them forcibly, holding to them with tenacity, and no man questioned where he stood on any public or personal issue. His friends are legion and his enemies zero.

His were the characteristics of those men who have always directed empire in its progress and who made the world and the community richer and better for his presence in it, all too short as it was, and his passing will be felt as a universal loss by all. He provided well for his family and reared his children to be substantial citizens and credits to the communities in which they lived, leaving them a heritage of staunch character, and substantial, unsullied, loyal citizenship that might well be the ambition of the younger generation of today to emulate.

One dismal April day they put the "closed" sign in the window of Donahue Grocers and headed home for lunch. John handed Bess the sack with the cheese and bread. "I'll stop to see if we have any mail. Why don't you go along and get lunch started?"

At the house, she washed up, set out the cheese, pickles and vegetables, and was slicing bread when John came in. She looked up to see his furrowed brow. "What is it?"

He held several envelopes. "Letters from Mary and Ella for you. And this one postmarked from Chicago from Craig." He sat down heavily. "What is he doing in Chicago?"

"Oh, John, you always think it's bad news." She came over and put her hand on his shoulder. "Open it." He pushed the letter toward her on the table. She picked it up and slit it with a kitchen knife. With careful fingers she took out the single sheet and handed it to him. She leaned over his shoulder while they read it together.

April, 1927

Dear Mother and Dad,

I have left the university. I have married and am living and working at the Tribune *here in Chicago. Please do not be angry with me. Irene Liddell is a wonderful woman, and I know you'll love her as much as I do when you meet her. With or without a degree, I can get a good job. I am enjoying the work in the newspaper. I write this letter hoping that you are both well and that the Donahue Grocers is prospering.*

Love,
Your son, Craig

Confused, they looked at one another. "How could he do this to us?" John moaned.

"He says nothing about a wedding," Bess said, perplexed. "Do you think they married in a church? Liddell doesn't sound like a Catholic name to me."

"How could he marry without us? If he married in a church he'd have to send for his baptism record." He stood slowly. "A week ago he was at the university." He pointed toward Craig's last letter on the desk. "Bess, there wasn't time to announce wedding banns. What are we to think? He never mentioned a woman in any of his other letters."

"It must be that woman." She frowned at the letter. "I wonder if she's carrying his child."

"What have we done wrong, Bess? All those years of study gone. And then to write," he read from the letter, "'With or without a degree I can get a good job.' We always believed him to be so levelheaded. I don't understand it."

"Well, it's his life. He'll have to live with what he's done." She went to the stove to pour the tea. "A month away from graduation, and he's throwing it away! Notre Dame wouldn't let him stay with a wife. They were probably married by a justice of the peace." She wiped her hands on her apron, took the letter from him, folded it, and returned it to its envelope. "Let's eat our lunch and get back to the store. We've got work to do." She put it with the other mail still unopened.

He muttered to himself. "Didn't we raise our children as Catholics? Didn't we send him to the best Catholic university in America?" He ran his hands through his hair and looked blankly at the food on the table. "I can't eat anything."

"Yes, you can. And you will." She took her place and began eating. After a few minutes, he joined her and began to eat automatically. Neither spoke.

"That woman is probably some Jezebel." He stabbed his fork into the pickled cucumbers. "Craig is too young to be tied down with a wife and family – he's not even twenty-one." They fell silent. "Perhaps we can have the marriage annulled. Who knows? Perhaps they're not even married, just living together."

She had no answer. When she finished, she cleared the table. "Why don't you stay here for a while? I'll go back and open the grocers. Wash up the lunch things, why don't you, and then join me?"

He looked at her. "How can you take this so calmly?" She didn't answer him, but donned her jacket, hat, and gloves and left. He wondered why this was happening. *How could they hold their heads up? How could they face their neighbors and say their son couldn't finish college? Craig had to get married.* As he sat and stewed, he felt like he did as a child taunted and hated by his schoolmates because he was an orphan and different from the others – alone and rejected. He put his head down in his arms on the table. Tears came, and then wrenching sobs. It was some minutes before he could compose himself. When he stood, he set to the washing up. *No, our children are beautiful. It's that woman who led Craig astray, who made him leave his studies and take a job in Chicago.* He washed his face, rolled down his sleeves, and put on his jacket. As he walked down the street, he straightened his shoulders. When he entered the store and saw there were no customers, he took her hands and gently squeezed them. "We'll face this together, Bess, you and I. Thanks for staying calm."

"No use crying over spilt milk. It'll serve no purpose if we try to stop this marriage." When the door opened and a customer entered, John stepped forward and with his usual cheerfulness said, "How may I help you?"

John, Bess, and Kathleen shared supper on a warm August day. Kathleen had received her teaching certificate several months earlier and had applied for a position. "School starts soon, Kathleen," John asked,

"You haven't heard of a position yet?"

"Oh, yes." She ducked her head, looking chagrined. "I did. They gave me a school near Hill City." She looked up at him and almost pleaded, "Will you drive me there next weekend?"

Exasperated, Bess scolded her, "How long have you known this? Why didn't you tell us?" She said to John, "Hill City is in the Black Hills. That's an all-day journey."

"You've been so busy and … I wasn't sure I wanted to go that far … and I hoped there'd be something else … and …" she trailed off. "Sorry."

Bess went on, "Honestly, Kathleen, why didn't you tell us? You've agreed to take it?" Her daughter nodded. "What if your father couldn't take you? What if he were busy?"

"I could take the train," she said lamely.

Her mother shook her head. "A one-room school?"

"Yes, I'll get the papers to show you." Kathleen jumped up to retrieve the papers. When she returned out of breath, she opened the envelope and read, "A one-room school in Gillette Prairie near Hill City. The board said I can live with the Kindler family, who live about two miles from the school." She handed the papers to her father, adding apologetically, "If you can't take me, I can go by train."

"No," her father said. "You will not take the train. I'll drive you Saturday. If you're going to be there all year, you'll need all your things. You won't be able to come home for the weekend." They sat silently, finishing their dessert. He warmed to the idea. "Besides, I want to see what kind of place you're going to be in for all those months. And, I'll have time to spend with my favorite girl."

"Thanks Dad," she said gratefully, then turned to her mother. "Will you come along for the ride, Mother?"

"I'm afraid I can't. With the boarder moving in on Saturday, I'll have to be here to help her get settled." She took the papers from John and perused them. "Dad, you'll have to stay overnight. You can't drive both ways in one day."

"Right, and if the Kindlers can't put me up, then maybe I can find a room in Hill City. I'll return to Ethan late Sunday."

"Good enough," she said.

"Thanks, Dad, Mother," Kathleen smiled.

Several days later Bess helped her daughter pack. "You want to be ready so your father can get an early start. Make sure you have everything. Do you have a list?"

"Yes, Mother." Kathleen gestured to a paper on the dresser as she folded a skirt and stuffed it into the satchel.

Bess took the skirt out and refolded it. "If you fold it properly, it won't get wrinkled."

"But it has to be ironed again any way."

"Not if it's packed properly. You should learn to do it right." She looked in despair at her daughter. "Oh, never mind. I'll take care of your outer garments. You do the rest."

"Where's my red scarf?"

"Look in your coat pocket. You probably left it there last winter. And don't forget your wool sweaters and socks – you're going to need them."

On Friday Kathleen rushed through her supper. After she took a last hurried bite, she said, "I'm going out with Clara and Esther for a while. Don't wait up for me."

"Is that wise?" her mother asked. "You'll leave early. This is farther than Aberdeen." She looked at John. "And she's not finished packing yet." She turned back to her daughter, "When will you do that?"

"Oh, let her go, Mother," John said. "She's young. She'll be ready in the morning."

"Thanks, Dad." Kathleen gave him a bright smile and hurried to the door.

The next day, he rose before dawn to prepare breakfast. When everything was ready, he went up to Kathleen's room to rouse her. Returning to the kitchen, he found Bess drinking her coffee. She put her cup down and asked, "Is she up?"

"Yes, but not packed. I thought you helped her."

"I did. But you know her. She's just not organized."

In a few minutes, Kathleen, fully dressed with her hair neatly combed, entered the kitchen. "Good morning," she said brightly.

"You sound chipper this morning." Bess said, surveying her daughter. "Your father says you're not ready to go."

"It won't take me long. I just have a few more things to do."

John looked at her glowing face. "Are you nervous?"

"I'm too nervous to eat." She looked at her mother dishing out cereal at her place. "Well, I'll eat the oats. It may be a long time before lunch."

When they were ready to leave, her father carried the bags out to the Chevrolet, then stood waiting while Kathleen said goodbye to her mother. "Do you have everything?" Bessie asked.

"Yes, Mother," she said, holding up a small handbag. "The rest is in here. Directions to Hill City, to Gillette Prairie, and to the Kindlers."

"What about the instructions for the school and for the program of studies?"

"Oh, no. I think those are upstairs." She clapped her hand to her mouth and bolted back into the house. She came back, carrying the packet of papers. "Now I have everything. I looked all around the room to make sure." She hopped into the rider's seat. Bess followed them, standing by the open car window, repeating all kinds of reminders. "I'll be fine," Kathleen assured her. "Don't worry."

The ride was long, but father and daughter amused themselves part of the way by singing all their favorite songs at the top of their lungs. They drove miles without seeing another living soul or any sign of human habitation. After they stopped for lunch, Kathleen took over the driving, but told her father, "When we get to Hill City, you can drive again."

"Fine, I'll sit back for now and admire the view." As they approached the Black Hills, he said, "Look how dark the hills are. No wonder they call them the Black Hills."

They ate supper in a little café in Hill City. John told her, "We don't know if the Kindlers are prepared to feed us. Did you write and let them know when we'd be arriving?"

"I told them either late afternoon or early evening and that you wanted to stay overnight." She added as an afterthought, "But they didn't answer my letter. It was late when I told the school department I'd take the school."

He patted her hand. "It's all right, Kathleen. If I have to, I'll just come back to town and take a room for the night." He pointed to a rooming house nearby.

At the farmhouse they met the farmer, Mr. Kindler, coming in from the barn. He greeted them warmly. He said he had boarded the schoolteacher for the past ten years. "My son Leo," he said with his thick Norwegian accent, "went through the school when we first came." Just as he mentioned his son's name, the young man joined them. Tall and blonde, he was about Kathleen's age. The men carried in her trunk and bags, and Mrs. Kindler showed Kathleen her room, small and pleasant, facing east with a view of the mountains. Mrs. Kindler said, "It's warmer on this side of the house in winter. When the north wind blows it gets fairly cold over there." She pointed to the opposite side of the house.

They did have an extra bed, so John stayed overnight, grateful he didn't have to take a room in Hill City. Like all farm families, the Kindlers retired early.

In the morning, after breakfast, John drove Kathleen to the schoolhouse where they spent several hours getting the place into some order. They knocked down cobwebs from the ceiling and swept up mouse droppings along the edge of the floor; they dusted desks and washed windows. John checked the stove and was happy to see that the families had left a substantial woodpile.

When they finished their cleaning and looked around, he said, "Considering that the place was empty for three months, it isn't bad at all. It helps that they have good strong windows here." They returned to the farmhouse, cleaned up, and had lunch. "I'll get home before dark if I leave now," he told them. He thanked the Kindlers and asked them to take care of his daughter. Kathleen walked out to the car with her father, kissed him goodbye. "Don't worry about me, Dad. I'll be fine."

"You write to your mother," he reminded her. "She'll want to know how you're doing." He climbed in behind the wheel. "Enjoy the children. We'll see you in December."

At the end of a cold November workday, John and Bess left the store and walked home briskly. He said to her, "So it's settled then. We spend Thanksgiving in Chicago."

"Yes. As much as we disapprove of that woman, Craig is still our son." After they walked another block, she asked, "How long do you think the drive takes?"

"Several hours," he said. "If we leave early enough we'll get there in early afternoon, depending on how much traffic we meet."

"We'll come back Monday?"

"Yes, Newton said he'd watch the store for us till Tuesday if we want. Isn't it great to have such good neighbors?" They went up the steps into the house, putting on the lamp as they passed through the sitting room and headed toward the kitchen. "Why don't we see how it goes?"

"I just don't know … I mean … that woman … I don't know how much of her I can stand," Bess said as she tied on her apron and sliced the bread for supper. "I told Craig I'd bring some mince pie and home-made breads. I imagine she's not much of a cook."

Several days later, as they made the return trip, Bess said, "That woman certainly doesn't know how to keep house. Did you see the way she had put things in the larder? No order at all." He didn't respond. After watching scenery pass by for several miles, she added, "Mercy! And not much of a cook either. Weren't her meals ghastly?" John still didn't answer but drove, lost in his own thoughts.

After a long pause he said, "At least we heard about Craig's work at the paper. And his future plans. The good news is he's straightening out his affairs at Notre Dame, and it looks like they'll give him his degree after all. His plan of coming back to Dakota, getting a teaching position, and studying in the summer to get a master's at Ohio State in Columbus is a good one. They can stay with her parents while he's in school." He maneuvered the auto around some construction work. "After all, he is still sensible. And he's our son."

"I'm glad. He can do much better than what he's doing at the *Tribune*."

"We always believed in him. Who knows? Maybe he'll become a college president instead of a newspaper editor?"

"He has to worry not just about himself and a wife, but soon a baby. He has responsibilities."

"Which I'm sure he'll fulfill."

They rode again for some miles in silence. She spoke first. "I wonder how Kathleen is doing. Her letters are too few and too short. Well, she'll be home soon for Christmas. I just wish she wrote more often."

"I hope she doesn't get involved with the farmer's son. I told you about Leo Kindler. Good looking man. We don't want her to marry a farmer. Especially one who lives so far away from us. Bad enough our son is far away. We don't want our daughter the same distance in the opposite direction."

"No, we don't. But our children will make their own decisions. And whether we approve or not, they have their own lives to live."

"If you remember, you and I chose on our own, and haven't we done fine?" The warm sun filled the auto.

The following April, when John came home from his day trip to Sioux Falls, Bess announced, "We have a grandchild." She was at her Singer in the sitting room. "Craig called about an hour ago." He stood in the doorway. "It's a girl. Both mother and baby are fine."

"And her name?"

"Joyce Elizabeth."

He picked up the portrait of Craig that sat on the piano. "So, her name is a Liddell name."

She smiled at him. "And the Elizabeth for me. I hope the baby looks like us."

"Will they have the child baptized, I wonder."

"I certainly hope so. When you talk to Craig, you tell him he must do his duty. That woman can't object to having her child baptized. After all, she is a Lutheran, and they believe in baptism."

"Well, Craig said she agreed that any children they had would be brought up Catholic. He'll do what is right."

The late afternoon sun peeked into the Donahue sitting room where John sat at his desk looking over the bills. Things indeed looked bad. He put his head in his hands and closed his eyes. After a few minutes he felt Bess' presence, even before her gentle touch caressed his shoulders. "How bad?"

He pushed his hair back from his forehead. "Fairly bad, I'm afraid. We're going to have to close the grocers." He gestured to the stack of bills. "The stock isn't going anywhere, and bills keep piling up."

Bess pulled a chair over and sat beside him with her hand on his arm. "Lord knows you tried! You've done everything you could to make a success of it."

"I don't know, but it seems since I lost the post office job, things have been going downhill."

"No, it was the auto accident that really hurt you. And I mean more than the physical damage. The store was open only a month when that car slammed into you."

"You're right. And I lost heart after that." They sat quietly.

Bess suddenly said in her no-nonsense, take-charge voice. "So, you'll close the store. Fine. You'll move onto something else."

"Maybe if I used a more aggressive ad campaign or worked harder. Maybe if I specialized."

"Nonsense. You did everything you could. For one thing you had too much competition. Besides, this town can only support so many businesses. Don't forget, the others were already established. And everyone knows it's impossible for someone new to succeed."

"You thought it a bad idea when I first proposed it."

"You wanted to open the store, and you had a good place. Many things contributed, not the least of which is that people have no money. That's the other thing. And I'm afraid that things will get worse before they get better."

"All right. So now what do we do? We have to pay at least some of these bills. If I sell the newspaper, we'll have some cash. And then, when the grocers is closed, we'll see if we can rent out the building and have some regular income."

"Good." She got up and straightened the doily on the side table. "Now put the bills away and come into the kitchen. Help me with supper." She stopped at the window and said in awe, "Oh, a beautiful sunset."

John rose to follow her and looked out also. "Yes, a golden sunset. Perhaps a promise of good things." He went into the kitchen and put on his apron. "At least we'll have plenty of food for awhile. We'll have a mammoth sale to move the perishables. But some goods we can use ourselves." A few minutes later he turned from the stove to say, "Thank you, Bessie, for not saying 'I told you so.'"

Chapter Twelve
The Drought Years

Kathleen taught for three years in three different school districts – in the Black Hills, in Baker Township, fourteen miles west of Ethan, and in the town of Dolton, fifty miles east – all rural one-room schools. In Dolton, several of her students had an older brother, Fred Kappenman, and by the end of the school year, they planned to marry. When she returned home to Ethan, he came with her to meet his future in-laws. The young couple sat on the sofa opposite her parents, who took the two chairs. Fred told them he'd take good care of Kathleen.

John looked at the dark-haired, good-looking man with his winning smile, weathered face and large callused hands and asked, "What are your plans?"

"I'll work with my father for now, but eventually I'd like to get my own place."

"So, you'll live with your folks when you marry?" Bess asked. "Will that work?"

"Well, since I'm the only boy – I have nine sisters – I have my own room. We'll be fine. It's a big rambling farmhouse. Ethel and Lorraine are married and are gone. Besides, the younger ones are still children. Three girls sleep in one room and four in the other. As I said, we have a big house."

"I had some of his younger sisters in school," Kathleen added. "And Ethel had her first baby before Mrs. Kappenman had her last one."

John, shifting uneasily in his chair, turned to Fred. "How far did you go in school?"

"I finished eighth grade. My father needed me on the farm. Just so much work to do."

"They work hard," Kathleen said in his defense.

"I know what farm work is," John spoke quietly. "Remember, I grew up on a farm. So did your mother. It's not an easy life. Do you have any idea what it's like being a farmer's wife?" This was not the kind of marriage they wanted for her.

She nodded. "I'm willing to learn."

When John and Bess had received Kathleen's letter in early April informing them of her plan to marry, they knew there was nothing they could do to prevent it. Now they saw her determination. She had written: *"He's from a good Catholic family, he's a hard worker, we love each other and want to marry. The woman Craig married wasn't even Catholic, and there was nothing you could do about that. At least I'm telling you about Fred and me. He'll bring me home in May so you can meet him."* After her name she had added a postscript, *"I want you to like him as much as I do."*

John asked some final questions of his future son-in-law, who answered them almost as if he had memorized the facts. "My father was born of German immigrants in Iowa, but came to Dakota when he was small – lived in Dolton most of his life. My mother's maiden name was Nugent. The Irish Nugent. She was born and raised in Bridgewater. They want to come and meet you."

The Enterprise
July 1, 1930

Local Woman Weds Dolton Man

Miss Kathleen Donahue, daughter of Mr. and Mrs. J. L. Donahue of this city, was united in marriage to Fred W. Kappenman of Dolton, at Holy Trinity church in this city Tuesday morning, July 1, at nine o'clock. The marriage was solemnized by the pastor, Rev. Fr. Eckl. The bride and bridegroom were attended by Miss Ruth Moran of Armour, cousin of the bride, and Raymond Kappenman, cousin of the bridegroom, of Dolton. The organ prelude and processional were played by Mrs. Albert Feiner as the bridal party proceeded down the aisle.

The bride's gown was of white traditional satin and lace, of princess design, with a full length skirt. She wore a hair braid, white picture hat, and carried an arm bouquet of tea roses. The bridesmaid was attired in an ensemble of ashes of rose colored lace and satin and hair braid, hat to match. She carried an arm bouquet of pink carnations.

A three-course breakfast at the home of the bride's parents followed the church ceremony, served by Mrs. John P. (Mattie) Moran, Mrs. Donahue's sister. Mrs. Moran was assisted by the Mesdames Gunner (Florence Schurz) Osen and Robert (Frances Schurz) Grady, her nieces, and Miss Bertha Schurz. Only the immediate relatives of the bride and bridegroom were guests. A wedding cake was the center of the bridal table. Garden flowers and tapers completed the decorative ensemble. Covers were laid for nine guests at each of two tables.

The bride's traveling costume was an ensemble of royal blue crepe with hat and accessories to match. A motor trip to the lake region of Iowa and other points are included in the honeymoon plans, upon which they departed that evening.

The bride was born and reared in Ethan. She is a graduate of the local high school and the Northern Normal at Aberdeen. She has been teaching since graduating from that institution. The bridegroom was born on a farm near Dolton. He is engaged in that occupation there, where they will make their home.

The Enterprise extends best wishes to the pair.

On a hot July day a year later John and Bess sat at the kitchen table sipping coffee, surrounded by the jumble of used cups and small plates littered with the remains of muffins. Through the window they watched the sun rise in the east. John heaved a sigh. "I guess the building is pretty much gone. Stockel thinks nothing can be salvaged."

"I thought it was just the bakery side."

"Oh, yes. You're right, of course. The east side can probably be repaired. So discouraging. The bakery rental was a good source of income. We'll lose that."

"Those people should have been more careful," she scolded.

They had awakened in the middle of the night to the wail of the fire alarm. They knew that the fire was near: the flames had lit up their room, and the acrid smoke had filled their nostrils. John rose, and when he stumbled sleepily to the window, he let out an anguished groan.

"What is it?" she cried, sitting up in bed also instantly awake.

"Looks like it might be the bakery." His voice was in a panic as he quickly pulled on his trousers. "I'll go see if I can help." She donned her robe, adjusted her hair in its bun, and followed him down the stairs. "I'll make coffee and muffins."

When he reached the group gathered on the street, Fred Tobey stopped him. "The firefighters have things under control. Best let them do their job, John."

Clarence Scheich joined them. "Charley Stockel went to the station at the first sound of the alarm and started the motor, so the pumps are going good. Amazingly, they've got plenty of water."

"What happened?" John asked. "Do they know?"

Fred said, "The bakers say the lard for the doughnuts boiled over and set the floor on fire. See them over there – by the fence? They got out pretty quick and pulled the alarm. Everyone was afraid the Bauer house might be in danger so they wet it down right away."

"Good thing there's no wind," John observed as he wiped his face with his handkerchief. "Then the story might be different."

The crowd watched as water continued to pour onto the building that had once housed the print shop and post office. When the fire was under control, John urged the bakery workers, onlookers, and firefighters to stop by the house for coffee. "Bess has it ready." He smiled to himself when he heard someone behind him say, "Just like Bessie Craig."

After everyone left, John and Bess sat on at the kitchen table. He looked bleakly at her and asked, "What'll we do without the rental income?"

"Now don't you start fussing about that. First, the insurance men have to look at it. We'll see what kind of settlement we get. Let's not worry until that's done."

After the fire, John and Bess did lose their rental income, but they continued to work. When Franklin Delano Roosevelt set up his New Deal programs in 1933, John worked for the Works Progress Administration in various supervisory capacities. At about the same time, *The Enterprise* owner, C. L. Flint, hired Bess to work with editor Harold Ronning at the print shop – mostly in setting type.

One August morning Bess stood in the doorway adjusting her hat. She paused to watch John, who stood at the kitchen table with his apron on. "Do you have everything you need?" she asked. She was heading out to work in the print shop; John would spend the day working in the kitchen.

"I'm all set here. You go off. I can find everything."

She hesitated, her hand on the doorknob. She watched him as he gathered the ingredients for the piccalilli: the pot of vegetables – peppers, tomatoes, and onions that they cut up last night. He was measuring out the brown sugar; the spices were laid out ready. Bess said, "The vinegar is in the larder."

"I know. I'll get it in a minute." He looked up at her, standing in the doorway. "Is there something the matter?"

She shook her head and said, "This is something else."

"What?" He concentrated as he stirred the mixture.

"It's just that you're working here, and I'm going to work at the print shop."

"We'll have to put it in the newspaper. Tell Harry I've taken over the domestic duties at the Donahue household. Most folks will be amused."

"I'll do that." And she was gone.

As if this were unusual. As if I haven't always worked in the kitchen – since childhood. Today, I'm here; most days I work for the WPA.

That evening, when she came in from work, she found their supper ready, and the jars of piccalilli lined up in rows on the sideboard.

"Mercy," she said, hanging up her jacket. "You certainly have made enough."

"That's just the vegetables you cut up last night. We have enough for the winter and we can give some away. Fred and Kathleen will take some. And we'll give some to Craig when he comes to visit."

"They'll enjoy it, I'm sure." He stirred the gravy for their supper. "We'll eat in a few minutes. The roast chicken and potatoes are ready."

"I'll be back in a minute." She went to hang up her hat and change her shoes.

He turned to survey the kitchen. Everything had been washed and put away – all the pots and pans. The kitchen, except for the jars of piccalilli, looked the way it always did. It was a long day, but the finished job satisfied him.

After their meal, as they cleaned up, she said, "Expect to see your name in *The Enterprise*."

"You told Harry?"

"I certainly did, and he had me write a short piece."

"I was joking. Everybody in town will be ribbing me."

"As if what other folks thought ever bothered you."

"You're right. Did you tell them that you did most of the work last night cutting up vegetables?" When she didn't respond, he went on, "No, you didn't." He wiped his hands and hung up his apron. "Just had this thought. We should have made piccalilli when we had the grocers. I bet folks would've bought it. Then maybe, the business would still be open."

"Harrumph." She filled the dishpan with hot water from the stove.

"You can scoff all you want, but this is the best piccalilli around. You mark my words – folks will be asking me for the recipe."

"Give out the recipe if you want, but don't give out jars of piccalilli."

"Yes, Mother," he laughed.

In June of 1934 John, acting as Ethan town representative at the annual Democratic Convention, stood looking over the crowd milling around the hotel ballroom in Sioux Falls. He'd made the two-hour train ride earlier in the day with Robbie Coyne, who was running for state representative. Suddenly, Rob clapped him on the shoulder. "Well, John, what do you think?"

"If you're asking what I think about the candidates for state representative, I think you'll be a good one." He smiled affectionately at his friend. "A year ago when you asked who was a good candidate for president, I named Roosevelt as the man who could do it – get us out of the economic mess we're in. And I think he's made a good start at helping the poor Middle American farmers who are suffering. I back good candidates for office. What do you think about your own chances?"

"I'll be elected. I'll campaign hard because I know nothing in this business can be taken for granted. And, John," he took his hand. "I want you and Bess to be at the state capitol when I'm sworn in next January."

"Wouldn't your father be proud! I'm sorry he didn't live to see this."

"Yes, he was a mover. He taught me by the way he lived to be involved in public service." He tapped him on the chest, "But you, John, also had your share in my pursuing a political career."

"Me? And your father? Neither one of us ever held an office."

"Come on, John. You and Dad talked about issues all the time. You were both so passionate, so I had two good models – strong in beliefs, service-minded, intelligent. Look at all you did when running *The Enterprise*. Especially during the war. You know I didn't have just one father to look up to. I had two. That's why I want you in Pierre. Sort of in Dad's place."

"Don't count your chickens before they hatch. Didn't you learn that from us, too?"

"Yes."

John looked at his watch. "We better get back to our seats. The next session begins in a few minutes."

They walked together arm in arm into the ballroom. "And Robbie, Bess and I will be proud to attend your inauguration."

John and Bess prepared their lunch of leftover turkey and trimmings on the Saturday after Thanksgiving. Bess said, "I missed Kathleen and the children this year. So good last year to have both Craig and Kathleen with their children together for the holiday."

"We can't be selfish. We have to share them with the Kappenmans. After all, we can see them any day we want to now that Fred is renting the Craig farm."

"Some years Craig may not be able to get here from Rockham. With an early storm it would be impossible. Glad he didn't stay in Chicago."

"It was quieter with just Joyce and Sheila, wasn't it? You must admit the place is livelier with the Kappenman children. Tom and Lois Ann are active. Wait until Jim starts walking and talking." They sat and began their meal.

"What are you thinking?" Bess asked when she saw John's amused smile.

"I don't know why, but I was remembering the year we went to the Clark farm for Thanksgiving. Must be fifteen years or more."

"It was 1917, because Kathleen and Rosemary were both nine. And even though Craig was older than James, those four children got along so well. Remember?"

"Kathleen looked so fragile next to Rosemary."

"It's a funny world. Rosemary taken at such a young age and Kathleen with three healthy children all these years later."

"It's the same funny world that brought me to Dakota." He took another bite. "I wonder if my sister is still alive, where they sent her."

"You'll never know."

"No. I'll never know."

"Did you have feasts at the orphan home in Boston?"

"Hardly. Nor at the Coynes. Oh, well, I mean, *they* had feasts on the farm, but I ate in the kitchen. And Mrs. Coyne always plated my food. Never gave me enough. Lots of times, she'd say, 'John doesn't like potatoes' and skip right over me to load up her children's plates. There was nothing I could do or say." Suddenly, he stabbed at the last piece of meat on his plate. "But even though I'm nice to them, I still get angry when I think of how they treated me." She said nothing. Just as suddenly he calmed down. "Robbie was always my friend. We had good times together."

"When you weren't working."

"When I wasn't working. You see what a wonderful work ethic I learned. Otherwise you might have a lazy bum on your hands." He sipped his tea. "But you and I have had many a feast. And the only reason I stayed with you all these years is you always let me have all the potatoes I want."

She laughed in spite of herself.

In April of 1935 John and Bess stood in their kitchen doorway, looking out at their three grandchildren, Tom, Lois and Jim, playing in the yard. He had returned home from his meeting in Mitchell and found her watching the children. "What's wrong?"

"Oh, John, Kathleen had a terrible accident. Fred took her to the hospital with horrible burns." She shuddered before going on. "She was rendering lard, using one of those surplus peanut butter pails." She shook herself. "I should start from the beginning." They moved away from the door to sit at the kitchen table; he took her hand in his. "Fred slaughtered a hog this morning; he was working right outside the house with his men. Kathleen had the fat heating on the stove. When she went to move the pail, the bottom fell out. The hot fat spilled down the front of her dress."

"How bad?" John sat forward, his face paling.

"Fairly bad. Fred took her to Mitchell to see Doctor Frank. I told him to take her right to the hospital. She's in a state of shock. And what may be worse than the burns, is she went berserk, screamed, grabbed Lois Ann and Jim. Ran and hid behind the door of the larder with those babies. Fred had to practically tear the door off its hinges to get to her."

"Where was the baby sitter, Janet?"

"She had the day off. That's why Fred brought the children here." They listened to the childish prattle. "Poor little tykes. They looked so frightened."

"Traumatic for all of them. Did you see her?"

"Yes, I was shaking out the rugs when they drove up. She was in the front seat. Fred bundled Jim into my arms, and the other two hopped out of the car and followed, but Kathleen stared straight ahead. Oh, John, she didn't even see me."

"Probably in shock. I should drive to the hospital to see how things are." They sat and listened to the children's chatter.

After a long pause, she said, "It's probably better to wait until Fred calls with word on where she is and what's happening."

"How was Fred through all this?"

"He was good – totally in control. He knew he had to get her medical attention right away. Once he saw what happened, he said he took her into the bedroom. Ripped the dress off her. He said most of the burns were on the front of her legs. I hope she doesn't lose the baby." Suddenly she stood and headed to the larder. "I'm going to get these children something to eat."

"I'll go out and tell them a story." He stepped outside and called them over to the back stoop.

Three months later John and Bess drove out to the Craig farm on a hot August day to see Kathleen and the new baby. Doctor Frank Tobin, Anna's son, was leaving the house. He put his black bag in his auto before turning to embrace them in greeting. "Aunt Bess. Uncle John. Good to see you."

Bess asked, "Frank, how are things?"

"Fine. Just busy as always." He folded his arms and rested against his auto. "Mom and Dad are fine. I saw them yesterday."

"No," she gestured at the house. "I meant Kathleen?"

"Oh, she's fine. And the baby is fine."

"I don't know why she doesn't go to the hospital to have her babies. Most women do nowadays. Lois Ann born in the auto halfway to Mitchell! That's no way to give birth!"

"Evidently, for this one she didn't have time either. She told Fred early this morning she thought the baby was coming; he went to get water at the well, and when he got back it was all over. The baby had arrived. I came out to check on her and found everything done. I just had to sign the birth certificate."

"So," John who had stood listening to their exchange asked impatiently, "boy or a girl?"

"A girl. She looks like what Kathleen must've looked like as a baby – very small."

John asked, "How are Kathleen's legs? Are they healing?"

"You bet. As I told her, she'll have scar tissue, but she's lucky it wasn't worse."

Bess said, "We're glad we saw you. Tell your mother I'll be up to visit soon."

"Gotta go. Another call to make." He embraced them, climbed into his auto, and drove off in a cloud of dust.

When they stepped into the kitchen, they found the children, finishing up their lunch. Fred leaned in the doorway smoking a cigarette. "It's a girl."

They greeted each of the children and then went into the next room, the children trailing after them. Kathleen lay propped up in bed, looking weary and weak. They looked into the crib at the latest addition to the family. Lois Ann pointed and said, "Baby."

Jim echoed her, "Baby."

Kathleen looked up in surprise, "Is that Jim? Is he talking?"

John said, "It *is* Jim talking."

"His first word," Fred said from the doorway. "About time he said something."

"She's a beauty," John looked at the infant. "Looks a lot like you did at birth. What's her name?" he turned to Kathleen in the bed.

"Judith Ellen. Like Lois Ann, she has a unique name. No Judiths around here. The Ellen is for your sister, Mother, and for Fred's mother; she's Rose Ellen also." As she started the explanation, Fred slipped out to attend to his chores.

John, seeing him go, followed him, leaving mother and daughter to talk. The children followed their grandfather.

In the car on the way home, Bess said, "I hope they're finished with having babies. Four are quite enough. Where did Fred go off to? Did you find him to give him the money?"

"Yes, found him. And yes, I gave him some money for food and for Janette."

"Do you think this drought is almost over? If it doesn't rain soon … I just don't know."

In the summer of 1937 John and Bess, Craig, Irene, and their two children, Joyce and Sheila, took a vacation on the West Coast. On the way, they camped for a few days at Yellowstone National Park before they continued on to California. In San Francisco they visited Tom's daughter, Pearl Donahue, who took them on a tour of the city. While in the area, they also visited the Coynes, who had moved to Oakland.

They drove on to Los Angeles where they stayed for several days with Bessie's sister Till and her family. One evening as they sat on the front porch, John said, "Such variety here. A place to make a life."

"You can really succeed here," Jim agreed. "We came before much of the development, got a good foothold, and we were ready. The real estate business has been good to us. You should've stayed with it, John."

Craig said, "It's the difference between what folks like you were able to do and what happened to the farmers who moved here in the last several years. We saw a few of the camps for the workers on the way."

"Too many of the big farms sent handbills all over the country advertising for help, never expecting the kind of response they'd get," Till said. "There just weren't places for all the workers who streamed into the state."

"Fred and Kathleen are struggling like the rest of the farmers?" Jim asked.

"Yes, but we won't tell them to come out here looking for work," John said. "They'd exchange one hardship for another."

When Bess and Till went into the kitchen to gather a late snack for everyone, Till said, "You worry about Kathleen."

"I do. And the children. Kathleen has so much to do. We remember how hard it is for a farmwife. Of course, she gets no help from Fred – no help with the housework or the children. From the sound of things his sisters waited on him hand and foot. They ironed his shirts, polished his shoes." After a few moments of silence, she said, "We'll be on the road tomorrow."

"We hate to see you go," Till said. "Who knows when we'll see you again?"

"We've got to get back. Craig has to get ready for school, John is scheduled again with the WPA, and I have my work to do. Not that we haven't had a wonderful time – really a marvelous vacation for all of us."

"Mother's right," Craig said as he stepped into the kitchen. "As wonderful as this is, we've got to get back to work."

John and Bess entered the Craig farmhouse. Though it was a hot August afternoon, Kathleen was in the kitchen baking pies.

"Fred took Tom on the tractor to check out the barley field," Kathleen told them. "Lois Ann and Jim are outside playing somewhere. And thankfully, Judy and Sharon are napping."

"We didn't see those two red heads. How did we miss them?" John asked. "I'll go find them. You talk to Kathleen, Bess."

Bess took an apron off the hook behind the door and began to help her daughter pare the apples. "Now, Kathleen, you want to cut these apples a mite smaller and add more sugar. You don't want the pies to be tart."

Her daughter stiffened and said, "Sugar is hard to come by."

"I know, but still you want to add just a little more," she spoke more kindly. "I'll bring you some when we come on Sunday." They worked side by side for a few minutes. "Your father and I think Tom should stay with us during the week for school. We know it will be hard for you or Fred to get him into town every day. Lord knows he's too small to walk across the fields, especially in the winter. Pack up a few of his things on Sunday, and we'll come get him. We'll bring him back here on Friday after school."

Kathleen sounded relieved. "That would be good. One less thing to think about. It's not too much for you and Dad?"

"Nonsense. We've had boarders for years." She began to pare another apple. "Dad and I can help him with his reading and numbers." When they finished, Kathleen put the pies in the oven. Just then, they heard the babies chatting. "What is that I hear?" Bess asked, brightening.

"Must be Judy," Kathleen sighed. "And she woke Sharon."

"I'll go check on them. Why don't you clean up here?" She washed and dried her hands before leaving the kitchen.

In a few minutes, she returned carrying Sharon, with Judy toddling behind her. "Where is your girl, Lorraine? She should help you with the children."

"She went to Mitchell for a few hours. She'll be back soon." Kathleen looked to the clock in the corner. "I miss Janet. She was wonderful."

"You give your help too much free time. With five children and all you have to do, it's important that you have help. And Kathleen, you have to be more forceful. Don't just let them decide what they'll do." She watched her cleaning up the table. "I'll see how Granddad is doing with the others. Come along, Judy. Come with me." After she stepped out of the door, she put Sharon down, and the two girls held hands as they walked to the small group sitting under the tree.

John was sitting on an upturned bucket, showing Lois and Jim "the cat's in the cradle" with a piece of string. As Bess and the two blonde girls approached, he put the string in his pocket, opened his arms to them, and sat one on each knee. She said, "It's all settled. Tom will stay with us. I told Kathleen we'd pick him up on Sunday." She hugged the children.

"Do you think we should head on home, John? We've got to get back."

"Whatever you say, Mother." He grinned and winked at the children. He eased himself up, setting the girls down gently. He hugged each of the four before he followed her to the auto.

John said, "Sure glad Kathleen had that fifth child. Sharon is a beauty."

She harrumphed. "You'll be spoiling her."

"You already spoil Lois Ann and Jim."

"How could I resist those two with their beautiful red hair – just like yours."

Now it was his turn to snort. "Judy sure looks like her mother."

"Well, Sharon looks like you."

"I wonder if any of these girls might look like my sister Mary. I wish I could remember her."

She reached over and patted his arm.

John arrived home after a long and tiring day at work. A cold blustery day and he was bone-tired and irritable. Bess presented him with a thick envelope. "Maybe this will cheer you up. A letter from Craig."

"Ah, do you think he found out anything?" He brightened, his voice reflecting the hope that Craig was able to get his birth certificate for him. He needed to apply for a Social Security card, part of the "New Deal" of

Roosevelt, but the agency asked for a copy of his birth certificate. He'd never had one.

She poured him a cup of tea. "This will hold you until supper." She remained standing beside him, holding the pot and watching him open the packet.

John took out a letter from Craig, as well as one from the orphanage and two birth certificates, his own and his brother Tom's. "Look at these, Bess," his voice catching at the sight of the letterhead from the Orphan Home.

She looked over his shoulder at the certificates. "That's what you need. Good."

He skimmed Craig's letter and turned to the letter from the Home for Destitute Catholic Children in Boston. He picked up the birth certificates and read aloud, "Father, John H. Donahue, mother Annie, birth date June 25, 1877." He shivered, full of memories. He sat still for a long minute. "Wait a minute! There's something wrong. I thought my birthday was in July." He looked at it as if he could change it. Suddenly, he became angry and slammed his fist on the table. The crockery rattled. "I can't believe this."

Bess looked at him mildly, ignoring his tirade, "Let it go, John." She had moved to the stove to attend to the vegetables.

He pushed away from the table, stood and paced the room, shaking the letter. "They robbed me of my sister. They robbed me of my childhood. They robbed me of my birthplace." He trembled in anger and looked out the window into the black winter night.

She said over her shoulder, "Read Craig's letter to me while I check on our dinner."

He turned around, "Did you hear me? A great wrong was committed." He waved the letter.

"I hear you, John," she spoke softly, "but it's all water under the bridge." She turned to watch him fume for a few minutes. "Who are you angry at, John? Who's to blame?" He scowled but did not answer. "The Coynes? They thought they were doing you a favor. The nuns at the Orphan Home? They thought that was the answer for the children. The railroad train that brought you here?" She waved her hand in frustration.

"It's just not right. I'm fifty-one years old and just discovering who I am, who my parents were, my actual *birth* date."

"You are who you are, and who you have been all your life, John Donahue." She went to him and forced him to look at her. "You're a good man. You're the same man I married thirty-four years ago, the father of our two children." She embraced him and held him to her; then after a few minutes she returned to the stove. "Let it go. There's no point. Read Craig's letter."

Soothed by her calm, gentle manner, he obediently walked to his place, sat, picked up the letter and read aloud.

Dear Dad,

I am enclosing the letter I received from the Home for Destitute Catholic Children in Boston, together with the certificates for you and Uncle Tom. I hope they will serve the purpose for which you wanted them. If they are not adequate, please let me know, and I will take whatever further steps are necessary. I imagine, though, that these documents will be satisfactory. I notice that the name is spelled "-hoe" instead of "hue" and that the date of your birth is, as I remember it, only a month away from what you had guessed to be. I thought you might be interested in the picture of the home which appears on the letterhead — would that be the same building you lived in?

John stopped reading and sighed. John H. and Annie Donahue almost became real. Bess stood at the stove watching him as he skimmed the rest of Craig's letter, then again picked up the letter from the Home, studying the picture on the letterhead. *Yes, that's where I was — inside that huge building behind its cold brick.* He read the names of the director and the board. He didn't need a letter telling him he'd been there. He remembered that big, cold place.

"We'll eat in a little bit, John," Bess interrupted his musings. "Why don't you relax in a more comfortable chair?"

John doggedly continued to examine the papers. "It says 209 Silver street."

"Is that all Craig wrote? Does he say how the children are?"

"Oh, yes, there's more. Sorry." He picked up the letter and read aloud:

Irene and the children are well. Joyce has had a cold, but she is back in school this morning. Irene's goiter has been bothering her a little — I think she has been working too hard. We have a big Christmas tree — about 7½ or 8 feet tall, I should judge — and the children can't take their eyes off it. I wish you and Mother could be here for Christmas.

I have been very busy, and I will be still busier from now on – almost too many things to do. I'm working for the ten-day week, though, and when that is arranged everything will be all right. Please write. Merry Christmas!

Love to all,
Craig

John put the papers back into their envelope. "I'll send Tom his birth certificate. He'll be glad to get it. What can I do to help with the dinner?"

"You can do the potatoes and carve the meat"

He took the masher from her and attacked the potatoes, muttering, "Never knew my right birthday. Bessie, I have a right to be angry. Think of all I've lost. Don't tell me anything different."

She patted him gently on the arm, "It's all right." She had heard this anger before and knew she'd hear it again. "At least, we'll have well mashed potatoes for dinner."

He smiled sheepishly.

Chapter Thirteen
Return to Massachusetts

John arrived home and poked his head into the sitting room. "Looks like the School Board needs someone good to straighten things out," he said as he hung up his hat and jacket. "I just met Edward Lynch, who said they need another member."

From her chair, Bess replied, "Don't tell me you're going back to that. You've had your turn. Besides you're too busy with the WPA work." After she took another stitch, she asked, "How would you fit in another meeting?"

"Something has to be done. Now that we have three grandchildren there, we have to be sure it's the best it can be." He stood in the doorway gazing at her, "Who could you name that would be good for the Board?"

"I don't know. The best people are already serving."

"Are they?" He gave her a mischievous grin, "What about you? You'd be good."

"Good? I've never done anything like that. You're the one who's been on committees and organized meetings for years. Not me."

"But you believe in education. You want what's best for children. And you're not afraid to speak your mind. If that's not enough reasons, your grandchildren need you to speak for them. What more reasons do you need?" He sat opposite her.

"I don't know, I ..."

"You'd be good at it. Really."

"Do you think the Board would take me? A grandmother?"

"Of course they'd take you! And they'd be darn glad to have you. You're a former teacher, and everyone knows you."

"I'll think about it," she said quietly, returning to her sewing.

But John knew she would join the Board. It was no surprise to him to hear that after attending several meetings, she was elected vice president. After she told him of one particularly lively session, he said, "I hate to say this, Bess."

"What's that?"

"I told you it was a good idea for you. From the sounds of things you're loving it. Admit it."

"I should have done this years ago for our children." She paused, and then shook her head. "Impossible. I couldn't have because you were on the Board."

He got up from his chair. "I'm going to the workshop to work on that cabinet."

She looked up to see him standing in the doorway. "Go along." John didn't move. "Don't you have something better to do than stand gawking at me?"

"Nothing better to do than look at the beautiful woman I married."

The summer of 1941 was as hot and dry in the Plains states as it had been for the past decade. Craig, Irene, and their children, Joyce, Sheila and Dennis, drove cross country from Springfield, Massachusetts, stopping first in Ohio to see Irene's family and on to South Dakota to visit the Donahues as well as other family and friends.

John and Bess were proud of their son with his beautiful family. He had received a doctorate several years earlier from Teachers College at Columbia University and was Director of Research in the Springfield City School System. The first day they arrived, after their supper, Irene and the children retired for the night, but John, Bess, and Craig stayed up talking.

"I want to show you something." Craig pushed down his sock to expose a mark on his ankle. "Remember how I wrote that Irene and I were struck by lightning? Look at this."

They saw clearly the scar on his leg in the shape of a cross.

"You wrote us about that. Tell us again what happened," John asked.

"We'd gone to New Hampshire to visit some friends. It's not terribly far from Springfield. The McKerleys – he's in the school office with me – have a summer home on a lake. The girls love to go because they have two girls about the same age. And, of course, they love the water." He leaned down to adjust his socks. "A storm was brewing as we drove, and just as we were getting out of the car, the lightning struck. Irene was evidently standing free of the car, but I still had one foot on the running board. We think it struck me and then bounced under the car to hit her on the other side. She fell to the ground and was unconscious for some time. I saw a flash of light and felt a burning on my legs. I ignored it because I had to get the children to safety and tend to Irene. Joyce was in the back seat, ready to hand Dennis out to his mother when it happened. Our friend Walter was standing in the doorway – he saw everything and came out to get the children into the house for safety. Then he helped me carry Irene into the house."

"Was it painful?" Bess asked.

"No," Craig shook his head. "Just a stinging sensation. That's all. Irene said she felt nothing. But I'm amazed at this odd mark." He patted his ankle.

"And Irene?"

"We had a doctor come to examine her; but he found nothing significant, said she'd be 'right as rain' in a few hours. No mark on her, although she was unconscious for an hour or more. Joyce and Sheila found the whole thing frightening. But let me tell you this gave me a wake-up call. I haven't been much of a church-goer." He paused, "Well, since I left Notre Dame. I've had the children baptized, the girls have made communion, and Joyce made her confirmation in May. Even though Irene's not a Catholic, she insisted. But since this happened, I try to be more faithful in going to church."

They sat in a comfortable silence for some minutes. "You'll talk to Fred?" John asked suddenly.

"Yes, I'm sure he could get a job in the Springfield area," Craig said. "I brought the Springfield newspaper with me. There's an article about how factories are gearing up for the war, and they're all hiring. It's just a matter of time before we join in the war in Europe."

John said, "Last war it took us almost three years before we got involved, and it was over quickly. But I'm afraid this war might last longer."

Bess said slowly, "I don't know if factory work is the best answer for Fred, but at least he'd have a steady income each week. Things have been bleak for farmers with the drought for more years than anyone can count."

Not long after this, with Craig's encouragement and the support of John and Bess, Fred and Kathleen made the decision to move to Massachusetts. Fred left six weeks before the family to take a course in machine shop training before he took a job. A few weeks later, on an October afternoon, Bess and John brought a covered dish and dessert to the farm for Kathleen and the children, who would board the train taking them cross-country the next day. They would join Fred, who had rented an apartment. With her parents' help Kathleen had had a farm auction – a success, selling household goods and farm animals and equipment, giving her some much-needed cash. The farm, however, was not sold; the Craig estate would continue to own and rent the property.

After the meal, John and the children (all except Terry, who already slept in the crib) went outside to look at the sky. Mother and daughter cleaned up the kitchen. Bess said, "It hardly seems possible that he's been gone almost six weeks already." They were all anxious about the separation, of the big move from South Dakota to Massachusetts. Kathleen with her six children faced a two-and-a half-day train trip the next morning. They wouldn't ship the furniture; they'd sold that. With the auction money, they'd buy what they needed in Massachusetts. Craig had helped Fred to find a secondhand furniture store in Springfield. All they would take with them were personal items, family treasures, and several suitcases of clothes. In truth, they didn't have much.

When they finished the few dishes, they stepped out to join John, who stood by the car as he chatted with the three oldest children sitting on the stoop. It was a warm, pleasant evening. The night creatures sang in the fields. The moon had risen high in the sky and the stars shone brilliantly. Judy and Sharon were running back and forth in the yard. "What about school for the children?" John asked Kathleen.

"Fred said there's a Catholic school just a few blocks away from the apartment, so the children will get a good education." They stood silently. Kathleen pointed at the row of trees in front of the house. "Fred planted those trees through the Civilian Conservation Corps. It's proved a good windbreak."

"Amazing how tall they've grown. In just a few years. Like your children. Growing so fast. They'll be all grown up before we see them again." Mother's voice broke, and the tears came.

"No, we'll come back to see you. The train isn't expensive."

John and Bess hugged them all before they got into the Chevrolet and drove back to Ethan. They would return in the morning to drive them to the depot. Bess was glad John had come home from Iowa where he was working. Because money was scarce, he took work wherever he could get it. This temporary job as supervisor with Ryan Construction was almost finished.

Barely a month later, John and Bess finally decided they would take the trip to Massachusetts – on a trial basis. However, instead of taking the train, they would drive cross-country so they would have an automobile. Both knew they would eventually leave South Dakota for good and settle near their two children on the East Coast, but they didn't speak of it. On a bleak and dark day John tied up the last bundle of books in the parlor. Bess worked in the dining room, packing china and silver. They would bring as many of their valuables as they could with them. They had found a renter for the house in their absence.

Bess poked her head into the parlor. "Are you almost finished?" She looked around and saw that indeed he was. "The things in the dining room are ready to be tied with a good stout cord. I packed the tablecloths and napkins around my good dishes so they won't break on the trip." She headed to the back of the house. "I'll start in the kitchen."

Very early the next morning, John and Bess looked around the house one more time as they moved from room to room. He carried the last two bags with their clothes, and she had the lunch and her purse. She asked, "Are we sure we have everything?"

"You bet," he said with false exuberance. "It was a good idea to pack the auto last evening. Makes it easier this morning for an early start." They stepped out to the car behind the house. After he opened the door for Bess and walked around to the driver's side, he patted the hood. *The tank's filled. Battery, fluids, and tires all checked.* He took his place behind the wheel. "We should have no problems on the road. Robbie will stop by later to check on things. With the ad in the paper, we should soon enough find a renter for the house."

As she settled into her seat, Bess shivered and pulled her coat more closely. "It certainly is cold." She picked up the plaid lap robe and spread it over her knees. She opened her handbag and took out the directions for the trip that Craig had mapped out for them. As they headed south to get onto the highway, they found the road practically empty. John kept a steady hand on the wheel. *I can make good time on these flat, straight roads.* After they had gone several miles, passing familiar landmarks, she said, "Now, John. There's no need to speed. It doesn't matter how long it takes us to get there. We don't have any deadline." She kept her eyes steadily on the road ahead of them.

"Don't worry," he reassured her, glancing down at the speedometer. "I'll drive carefully. You tell me when you need to stop." He thought of the route – through Iowa, Illinois, Indiana, Ohio, Pennsylvania, New Jersey, New York, Connecticut and finally, Massachusetts. They were giving themselves plenty of time with stops at roadside cabins for overnight stays. Craig had given them suggestions of places. John thought of it as no more daunting than his trips years ago to South Bend with Craig, or more recently in the opposite direction when they visited California.

They drove for miles into Iowa with cornfields (now empty and bare) on either side of the road. By noon a brilliant sun warmed the interior of the car. Bess folded the lap robe and placed it on top of the boxes in back. About noon they found a filling station where they stopped to refuel and eat the lunch they had packed. After they stretched and walked around a bit, they continued on their way.

Craig and Irene moved to Springfield in 1939, Kathleen with the children in October of 1941, the Donahues a month later. For the first several months in Massachusetts, John and Bess lived with Craig and his family. Once they determined that the stay would be permanent, they looked for and found an apartment on Washington street, several houses away from Craig. They decided that the Forest Park section was a lovely area of Springfield. They joined Holy Name Church, where John chafed at the pew rent added to the weekly collection.

They knew they had to work and followed Fred's example by enrolling in a trade school before finding a factory job. After their six-week course, they were hired at J. Stevens Arms in Chicopee. On their first day, the manager, Mr. Broderick, led them to their workstations. Bess took her place on the assembly line as an inspector. "Stacia will show you what to look for." He turned to the woman sitting on the next stool, "Stacia, this is the new girl, Elizabeth. Show her what to do."

"Okay, old lady." Stacia snapped her gum. "Let me show you what ya gotta do."

Bess sat straight in her chair and said primly, "My name is Elizabeth." She set her lips in a tight line.

"Yeah, sure, Queenie," she said, fingering Bess' lace collar. She grunted, and then hollered across the aisle to another worker, "Hey, Babs, we got ourselves a real lady here. Have some respect." She gave a coarse laugh. "We wore our lace today. This here is Queen Elizabeth, but we'll call her Queenie for short."

At supper when they shared stories of their first day, Bess complained, "That woman showed me three times what to do. Three times. I knew what to look for the first time she explained it. Then she watched me for twenty minutes to be sure I knew what I was doing." She put the stew casserole in the center of the table.

"You have to admit that most of the workers are somewhat duller than you are," he smiled as he sat down opposite her and helped himself to his dinner.

"Did you see the filth of the place? Dirt and dust everywhere." She made a face. "On the windows, floors, worktables. And the language of those women. I'd never believe I could hear such filth coming from women. And women wearing pants!" She snorted her disapproval. "I'll always wear my housedress." She arched her tired back, finally asking how his day went. "Are you very tired? You're on your feet all day. At least I do my work sitting."

"I think working as floor manager is easier than an inspector job. I move around. I talk to different people. I have variety." They ate in silence. After some time he broke the silence "It's certainly not like anything else we've done over the years. But beggars can't be choosers. We take what we can get." He took a few more bites, and then added, "And we'll be glad of our pay check on Friday."

One March evening Bess looked up from the newspaper. "Did you read this?"

"No, I'll read it after you finish. I want to plan this next project."

"Listen to this. 'Superintendent John Granrud announced yesterday that acting assistant superintendent of schools, Dr. T. C. Donahue; acting assistant director of the bureau of guidance, placement and adult education, H. S. Robbins; and acting director of the department of research, S. E. McKerley have received commissions in the navy and will leave soon for serving. The three hold important posts in the local school system.

'Dr. Donahue and Mr. Robbins have been commissioned lieutenants, junior grade, and Mr. McKerley, lieutenant, senior grade. McKerley and Dr. Donahue will leave Friday for preliminary training at Columbia university and Mr. Robbins will report April 22 at Chapel Hill, N. C., for a 30-day indoctrination program.

'Dr. Donahue became acting assistant superintendent of schools in September to fill a vacancy left by John L. McConnell when he entered the army. Since May 1940 he was director of research. Dr. Donahue had graduated from Notre Dame university, and did graduate work for three years at Ohio State university, where he received his master's degree. He studied for two years at the advanced school of education of Teachers' college, Columbia university, and was granted the degree of doctor of philosophy.

'After several years in teaching and administrative positions in South Dakota, Dr. Donahue came to this city in February 1939 to become an assistant in the central office of the public school system.'" She looked to see if he was listening.

"Well, we knew all that. Craig told us."

"I know, but it doesn't say who his wife and children are, or where he was born, or anything about his parents. Your little paper in Ethan was so much better than this." She shook the paper.

"We did have a good newspaper. But remember. You had a hand in it."

When John read in the *Daily Republican* that the Civil Defense Department was looking for air wardens to patrol neighborhoods in order to enforce the blackout during the war, he decided he'd do his part in the war effort. On Saturday, he reported to the center on Main street, and after the two-hour training session returned home with his badge and papers giving him the authority to enforce the blackout.

As they ate lunch, he told Bess, "They could've done that training in a much shorter time. Wasted so much time. We did things more efficiently in the last war with the Four-Minute Men."

"This is different. This war is on such a wider scale. And it's more dangerous living this close to the coast. All those war planes!" She shuddered before taking another bite of her sandwich. "I don't know why you want to do this. After working all day on your feet. And then walking the streets at night. It's too much for you." She had read the instructions and the names of the neighboring streets he would patrol.

"I'll be fine. I want to do this. Craig is off to do his part. I want to do my share. Simple as that." He had finished his lunch and was enjoying a cup of tea. "Look at what I did in 1918 with the Red Cross and Four-Minute Men and Home Guard. This is nothing."

Bess started gathering the dishes. "You were twenty-five years younger." She filled the dishpan and began the washing up. "Just don't complain to me how tired you are."

He dried and put away their few dishes. "I'll be good. No complaining. I'll get to know the neighborhood, and may even meet some folks."

A year and a half later, John stood in the bedroom, ready to close up his suitcase. He was returning to South Dakota to auction off their household goods. They wouldn't sell the house immediately because they relied on the rental income. But they had finally decided the move was permanent, and they would not return to live in South Dakota. He had sent the advertisement to *The Enterprise* announcing the auction and expected the furniture and furnishings to bring in good money because they were all in good condition. "Do you have everything?" Bess interrupted John in his musing.

He turned and smiled. "I think so. I'm only going to Dakota and back. I don't need much for such a short trip." She moved her hands from behind her back and handed him his razor and brush. "Oops." He took them and slipped them into his valise. "I would've forgotten. Call me at Fanny's if you need me. She'll know how to reach me if I'm not there." They walked to the door together. They embraced. "See you next week."

John boarded the bus in downtown Springfield less than an hour later. On the long ride, with his bag next to him, he looked out at the countryside. *I carried less than this on my first trip of Dakota. All my worldly goods. That time I stayed over fifty years, this time it's only for a few days.* He watched the changing landscape. He thought of that trip so many years earlier when as a child he was so bewildered, when he believed he was going to help farmers for a short time. Now he knew he had family waiting for him when he returned. To Dakota and back. That's what Tom had said to him on the train. Somehow he'd found his way back to Massachusetts.

When he arrived at the familiar depot in Ethan and got off the train (the bus had brought him to Sioux City, Iowa, and he'd boarded the train for the rest of the way), he felt a tug of the heart. He actually missed these familiar scenes and familiar faces.

Three days later, after the auction, John made the return trip to Massachusetts, satisfied with the sale. He patted his pocket. *This extra money will come in handy.* Most of the goods sold at a fair price, and Robbie would take care of the rest. While in South Dakota, acting on behalf of Bess, who was executor of the Craig estate, he also settled some other business affairs.

John rested on his first day back in Springfield. After lunch he stood in the spare room, staring out the window at the sugar maple and across the street at the neighboring houses. Bess sat sewing at her Singer. He turned and asked her, "You know what I miss most?"

"What's that?" she asked.

"The sky."

She echoed him, "The sky? What do you mean? The sky. We have sky." She turned from the machine to look at him. "Aren't you looking at it?"

"Come over here." He gestured to her. "Look out the window, and I'll show you what I mean."

"John, I'm busy here. I have no time for nonsense. I know what you can see."

"Humor me. Come and look out."

"Oh, all right." She put down the blouse and walked to the window.

He made way for her. "Tell me what you see."

"I see the blue sky with puffy white clouds."

He pressed, "What else?"

"Trees and the houses across the way."

"Would you see more sky at home in Ethan?"

"Maybe," she conceded as she looked sideways at him.

"Do one more thing. Close your eyes and pretend you're standing at the edge of Ethan."

"John," she protested.

"Please." He watched her reluctantly close her eyes. "What do you see?"

"I see sky and miles of land in all directions. From our farm you could see the church steeple in Dimock. You know," she said, finally taking his spirit, "I miss the smells, too – of newly mown hay – the heather – the outdoors – the good smells. That's what I liked when I moved to town."

"South Dakota is called the 'Sunshine State' for good reason. You can see the sky for miles around everywhere you look. Here you can't get the same feeling of openness. Hills, buildings, trees – you can hardly see the sky." Bess opened her eyes and returned to her work, but now she listened to him. "Last week I borrowed Herman's car and drove out to the old Coyne farm. I just stood there looking in all directions. We can't do that here. If I remember it rightly, we couldn't see the sky in the Orphan Home either. Windows were up high near the ceiling. Somehow, believe it or not, when I got to Dakota I felt free. As sad as I was, I mean … even though I had to work, there was a kind of freedom because of the space and the sky. Don't you feel cramped here?"

"Well we are. The houses are built closer together. And look at us. Cramped into a house with three other families." He moved to the end of the bed and sat. "Yes," she conceded again. "You're right. We have less sky here. Too many buildings and trees."

"And you know what that means? It means we have less freedom and less beauty. Life was so much easier when we were younger."

"We did all right for ourselves."

"Part of it is the factory work, but the other part is the reason we do this work. This war is worse than anything we ever saw. Such horror is too much to take in." He stood and looked out the window again.

"The other thing we miss is our garden. We should be growing our own vegetables in a garden. And have flowers. Just no space in that sad excuse for a back yard here. Anyway we don't have the time to put into a garden. But wouldn't it be lovely if we could have a victory garden like we had in the last war." She stopped her work. "Were the fields as dry as ever?"

"No, the crops looked good this year. I saw some good ones." After a minute he shook himself and stood. "I'm going to the workshop to see if I can finish up the clothes hamper for Kathleen."

"When do you think you'll finish?"

"I just have to do the cover. And paint it. I'll add the hinges when the paint dries."

"Not by tomorrow?"

"No, afraid not. Next week. I'm behind in my work."

"Kathleen will be glad when she gets it. I'll have Lois Ann's frock ready for tomorrow, but the other two girls will have to wait till next week for theirs. God knows they need them! I'm behind in my work, too. And I didn't take time out to go to Dakota."

"I'll be back up for lunch."

"Fine."

Suddenly, he turned back. "Why don't we go to Forest Park this afternoon?" Surprised, she looked up. "We can look at the flowers, the grass, and the trees."

She looked at her sewing in exasperation, thought for a moment, then said, "Why not? It may do both of us good. I want to see how the roses are doing. We may even see more of the sky." They both laughed.

The war was finally over in 1945, but it was almost a year before Craig returned home from the navy to take up his work again at the school department. He'd been appointed acting superintendent, but he knew that Springfield, founded by the Puritan John Pynchon and very much anti-Catholic, would not hire an Irish American Catholic to run its schools. When he visited his parents on a warm August afternoon, he told his parents his decision. "You're the first to know that I'm leaving Springfield, of course, after Irene and the children. I'm taking a superintendent position in Eastchester, New York. I'll hand in my resignation here tomorrow."

"Good. This job is not what you want to fight for," Bess said.

"No," Craig said, "They don't want an Irish Catholic heading the department. Looks like the city may elect an Irish Catholic mayor, but in the schools it's different. See what you've done by giving me such an Irish name. Some folks hear Terence Craig Donahue, and they inwardly shudder. More than they can bear."

John said, "To say nothing of the Irish face and the red hair. With your intelligence and Irish wit, you're doomed on all sides. New York is offering a good contract?"

"Indeed. The school committee members couldn't have been more affirming."

"Have you looked at a place to live?" Bess asked.

"They suggested Scarsdale, and it looks like a good area to bring up a family. Nice section of New York. I drove around after the interview last week. Lovely homes. I'll contact a real estate agent and see what's available. Irene and I are ready to purchase a home. If this school system is as good as it seems, we'll settle there."

"How did the children react?"

"Fine. They're accustomed to moving around. Joyce and Sheila remember South Dakota and New York. And all three have spent some time both in Springfield and in Davenport, Iowa, when I was in the service. They all make friends easily." He meditated, puffing on his pipe. "Of course, Joyce is off to college in the fall, Sheila's just entering high school, and Dennis in second grade will adjust just fine. The good news is that the drive isn't too far. You can come visit anytime, and I'll probably come this way once in awhile." He smiled at them, looking from one to the other. "I'll come and visit my parents so they won't forget what their son looks like."

Chapter Fourteen
Final Years

John sat in St. Augustine chapel, South Boston, 1948. *Full circle. This is where I was baptized. This was my parents' church.* He thought back to the day ten years ago when he opened the letter from Craig with his birth certificate and the letter from the Orphan Home and how angry he'd been. Today he walked along Silver street and saw the house of his birth. Just as he imagined it – a large three-tenement building. He knew his mother died and was buried in the nearby cemetery. He thought with a pang of his father and his sister. *What had happened to them?*

Early that morning he had awoken strangely elated and nervous. In one of his recent visits, Craig had promised to drive him to Boston so he could see these places. "I just want to see where I came from," he'd said. Now that they lived in Springfield, they could easily make the trip. He'd risen quietly so as not to disturb Bess, put on his robe, and went into the kitchen to start breakfast. He'd looked up when he heard Craig.

"Good morning. Looks like a fine day." Craig took butter, jam and cream from the icebox; then he stepped into the pantry for the plates and bread. "Mother's sleeping?"

"Yes, her cold knocked her for a loop. Hopefully, she'll get a good rest with us away for the day. She can heat up chicken soup later. How do you like your eggs?"

"Over easy."

After they ate, Craig said, "Why don't you get dressed and I'll do up these dishes?"

John dressed quietly. When he put on his suit jacket, he heard Bess stir in the bed. When she looked up at him, he asked how she felt.

"Better. I think I can eat something this morning."

"Craig probably has it ready. Good hot oats."

John was happy to spend the day with his son. In South Boston Craig maneuvered along Silver street – more like an alley than a city street. John tried to picture what it might have looked like some seventy years earlier. Perhaps it had been only a dirt path or cobblestones. Craig said, "Look to the right, Dad. The odd numbers are on the right. There it is. See the number – 209." He pulled in front of the brown three-story apartment building. "Do you want to get out?"

"Yes, I think I will." John gazed at the dilapidated building – his birthplace.

His son appeared at his elbow. "Do you want to see if we can go inside?"

"No, I just wanted to see it. I wonder what floor we lived on." He walked along, slowly facing the structure. "Perhaps up to six families lived here. Of course they probably didn't have indoor plumbing in the 1870s." He examined the house and yard with a critical eye. "The house may have looked better then." After staring in silence, he said, "They could do something with this yard. Put in a garden."

When Craig suggested, "You and I could fix up this place," he nodded. When John headed back to the auto, his son said, "Now to St. Augustine church. Just around the corner."

They examined the 1880 cornerstone before they went in to make a visit. Later they walked up the street a block to the St. Augustine chapel, the original church with its cemetery. "Since the church was built three years after I was born, I imagine I must have been brought here for baptism." They walked among the tombstones wondering where his mother might be buried.

"I imagine they wouldn't have had money for a stone." But still they wandered reading names and dates.

When they left Dorchester street, Craig headed for Harrison avenue to look for the Home for Destitute Catholic Children. When they pulled up opposite the large brick building, John said, "I won't get out here. I can see all I want to from here. No desire to go in, nor to see children or nuns living here now." It looked as forbidding as he remembered. After a bit he said, "I think I've seen everything. Thanks for bringing me."

Craig patted his arm. "It must be painful." He pulled the car slowly out into traffic and headed toward downtown Boston where they ate lunch. Later they stopped and picked up another copy of his birth certificate and visited some of the historical landmarks.

That evening they found Bess improved and with dinner ready for them. Hours later, before John and Bess went to sleep, he told her, "It's odd. I feel a sort of peace. Just seeing where I was born and baptized and the Orphan Home. Somehow I have a sense of wholeness. I feel I can finally let it go."

She touched him gently and said, "I'm glad."

On a hot July day in 1949 John and Bess visited Craig and Irene, bringing two of their grandchildren, thirteen-year-old Judy and twelve-year-old Sharon, for a week's visit.

One day while there, John and Bess sat chatting quietly in the parlor, each with a book. Suddenly Sharon stalked in to report in tears, "Judy and Dennis are playing with his chemistry set, and they won't let me play. They say only two can play."

John said, "Sometimes that happens."

"Will you tell them that they have to let me play?" she pouted.

"No, Sharon." He pulled her onto his knee. He pushed her blonde hair off her face. "Let me tell you that when no one wants you, when others shut you out, you have to go your own way. Learn that sometimes you have to make your own fun."

"It's not fair," she sniffled as she snuggled into him.

"Remember you have to be happy alone before you can get along with others." He took out his handkerchief and wiped her eyes. "Find something else to do by yourself. Go and look at the books in Joyce's room. I'm sure you'll find something just as good as a chemistry set."

"All right," she said slowly.

That evening, while the children played in the yard, Craig played some light tunes on the piano. When he finished, John said, "Thanks. It's good to hear you play again."

"Terry plays every song in three-quarter time," Irene commented.

He left the piano bench to sit beside her on the sofa. "Just glad to have a piano in the house again."

Bess said, "We enjoyed that. Thank you, Craig."

The next day they said their goodbyes and headed back. After they drove the girls home to West Springfield, John and Bess continued their drive to their own home. Bess said, "Well, at least you don't have to get up for work tomorrow. We can rest. I was remembering the argument we had before you finally gave up work."

"Not an argument," he said, "A friendly disagreement."

Last year, after she had harped for months about his retiring, he had finally asked, "And if I give up the work at the factory, what will I do?"

"You'll have time to work on your projects. Certainly you won't wander around here doing nothing." She had started to set the table for their supper. She stopped to look at him. "Just do it. Tell Mr. Spence you're leaving. It's ridiculous that you're still working at your age." She shook her head in exasperation. "You come home every night so tired you can hardly eat your supper. Tell them you're quitting. Enjoy some leisure. It's time for a rest when you're seventy years old."

He added more flour to the gravy. "I don't know. Mr. Spence said to me the other day he didn't know what we'd do without me."

"Of course, they don't want you to quit. You're a good worker.

Really, you're doing his work."

"That's not true. He works hard."

"Another thing. You give altogether too much attention to that young fellow, Bobby. You don't have that kind of time for your own grandchildren."

He turned away from the stove. "Now, that's not true. I can't spend time with them when they're in school. I see Bobby at work. You can't begrudge the fact that I have a young friend."

"No, I don't. It's just that I know how tired you are. We could enjoy one another and our grandchildren. I know I have more energy now that I'm no longer following that horrible schedule of eight hours of boring, back-breaking work in a factory."

"We need the money."

"We'll get by."

"I've been working since I was eight years old. I don't know what I'd do with myself."

"Do with yourself! How many projects have you started in your workroom? You have plenty to do."

Not too long after that John told her that he had finally handed in his resignation at work. "You know I sort of drifted into things all my life. Now I'm drifting out. And, you know, remarkably I've done well at all the work I've done. Not one to sit on my hands. I'll keep myself busy and not get in your way."

She put her hand on his arm, "I'm glad. Time to just enjoy life."

A week before John and Bess's fiftieth wedding anniversary, John looked out the window at the buds on the tree. "Spring and new life. Remember before we married how we believed we could do anything?"

"And we did. We've accomplished a great deal in our lifetime."

He turned from the window. "No great deeds, no discoveries, no major changes, no fame or fortune."

"We've had all of those." She took a seat on the davenport, inviting him to join her. "We discovered each other. We had two children who gave us ten beautiful grandchildren, and now we're on to the next generation. That's all either of us wanted. Not to be rich, not to gain fame or honors. Just to live a good life."

"We survived two world wars."

"Yes. That, too. Look at all you did during the first one with your work at the newspaper and for the Red Cross and the Four-Minute

Men."

"And during the second war we lent our son to the navy. And what would I have done without you?" He took her hand in his. We made a great team. The early years were the best years. Living in Ethan, raising our children, working for the community."

"The only time we've been apart in fifty years is when you were in the hospital. And I've never even had to go to the hospital. Amazing."

"They wouldn't take you. Such a fine specimen of woman."

"You can laugh all you want. I've kept my health."

"I know what I'm proudest of. Choosing you as my bride."

"Oh, you."

John had his share of health problems in the early 1950s with surgery followed by radiation treatment and the subsequent radiation burns. At the same time they were forced to move several times. In 1952 they received an eviction notice because the house on Washington street was condemned. They found a tiny apartment on Jenks street in the North End where they lived for six months, and finally moved to an apartment on George street in West Springfield where they would live till John's death in 1963. Again they had space for their projects, their hooked rugs, her sewing, and his carpentry workshop. And best of all, they had a yard where they could have a garden.

In his later years John was diagnosed with diabetes and because he remembered the bad experience in the hospital of ten years earlier – the cold unfeeling doctors and nurses, as he said – he refused to go back to the hospital. Bess kept her health, not declining perceptibly till after his death.

However, in spite of his physical difficulties, he continued to approach life as he had all his years. He and Bess continued to work together – cooking and cleaning, working in the garden and on their projects. They had started as a team; they continued as a team to his end. They enjoyed their grandchildren, attended their weddings, and rejoiced in the birth of each of their great grandchildren. They kept in touch with folks in South Dakota by faithful letter writing, especially with Bess's sisters and their families.

On a cold March day of 1955 John came into the house carrying several bundles. Bess bustled over and, while he removed his jacket, emptied the sack. He had walked the several blocks to the discount fabric store. "Perfect. These colors are absolutely right: purple, lavender, and the light green." She fanned out the various small bolts of material. "We've already got enough yellow and dark green. Oh, and the material is fine. You didn't spend a lot of money?"

"No, that place has good sales. Where's the wrapping paper? I'll get started on the design while you cut the cloth into strips." She went into their bedroom and returned with the pansy wrapping paper. While she was gone, he had cleared off the kitchen table so he could work there.

Bess said, "Won't Sharon be surprised! I was delighted the other day when she gave us our anniversary gift and told us she bought the wrapping paper because pansies are her favorite flower. A perfect design for her hooked rug. We want to give her something special for her wedding day."

"She's someone special. What would we do without her?"

Bess spread out the material. "Let's see. We need mostly purple. Not as much of the lavender and green." She divided the cloth into several piles.

John set to work by plotting out the flower design with a sketch on brown paper. "Yes, this is grand. I can transfer the design right onto the canvas. Should work nicely." After some time of working, he added, "As soon as we finish this we've got to start thinking about one for Lois Ann. Looks like she'll marry that Sam fellow."

"Will Sharon take you shopping on Saturday?" When he nodded, she said, "I'm sure glad you stopped driving."

"Don't harp on that." As he continued to sketch, he thought of the day several months ago when he had come out of the grocers and was assaulted by ruffians who had knocked him down and took his sacks from him. That was the final straw. Sharon took him to the police department where he reported the robbery, but he knew with this attack his independence was slipping away. The attack did more than hurt his knees. It made him realize how fragile he was and that he had to rely on someone else. Too many physical ailments. Too many accidents. Too many traffic violations of going through red lights and down one-way streets the wrong way. He finally had said, "Enough. I'm not driving any more. I'll turn the auto over to Jim. He sure can use it."

"You've had other accidents. You'll get over this."

"No. This is different. It's not the same as when you fall off a roof or a ladder or have another car slam into you because of a dust storm. These hoodlums deliberately attacked me because they saw me as old and weak." He stared at the floor. After a few minutes he lifted his head. "I hate being old."

She came over and put her hand on his shoulder. "No, it's no fun being old. But keeping active and doing things for our grandchildren helps." She gave his shoulder a light squeeze.

When they finished Sharon's wedding gift of the hooked rug, they began one for Lois Ann, following the same procedure, this time with a design of blue bells. A year later they went to work making crib quilts for the coming babies. For Judy, born to Lois in July, they made a Sunbonnet Sue, and for Rick, born to Sharon in August, a Dungaree Boy. Most of the work was done before the births. They needed to add the figure when they knew whether the newborn was a boy or a girl.

Another April several years later John and Bess sat on the sofa, facing their wedding portrait. "Truly a handsome couple," he said and squeezed her hand lightly. "Certainly the most beautiful bride ever. Being together for fifty-five years is certainly an accomplishment."

"It's more than an accomplishment. It's been good."

"We've had our ups and downs."

"True. But not the tragedies some families experience. For the most part we've got along fine. Our children remained healthy, and they've given us wonderful grandchildren."

Suddenly he grew very quiet. "And now what do we have? Just the prospect of the end."

She jumped up. "The end! What are you talking about? The end! We've got too much to do. The first thing is seeing about supper." When he sat on, she said, "We've got to start on the garden tomorrow. The seeds and seedlings are all ready to go into the ground. And these geraniums." She pointed to two pots. "They look good. Survived the winter." She walked over to the table and picked up a book. "And this lovely new book on gardening will help. I want some fuchsias and zinnias this year. And, of course, marigolds." She looked to see if he was listening. She scanned through the seed packets. "The iris will add height in the back. The tomato plants will be ready soon. We'll have cucumbers and squash. We've got to organize these." She fanned out the seed packets. "Decide what goes in the ground first. And we have to work on getting that rug done for Kathleen." She put the gardening book down. "You stop talking about the end. We'll just keep going. You're not even eighty years old yet. What are you thinking?"

He hadn't moved but sat still. "I don't know how long my father lived. Maybe my time is already up."

"Your time is up with moaning and groaning. Come and help me with supper."

John got up slowly. "Remember the garden we had in Ethan?"

"Yes." She turned and saw that he made no move to follow but stood in front of the sofa. "You can remember in the kitchen. Come along."

With this urging he shook himself and followed her slowly.

In 1963 John suffered his last illness. A week before his death he sat up in bed with pillows propped around him. Cantankerous his last months, he belied his lifelong behavior as calm, patient, and benevolent. Bess knew that this man was not the John Donahue she had married almost sixty years before. He snapped at her, was rude to visitors, and complained about everything. In the face of his final illness, Bess grew strong, calm, and fully in control.

One day Sharon stopped for a short visit with her three boys on the way home from school. John became agitated. "Who are these people?" he demanded of Bess. "Did you tell Evelyn she could come today?"

"This is Sharon," Bess told him patiently. "You know Sharon Marie, your favorite granddaughter. She brought her boys to see you. Ricky, John, and Joe."

"Don't tell me. This is Evelyn, and I don't want her here. Tell her to go away. She's been looking in the window all day." Bess looked at Sharon.

Seven-year-old Ricky stepped forward. "Grandfather, we brought you some flowers."

"Who is this little man?" he asked crossly.

"I'm Ricky. We brought you some flowers," the child said evenly, not taking his eyes off his great-grandfather. Bess took them from him and put them on the bedside table.

John looked at Sharon and demanded, "Who are you?"

"Sharon, Granddad, and these are my boys, Ricky, John, and Joe, your great-grandchildren."

"Too many children, Sharon." Suddenly lucid, he looked wearily at her. "Don't have seven children like your mother. It's too many. Three are quite enough." He closed his eyes and dozed. Almost immediately he opened his eyes again and said, "Bess, I don't want these people here. Tell them to go away."

"They came to see you," Bess said gently.

"See me! They look at me all the time. I see them peek in the windows." He became agitated, pulling on the bedcovers. "Close the blind. How many times do I have to ask you to close the blinds?"

"Close your eyes and rest, John," Bess said as she patted his hand. She turned to Sharon. "You'd better go."

Five-year-old John said, "Goodbye, Granddad."

John opened his eyes and said crossly, "Granddad. Where did you get that word? I'm your grandfather."

"Goodbye, grandfather," Ricky said, patting his hand on the coverlet. "We'll come again to see you."

Four-year-old Joe patted his hand in imitation of his brother but said nothing.

Bess walked to the door with them. "He doesn't know people anymore."

Sharon said to her sons, "Go, wait for me in the car. I'll be there in a minute." She watched them go. "He knows you, though." She turned to Bess, holding her hands.

"He'd better know me. We've been together a long time. And he knows your mother. But everyone else is someone from Ethan. People we knew long ago."

Sharon said sympathetically, "This is hard on you, Grandma."

"I can't complain. No finer man than your grandfather." She squeezed Sharon's hand and said, "My mother told me that before we married." They stood together in silence. "I can put up with this. He wants to die at home, and I'll let him have that."

"How's his leg?"

"Fairly bad. Doctor Connery comes in to dress it daily. He's the only one he'll see. Just refused for the last several years to go to a doctor. Said he already suffered enough at the hand of doctors. He had such a bad experience ten – twelve years ago. Just wouldn't let me take him to see what was the matter."

"What does the doctor say it is?"

"The result of untreated diabetes. Says it often comes to the elderly. Gangrene. Just a matter of time. He's ready to go. Lived eighty-seven years, and when he's himself he says he had a good life."

"Would you want someone to come and stay with you?"

"No, I'm fine. I rest in between. He's not a demanding patient. He just has this obsession that someone is spying on him. I don't understand. But what bothers me is that he doesn't know people. People like you. People who were so close to him."

They heard the car horn. "That's one of the boys. I gotta go. I'll bring mother tomorrow. I'll have my mother-in-law watch the boys." The horn tooted again more insistently. "Those boys!" I promised them ice cream if they were good."

"Enjoy them. They're beautiful boys." They embraced. Both women had tears in their eyes. "Go, get them their ice cream."

The next day when Sharon and Kathleen left after their visit, Sharon said, "A tower of strength. Grandma is a tower of strength."

Kathleen was too overwhelmed to speak.

As John lay dying, Bess stood at his bedside looking at him. She went over in her mind all their years together. John, the handsome young man who'd courted her. Her helpmate. Their laughter and tears, joys and sorrows. She thought how right from the beginning they fit together. So compatible. Most men, averse to work in the house, left such tasks to the womenfolk. Not John. He set up the pattern as soon as they wed. "You dust, I sweep, you cook, I do the dishes, we both cook, we both do the cleaning up, you do the laundry, I iron. We'll work in the garden, we'll care for the children together." Then too, Bess helped in whatever endeavors he pursued: in the print shop, post office, grocers. And at the end they both worked in the factory. They shared the same interests, both were voracious readers, and they discussed all the topics of the day. He had his woodworking projects, she her sewing.

When she knew he was gone, she smoothed his hair and traced his features with her finger. Handsome, intelligent, gentle, and good. "Thank you, John, for a good life. I will miss you." She leaned over and kissed him gently. Still warm. "What do I do now?" she said aloud. And no one was there to answer her.

John Donahue died of complications from diabetes on April 27, 1963, at the age of eighty-seven.

Utterly bereft at the loss of her husband, companion, and friend of a lifetime, Bess was lost. She refused to stay alone, but immediately moved in with Kathleen. "The only time I've been alone in my life is the few days he was in the hospital. No, but even then when he was sick in the early 1950s Lois Ann stayed with us. And when we lived in Ethan, we always had a boarder or one of the grandchildren. I won't live alone."

After six months she went to Scarsdale to stay with Craig and thus began the pattern she followed for the last four years of her life. Bess died April 20, 1967. John and Bess were buried side by side in St. Thomas Cemetery in West Springfield.

Orphan Train Riders

The story of the "orphan train riders" is a forgotten fact of our history. Between 1854 and 1930, hundreds of thousands of children between the ages of five to fifteen were sent from the United States cities in the East to rural areas (first in nearby farming communities and then, gradually farther west) to become indentured servants. Boys were most often sent to farms, while girls worked as domestic help, either in private homes or hotels. The children were orphans, or if the parents were alive, unable to care for them. In any case, the practice of relocating children by social and religious agencies was the answer to child or foster care for at-risk children. Sometimes the family adopted the child. In many cases the family treated the child well; in others the child experienced coldness or alienation; in still others, abuse.

Because the last of the "orphan train riders" began to age and die in the 1990s, people began to document their stories, in order not to lose this valuable piece of our history. Thus, books of fiction and memoirs, videos, and documentaries began to take on a prominent role in telling this little-known and mostly forgotten historical social phenomenon. In some states "orphan train riders," now adults, gathered in reunions and told what had happened to them. A Web page on the Internet was developed to chronicle their stories, and many searched for living members of their birth families.

Stephen O'Connor tells the story of the practice in his book published in 2001 called *Orphan Trains: The Story of Charles Loring Brace and the Children He Saved and Failed*. Several factors led to the child welfare system called family placement or out placement – not orphan train riders, a term which came into use much later; in fact, after the phenomenon had stopped. The clergyman Brace whose story is told in the above-mentioned book began the practice in New York; other child advocates, mostly religious groups, followed suit, finding placement with farm families for vagrant or homeless children. One factor contributing to the idea was the expansion of transportation in the United States, most notably the opening of the Erie Canal and the railroad, which stretched across the country. Another factor was the flood of immigrants who came to America seeking freedom and a better life. The large cities of the East – New York, Boston, Philadelphia – became way stations before the newcomers headed west to homestead on the prairie or to seek a fortune in the California gold mines.

Another factor having a significant impact was the indenture system. With its long history of reform and removal of undesirable or potentially criminal children, Brace found a logical way to deal with large numbers of wayward children. However, he reinvented the system by stressing that the child be incorporated into the family. Adding to this was the need for cheap labor, and the belief in the 1800s that it was good for children to work; also long hours for all workers were the norm. Brace established the Children's Aid Society in 1853 with the goal to be "the means of draining the city of these children, by communicating with farmers, manufacturers, or families in the country who might give the children jobs and put them in the way of an honest living."

Other agencies, mostly religious, followed the same pattern. Groups established orphan homes as temporary places for children to stay during a family crisis. Few children stayed more than a year or more because the goal was to find placement with a family. One sad aspect of the time was that agencies were oblivious to any emotional problems of children; also they seldom considered the family tie important. Thus, the separation of siblings became inevitable and routine. Stories are frequently told of brothers placed on farms twenty miles apart – a distance not easily covered; thus, they rarely saw each other. Child placement by transporting children to rural areas took place in European countries as well: Germany, Norway, Sweden and others. But England was most enthusiastic, sending thousands to Australia and Canada.

About the Author

Judith Kappenman was born in Ethan, South Dakota, and moved to West Springfield, Massachusetts, at the age of six. She attended local schools and entered the Sisters of St. Joseph after she graduated from high school. She received her bachelor's from Elms College, an education degree from Worcester State College, and a CAGS from Assumption College. She taught school for 42 years, eight in an elementary classroom and 36 as a high school English teacher. After retirement from teaching, she has worked as  director of the Irish Cultural Center at Elms College. She sings with the Springfield Symphony Chorus and St. Michael's Cathedral Choir of Boys and Adults. She serves on the board of Billy's Malawi Project, a non-profit organization dedicated to raising funds for an African clinic founded by an Irish woman in memory of her son.

Made in the USA
Middletown, DE
13 July 2023

35109283R00154